CAMBRIDGE COMMENTARIES ON
WRITINGS OF THE JEWISH AND CHRISTIAN WORLD
200 BC TO AD 200

VOLUME 7

The Jewish and Christian World
200 BC to AD 200

CAMBRIDGE COMMENTARIES ON
WRITINGS OF THE JEWISH AND CHRISTIAN WORLD
200 BC TO AD 200

General Editors:

P. R. ACKROYD

A. R. C. LEANEY

J. W. PACKER

THE JEWISH AND CHRISTIAN WORLD 200 BC TO AD 200

A. R. C. LEANEY

Formerly Professor of Christian Theology
The University of Nottingham

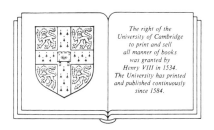

The right of the
University of Cambridge
to print and sell
all manner of books
was granted by
Henry VIII in 1534.
The University has printed
and published continuously
since 1584.

CAMBRIDGE UNIVERSITY PRESS

Cambridge
London   New York   New Rochelle
Melbourne   Sydney

Published by the Press Syndicate of the University of Cambridge
The Pitt Building, Trumpington Street, Cambridge CB2 1RP
32 East 57th Street, New York, NY 10022, USA
296 Beaconsfield Parade, Middle Park, Melbourne 3206, Australia

First published 1984

Printed in Great Britain at the
University Press, Cambridge

Library of Congress catalogue card number: 83-7189

British Library Cataloguing in Publication Data
Leaney, A. R. C.
The Jewish and Christian world, 200 BC to
AD 200. – (Cambridge commentaries on writings of
the Jewish and Christian world, 200 BC to AD 200; 7)
1. Judaism–History–Post-exilic period,
586 B.C. – 210 A.D.
I. Title
296'.09'01   BM165
ISBN 0 521 24252 5 hard covers
ISBN 0 521 28557 7 paperback

CS

To my son
John

Contents

Contents

Contents

Contents

General Editors' Preface

The three general editors of the Cambridge Bible Commentary series have all, in their teaching, experienced a lack of readily usable texts of the literature which is often called pseudepigrapha but which is more accurately defined as extra-biblical or para-biblical literature. The aim of this new series is to help fill this gap.

The welcome accorded to the Cambridge Bible Commentary has encouraged the editors to follow the same pattern here, except that carefully chosen extracts from the texts, rather than complete books, have normally been provided for comment. The introductory material leads naturally into the text, which itself leads into alternating sections of commentary.

Within the severe limits imposed by the size and scope of the series, each contributor will attempt to provide for the student and general reader the results of modern scholarship, but has been asked to assume no specialized theological or linguistic knowledge.

The volumes already planned cover the writings of the Jewish and Christian World from about 200 BC to AD 200 and are being edited as follows:

1. *Jews in the Hellenistic World* – J. R. Bartlett, Trinity College, Dublin
2. *The Qumran Community* – M. A. Knibb, King's College, London
3. *Early Rabbinic Writings* – H. Maccoby, Leo Baeck College, London
4. *Outside the Old Testament* – M. de Jonge, University of Leiden
5. *Outside the New Testament* – G. N. Stanton, King's College, London
6. *Jews and Christians: Graeco-Roman Views* – M. Whittaker, University of Nottingham

A seventh volume by one of the general editors, A. R. C. Leaney, *The Jewish and Christian World 200 BC to AD 200*, examines the wider historical and literary background to the period and includes tables of dates, relevant lists and maps. Although this companion volume will preface and augment the series, it may also be read as complete in itself and be used as a work of general reference.

P.R.A.
A.R.C.L.
J.W.P.

xi

Author's Foreword

This book is intended as a student beginner's guide to the history of Judaism and Christianity in the period 200 BC to AD 200, and to the literature associated with both the Jews and Christians which falls outside the list of accepted books of the Old Testament, Apocrypha and New Testament.

The book is divided into two parts. The first is concerned with the history of the peoples where Jews lived, and of the Jews themselves in those places, covering the Mediterranean world, Mesopotamia and Egypt and part of Europe and North Africa. This has involved an outline history of Rome from 264 BC to AD 284, necessary also because of its importance for the history of so many other peoples.

The second part deals with the literature which arose from Judaism. It discusses the Jewish scriptures – the Law, the Prophets and the Writings – and the New Testament, almost wholly as formed collections, and mentions only briefly individual books among them. For information about these the reader is referred to the Cambridge Bible Commentary Series based on the New English Bible. The literature discussed here is the non-canonical writings of both Judaism and Christianity, of which most students of the Bible are perhaps only dimly aware, while conscious of their importance. Besides ★Jewish writers in the hellenistic world, these are the ★Pseudepigrapha (for the term see p. 158), the ★Qumran writings, ★early rabbinic Judaism, and ★non-canonical Christian writings. In addition, the lists at the end of the book include ★non-Jewish and non-Christian authors of the Roman Empire. (Separate volumes on all the subjects marked with an asterisk, giving examples in English translation from representative authors with commentary, are being published in the same series as the present volume.)

The author acknowledges with sincere gratitude the hard work contributed by his fellow-editors, Professor P. R. Ackroyd and Canon J. W. Packer, the former having supplied important parts of the material and the latter having undertaken a full and thorough final revision. He is most grateful also for essential constructive criticism from the Revd J. R. Bartlett, Professor M. de Jonge, Dr M. A. Knibb, Mr Hyam Maccoby, Professor G. N. Stanton and Miss M. Whittaker. Mr Roger Coleman of the Press has given to the task much hard work and patience. While the author accepts full responsibility for the final product, he thankfully recognizes the corporate discharge of a varied task.

Abbreviations

Standard abbreviations for the books of the Bible and the Apocrypha are given on p. 229, those for the Qumran documents on pp. 233f., those for the Pseudepigrapha on pp. 231f., and those for certain rabbinic writings on pp. 234f. The following occur in the text:

ANET	*Ancient Near Eastern Texts Relating to the Old Testament*
AV	Authorized Version of the Bible
b.	In Jewish names 'ben' (= 'son of'); elsewhere 'born'
c.	*circa*, Latin for 'about', used for approximate dates
CBC	Cambridge Bible Commentary
CPJ	Corpus Papyrorum Judaicorum
d.	Died
DOTT	*Documents from Old Testament Times*
fl.	i.e. *floruit*, Latin for 'he flourished'. Used with a date to indicate the most active period in the life of someone whose dates of birth and death are unknown
Hist. Aug.	*Historia Augusta*
JTS	*Journal of Theological Studies*
LXX	Septuagint, the Greek version of the Old Testament
Making	E. B. Mellor (ed.), CBC *The Making of the Old Testament*
M	Mishnah
NEB	New English Bible
P. Ox.	Oxyrhyncus Papyrus

Aquileia

Luca

R. Rubicon

ILLYRICUM

R. Danube

Rome

SARDINIA

Puteoli
Neapolis

Pompeii

Hadrianopolis
Philippi

MACEDONIA
Thessalonica

Carthage

Zancle-
Messana

Rhegium

SICILY

Thapsus

EPIRUS

Actium

THESSALY

Hellespont

R. Granicus

Adramytt
Pergam

Thermopylae

AETOLIA

EUBOEA
Chalcis

Sa
P

Delphi

Athens

Marathon

Ephesus
del

Corinth

Samos

Cenchreae

BOEOTIA

Tra

ARGOS

Delos

Milet

Sparta

Halicar

Cos

Rh

CRETE

M e d i t e r r a n e a n

Ptolemais
Arsinoe

Apollonia

Cyrene

Berenice

CYRENAICA

LIBYA

Oasis of
Siwah

MACEDONIA Country or Province
<u>Alexandria</u> Metropolis

0 ———————— 500 km
0 ———————— 300 miles

Map 1   The Diaspora. After S. Safrai and M. Stern (eds.), *The Jewish Peop*

xvi

CHERSONESUS

KINGDOM of BOSPORUS

Black Sea

Caspian Sea

• Sinope

BITHYNIA PONTUS

• Zela

Ancyra

ARMENIA

• Artaxata

GALATIA

CAPPADOCIA

HYRCANIA
PARTHIA
MEDIA

Apamea
Laodicea
Iconium

Caesarea
Mazaca

COMMAGENE

Samosata

Nisibis

R. Lesser Zab

Lystra

Zeugma

Edessa

Tigranocerta
Nineveh

• Arbela

Tarsus

Carrhae

MESOPOTAMIA

ADIABENE

Side

Antioch

SYRIA

OSROENE

R. Tigris

Seleucia

Ebla

Sura

CYPRUS

Ugarit

• Hamath

Dura
Europos

Aradus
Tripoli

• Emesa

• Palmyra

Ctesiphon
Seleucia

Berytus
Sidon
Tyre

Byblos

• Damascus

Pumbeditha
Nehardea

BABYLONIA

ELYMAIS

Zarephath

Babylon

Susa

Alexandria

Pelusium

• Jerusalem

R. Euphrates

Naucratis

Raphia

Spasinou Charax

Leontopolis

ARABIA

(Persian Gulf)

Memphis

• Petra

Arsinoe

Sinai Peninsula

• Oxyrhyncus

• Hermopolis

NABATAEA

R. Nile

Red Sea

Abydos •

Thebes • Luxor

Apollinopolis •

Elephantine • Syene

First Century, Vol. I, Van Gorcum (Assen), 1974

Map 2 Asia Minor. After L. H. Grollenberg, O.P., *Atlas of the Bible*, Nelson, 1956

Map 3   Palestine after death of Herod. After S. Safrai and M. Stern (eds.), *The Jewish People in the First Century*, Vol. I, Van Gorcum (Assen), 1974

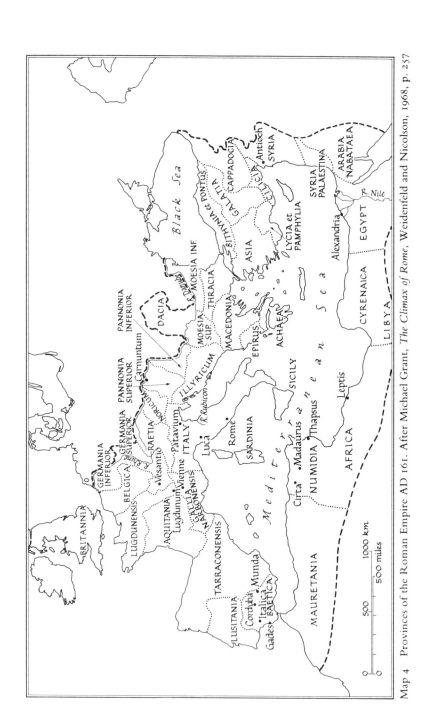

Map 4 Provinces of the Roman Empire AD 161. After Michael Grant, *The Climax of Rome*, Weidenfeld and Nicolson, 1968, p. 257

BRITANNIA

GERMANIA INFERIOR
GERMANIA SUPERIOR
BELGICA
LUGDUNENSIS
AQUITANIA
Lugdunum
Vienne
GALLIA NARBONENSIS
Vesantio
RAETIA
NORICUM
Patavium
ITALY
Luca
R. Rubicon
Rome
SARDINIA

PANNONIA SUPERIOR
Carnuntum
PANNONIA INFERIOR
ILLYRICUM
DACIA
MOESIA & Danube
MOESIA INF.
MOESIA SUP.
THRACIA
MACEDONIA
EPIRUS
ACHAEA

Black Sea

BITHYNIA & PONTUS
GALATIA
CAPPADOCIA
Antioch
SYRIA
CILICIA
ASIA
LYCIA et PAMPHYLIA
SYRIA PALAESTINA
ARABIA NABATAEA

SICILY
Leptis
Mediterranean Sea
Alexandria
R. Nile
EGYPT

TARRACONENSIS
LUSITANIA
Corduba
Munda
Italica
Gades
BAETICA

MAURETANIA
Cirta
Madaurus
NUMIDIA
Thapsus
AFRICA
CYRENAICA
LIBYA

500
1000 km
500 miles

Part I

1. Historical Outline: Exile, Restoration and Diaspora

The period covered by this book is effectively *c*. 200 BC to *c*. AD 200; but to begin our outline at 200 BC would be to plunge into a situation which must be described very largely in the light of the previous centuries. In fact the Exile of the Jewish people (597 BC) provides a natural point at which to begin. For centuries this event has been regarded by Jewish scholars as beginning the period of the Talmud, and by others as beginning the formation of 'Judaism', thought of as a system of belief and practice founded on God's dealings with his people in the past.

The period therefore begins with a disaster; it was followed by a measure of recovery, but the disaster produced the permanent effect of the dispersion (Gk *diaspora*) of the Jewish people. Our outline must therefore begin with the Exile, Restoration and Diaspora.

EXILE

The biblical account of the events leading to the Exile is narrated in 2 Kings 17 and 23–5. In 721 BC the majority of the inhabitants of the northern kingdom of Israel were taken into captivity by the Assyrians, who, in their Annals, claimed to have transported 27,290 of them as booty (see *ANET*, p. 285). In 597, 587 and 582 much the same fate befell the southern kingdom of Judah at the hands of the Babylonians, though Jeremiah's total of 4,600 (Jer. 52:28–30) probably refers to adult males only. The narrative says very little of the subsequent history; 2 Kings 25:22–6 tells briefly of the governorship on behalf of the Babylonian Empire by Gedaliah and of his assassination by Ishmael. The people remaining in Judah (or Judaea), fearing vengeance at the hands of the Babylonians, fled to Egypt. A fuller version of these events is given in Jer. 40–1. 2 Kings ends with a brief notice about King Jehoiachin, taken prisoner in 597 (2 Kings 24:15); in the thirty-seventh year of his captivity he was released by Evil-Merodach (Amel-marduk) when the latter succeeded Nebuchadrezzar, i.e.

in 562 (2 Kings 25:27–30; cp. Jer. 52:31–4). The captivity of Jehoiachin is reflected in records on cuneiform tablets found on the site of ancient Babylon. They are known as the Weidner Tablets. (See *DOTT*, pp. 84–6; *ANET*, p. 308.)

RESTORATION

Subsequent events are difficult to follow. There was a return of exiles, after Babylon had fallen to the Persian king Cyrus, in about 538 BC, but of how many is unclear. There was a restoration of the Temple, but when, by whom, and how far successful – all are again unclear. To speak of the 'Return' implies too confident and too sweeping a claim, with its suggestion of a return of all exiles and a complete reversal of the disaster of the Exile. It is better to use the term 'Restoration', since there was eventually a restoration of the Temple, of its worship, and of the worshipping community centred upon it.

For information about this restoration we are dependent on the Chronicler, the scribe who brought together and no doubt wrote part of the books 1 and 2 Chronicles, Ezra and Nehemiah. The problems raised by his writing and by his material are many and complex. To discuss them adequately would demand more space than is appropriate in this volume; but the main facts and a few of the more important problems may be briefly indicated.

2 Chronicles does no more than allude to the exile of the northern kingdom's inhabitants and in ch. 36 gives a condensed account of the last years of Judah before the Exile of 587. This narrative stresses the theme of divine punishment for apostasy, and the death or captivity of all the inhabitants at the final capture of Jerusalem, claiming this as a fulfilment of the prophecy of Jeremiah (Jer. 25:9–12). Gedaliah is not mentioned, and the comforting ending of 2 Kings 25:27–30 about Jehoiachin is also absent. Instead we have as ending a short passage (2 Chron. 36:22–3) to the effect that 'in the first year of Cyrus king of Persia' the Lord inspired Cyrus to proclaim that 'the LORD, the God of heaven' had given him 'all the kingdoms of the earth' and charged him to build a Temple for him in Jerusalem and that any who wished to go thither should do so.

The repetition of this passage at the opening of the book of Ezra (1:1–3) links what now appear as the books of Chronicles, covering the period of the monarchy, with the material concerning the restoration of Judah utilized in the opening chapters of the book of Ezra. It also provides a hopeful ending to the otherwise dark description of the downfall of Judah. The book of Ezra begins on the same optimistic note.

The subsequent course of events is far from clear. The material used in the books of Ezra and Nehemiah is of mixed character and raises considerable problems in attempts at reconstructing the history. Two parts of Ezra are in Aramaic (4:8 – 6:18 and 7:12–26) and were apparently official documents. The remainder, in Hebrew, contains lists (Ezra 2, cp. Neh. 7; and Neh. 11–12), which are almost certainly not of the Chronicler's own composition. The same must be said of the first-person material in Nehemiah (1-2; 4:1–7; 5; 12:27–43; 13:4–31) whether actually memoirs of Nehemiah or not.

These textual difficulties are inseparable from the historical problems. For example, what was the character of the actual return from Exile? Did Cyrus authorize a mass migration, as seems implied by the form of his decree given in Ezra 1:2–4, or only the rebuilding of the Temple, as in 6:3–5? The famous Cyrus Cylinder (p. 21), which does not mention the people from Judah, suggests the latter, that is that he encouraged only the restoration of the Temple. What is known from elsewhere (including the Jewish historian Josephus – p. 76) makes it virtually certain that though a considerable number of people returned, and some in the course of time were able to go to and fro, the majority of the exiles remained permanently in Babylonia (p. 22). Another problem is how to date, relatively to one another and to known dates such as the rules of Persian kings, the two personalities Ezra and Nehemiah. Both are placed in the reign of Artaxerxes (Ezra 7:7; Neh. 2:1); if this is Artaxerxes I (465–424), Ezra is dated 458 and Nehemiah 445; but the lack of cross-references from the one to the other suggests that they were not contemporaries. Was then the Artaxerxes of Ezra Artaxerxes II (404–359), dating Ezra to 398? Many think that this is the case, but an important reference, Neh. 8, does make the two contemporaries, for in that chapter Ezra proclaims the law while Nehemiah is governor. Evidence from the Elephantine papyri (*Making*, pp. 38–40) seems to support the view that Nehemiah was active under Artaxerxes I in 445, and Ezra probably under Artaxerxes II, since they give names of persons known to be contemporary with each, and place them in these respective periods. But this evidence

3

is not as certain as it was thought when first examined. For example, the papyri mention the name of Nehemiah's adversary Sanballat in circumstances fitting well with the date of 445 for Nehemiah; but the 'Samaria papyri' (discovered in a remote place near Jericho but apparently brought from Samaria) provide evidence of recurrence of the name of Sanballat, and of one bearing this name in the fourth century. (See F. M. Cross, *Biblical Archaeologist* 26 (1963), 3, pp. 120–1.)

One of the most important questions, perhaps the most important, is: When did the rebuilding of the Temple begin? Here the books of Haggai and Zechariah offer some evidence; Hag. 1:1–10, dating itself to 520, reproaches the people for living in houses with roofs while the Temple is in ruins. In ch. 2, in an oracle dated a month or more later, Zerubbabel the governor is encouraged to begin building, and Zech. 4:9 prophesies that Zerubbabel, who laid the foundation, will finish it. Ezra 3:8 is consistent with this (though perhaps suggesting a different date) but Ezra 1:8 and 5:14–16 suggest a beginning under the earlier governor Sheshbazzar, this attempt being apparently thwarted by enemies (Ezra 4:1–5). A probable interpretation seems therefore to be that the Chronicler has exaggerated both the numbers of those who came to Judah and their zeal in rebuilding the Temple, while retaining evidence which allows us to see this exaggeration at work. By the way in which he tells the story, he suggests that the worship of Yahweh and the future of his people lay wholly with those who returned to Judah and their descendants, and that the history of the Jews of Babylonia was of no importance. We shall see that this was to be disproved by events; indeed, it is necessary to restore the balance and in due course to give some account of the Jews in Babylonia and in other countries distant from Judah and from one another. This brings us to the Diaspora.

DIASPORA

The Greek word *diaspora*, which means 'dispersion', is often used to denote this phenomenon of the spread of the Jewish people to so many different places in the world. Dispersion suggests diffusion from a centre; such it was, for it was diffusion from Judah and Jerusalem. Respect for Jerusalem was never lost, but the sense of being a distant colony of a people whose true home was elsewhere was bound to disappear under the influence of the natural tendency to regard as home the place where one has always lived. Respect for Jerusalem did not discourage pride in, or loyalty to, local authority, even for religious matters. The book of Esther, for example, clearly belonging to the eastern Diaspora, at no point suggests any idea of return to Judah; its problems are centred on the life of Diaspora Jews in an alien and sometimes hostile environment.

For lists of places where Jews lived in the ancient world during the period of our study we can turn to Philo (p. 140) and the book of Acts. Philo gives his list in his *Legatio ad Caium* (281–2), beginning it with the country where he lived: 'Egypt, Phoenicia and Syria, Pamphylia, Cilicia, most of Asia as far as Bithynia and remote corners of Pontus; and similarly in Europe, Thessaly, Boeotia, Macedonia, Aetolia, Attica, Argos, Corinth and most of the Peloponnese Islands also contain colonies, e.g. Euboea, Cyprus, Crete.' Asia is what we call Asia Minor. Philo has here apparently limited his world deliberately, for he omits Rome (which he visited) and remarks at the end of the list we have quoted, 'I say nothing about the regions beyond the Euphrates.' This famous river was a natural boundary, though not always recognized as a political boundary, between Rome, the great power in the west, and Parthia, the great power in the east during our period (see map p. xvii).

The list in Acts 2:9–11 is shorter but represents a wider spread. The first name reflects the Parthian supremacy east of the Euphrates from *c.* 140 BC to AD 226, the 'Parthian period' of Jewish history. The Parthian Empire extended over almost the same territories as the older Persian Empire and included the second, third and fourth countries in the list – Media, Elam and Mesopotamia, thus emphasizing that unlike Philo it gives pride of place to 'the regions beyond the Euphrates', and this means to Babylonian Jewry. This was the term used to denote the eastern Jewish communities which derived from ancient Babylon since the Exile; it shows consciousness of this origin, for Babylon ceased to be important politically in 539. The eastern countries are followed by Judaea, Cappadocia, Pontus, Asia, Phrygia, Pamphylia, Egypt, Cyrenaica, Rome, Crete, Arabia. The presence of Judaea in this list makes it look like one compiled by a non-Jewish historian who sought to answer the question: Where are Jews to be found? It is strange only in its context, which makes it part of an expression of astonishment from the mouths of a crowd in

Jerusalem. This contrasts with Philo who prefaces his list by referring to Jerusalem as the spiritual capital of all these districts.

Our primary task in this historical outline is not to elucidate the
story of the 'Return' from Exile, not even the details of the
Restoration of life and worship in Judah, although that is part of
the history of the most important land where Jews were to be
found. It is rather to outline the history of the Jewish people from
the sixth century BC onwards, wherever they happened to be; to
describe their religious and social organization; and to summarize
the literary activity associated with it. Our perspective is derived
from the well-known concept of the Fertile Crescent and from a
condensation of the lists of Philo and Acts. The exact shape of a
crescent cannot indeed be maintained: it can be described from
east to west, sweeping north from Babylonia through Mesopotamia, and south through Palestine to Egypt; but it must be
imagined as throwing out an extension from its most northerly
point westwards into Europe. The areas to be considered are
Babylonia and Mesopotamia, Asia Minor, Greece, Italy, Syria
and Phoenicia, Palestine, Egypt, Cyrenaica (see map pp. xvi-xvii).

2. Diaspora: The Historical Background

MAIN PERIODS OF HISTORY

The traditional 'Persian/Greek period' of Jewish history is 539–140 BC and subdivides into: Persian Empire 539–333 (this latter date is approximate); Macedonian Empire of Alexander the Great, *c.* 333 to 320; Seleucid period *c.* 320 to *c.* 140. The Parthian period has been traditionally held to extend from *c.* 140 BC to *c.* AD 226, when the Parthians were overthrown by the new Persian dynasty, the Sassanians. For Babylonian and Mesopotamian Jewry these divisions can be accepted as useful guides. For Jewish history in other parts of the world, dates shared with Greek and Roman history are more appropriate. (See the tables on pp. 221–5).

The Diaspora of the Jewish people took place within the context of historical events involving many different nations. These can be located easily in the Fertile Crescent and its westward extension, but before any account of the Diaspora is attempted, a very brief sketch of the main events is necessary.

In 520 BC, when our sketch begins, Darius I had established his position as king of Persia in spite of some disturbances; he ruled over a vast empire, which he had largely inherited from his predecessors Cyrus the Great and Cyrus' son Cambyses, and to which he had added. It stretched to the valley of the Indus on the east and embraced the whole of the Fertile Crescent, including Egypt and Libya, while the extension to the west included Asia Minor and Thrace. Persian power threatened, but as yet did not attempt to embrace, mainland Greece. Darius and his successors attempted to include it, but the effort proved that the Empire was too large to hold together the extremes of east and west. Failure to conquer mainland Greece led to the loss of Asia Minor and eventually to Greek counter-attack under Macedonian leadership. The enormous conquests of Alexander the Great of Macedon, leading a Greek army, inaugurated a new age. In 333 his victory at Issus enabled him to turn south through Syria, Phoenicia and

Palestine to Egypt before the series of triumphal advances into Persia itself, for a brief spell transforming the Persian Empire into an even vaster Greek Empire. It was indeed a brief spell: Alexander died in 323, and the date marks the beginning of another age. The classical Greek period was closed and succeeded by an age which saw the gradual breakup of the huge oriental empire which had in turn been Babylonian, Persian and Greek. This new age witnessed the spread over a very great area of the influence of the Greek language and of miscellaneous Greek ideas, and for that reason might have been called Hellenic (for the Greeks called themselves Hellenes). The days of creative greatness, however, had largely gone, and the new civilization has always seemed to historians, perhaps unjustly, to be derivative, finding its inspiration in past models rather than in a creative spirit. For this reason the period which followed the death of Alexander has been called hellenistic.

Alexander's great empire was divided after his death between his generals. These have been often called the Diadochi (i.e. successors). Antigonus was left with Macedonia, whose history now hardly concerns us. By 285 Ptolemy ruled over a thin coastline, and accompanying islands, of south-western Asia Minor, Lycia, Cyprus, and above all Egypt. He was in fact Ptolemy I (304–283), founder of the Ptolemaic dynasty. By far the greatest area was ruled by Seleucus I (312–280), and consisted of the remainder of the large territories to the east which had been Persian, extending to the west coast of Asia Minor. Its administrative centre was Syria, with Antioch (founded in 300 BC by Seleucus) as its capital. For a few years after the death of Alexander the position of Phoenicia and Palestine was uncertain, but by the turn of the century they were securely part of Ptolemy's empire. This lasted until the Seleucid conquest of Palestine in 200–198.

Rivalry between Seleucids and Ptolemies constitutes the main background of events for the history of the Jewish people in the very poorly documented but important third century BC, until the Maccabaean revolt against the Seleucids brings a sharper focus and the books of the Maccabees give us the story from about 175 BC. By then Rome's involvement in the Middle East had already begun, after her conquest of Carthage in 202. Rome was culturally so deeply influenced by the Greece she conquered that from some points of view the period of her ascendancy could be included in the hellenistic period. The years 200 BC to AD 200, with which this book is concerned, are part of what is known as the Graeco-Roman period, and may themselves be called the hellenistic–Roman period. In this period Christianity emerged, and Judaism, in anything like the modern sense, became articulate and literary, producing at the end of the period the Mishnah (p. 197). Hellenistic–Roman also denotes most of the area embraced by the Fertile Crescent and its western extension across Asia Minor and Greece into Italy. Only one of the spheres inhabited by Jews lay outside the hellenistic–Roman area, being for this four-hundred-year period ruled by Parthia. This was the area of Babylonia and Mesopotamia.

This is the area with which we begin our outline of the Diaspora. When describing it and the other areas, we shall begin with a sketch of the history of the country and of its own culture, and then give some account of the Jewish people living in it.

Babylon and the Persian Empire

The Neo-Babylonian Empire (so-called to distinguish it from the early flourishing period *c.* 1830–1530 BC) lasted only from 626 to 539. Its conquest by Persia at this latter date did not altogether obliterate its culture or learning. It is now not easy to determine how much we owe to Babylonia, but the profession of scribe was the most typical among wealthier members of the community, and great scholarly activity was obviously necessary to produce and to preserve the considerable body of literature which has survived and which has helped to illuminate Old Testament studies. It is debatable how much these scholars discovered; for example it is known that they anticipated Pythagoras' famous theorem, but not whether they developed the knowledge which it implies. They certainly devoted much time and zeal to the collection and recording of magic lore and omens, a sphere in which the Greeks regarded them as experts.

The Jewish exiles lived under native Babylonian rule for only a short time. The conquest of Babylon in 539 was a relatively late event in the career of Cyrus, king of the Persians; they and he were newcomers on the power scene in this part of Asia round the Persian Gulf, which had for long been the empire of the Medes. In October 539 Cyrus was proclaimed king of Babylon, and he adopted its administrative organization. These facts witness to the pride which he felt in taking his place in the traditional line of supremacy in the area. He thereby conformed to the established custom of the Neo-Babylonian Empire, and indeed corrected some of the eccentricities of its last king, Nabonidus. Cyrus was not in fact the first king of Babylon to send back the images of foreign deities to their native sanctuaries, a courtesy not only to them but also to the Babylonian deities whose temples they desecrated (Cyrus Cylinder, p. 21).

Cyrus (550–530) was one of the great kings of antiquity. He established a vast empire stretching from as far east as northwestern India to as far west as Asia Minor and the Greek islands (which with the coastlands became the satrapy of Ionia). His son Cambyses (530–522) extended this empire to include Syria–Palestine and Egypt, so that almost the whole of the area, which we have described as the Fertile Crescent with an extension to the west but excluding Italy, became the Persian Empire, but with a further extension to the east. The years 522–520, following Cambyses' death, were marked by unrest in several parts of the empire which included Babylon and Palestine. Whether Zerubbabel, apparently the governor in Jerusalem and a grandson of Jehoiachin, was involved in this unrest remains obscure. (See Hag. 2:4–9, 20–23; Zech. 4:6–10.)

Darius I (522–486) showed great ability in establishing peace and his own position as king by 520 and he commemorated his triumph by a large trilingual inscription on a rock face at Behistun. It is unfair to his reputation that he should be known best as the king whose army was defeated by the outnumbered Athenians at Marathon in 490. This famous event reminds us of the fact that the Persian kings, largely because of attempted revolts by the Ionian Greeks, were drawn into over-extended lines of communication in trying to subdue not only Ionia but even mainland Greece. The destruction of Athens after the battle of Thermopylae in 480 was the work of Xerxes (486–465), son of Darius, whose huge army seemed more than adequate for the destruction of the whole of Greece. But the Persians lost the subsequent battles by sea and the delivered Athenians recovered to build not long afterwards on their Acropolis those monuments which speak of the emergence of a totally new world from that which the Persians had destroyed.

After Salamis (480) the Ionian revolt took a definite shape and tried the strength of the contestants to the uttermost, producing instances of disloyalty on both sides. In Egypt the satrap defeated an army of Egyptians and Athenians in 455; this was an interesting event because we know that he employed Jewish mercenaries, who had been in the country since before the conquest by Cambyses (525). There seems to be nothing to connect this military force with those Jews who took refuge in Egypt, taking Jeremiah with them, in 587 (Jer. 41:16–18; 43:5–7). For a time it seemed, especially after the victories of the Athenian Cimon, that the Persian Empire might break up with his destruction of the Persian fleet in 450, but strength and the will to press home advantage in battle diminished alike on both sides. The Peace of Callias in 449/8 gave independence to the Ionian Greeks and banished Persian ships from the Aegean, and this might seem to have been a great victory for the Greek spirit, but divisions among the city-states and the exhaustions of war made the future both less secure and less glorious than the artistic triumphs of Periclean Athens suggest to later ages.

If the Persian Empire was too far-flung for constant adequate defence, it still needed a well-organized and brilliantly sustained attack to dissipate it altogether. Such an attack was soon to come from the unexpected quarter of Macedonia in northern Greece, a country and people thought of as nearly or quite barbarian by the ancient city-states of the classical period. By the end of the fifth century the latter had worn each other out in foolish and unnecessary wars, even though they had recovered much of their liveliness by the middle of the fourth century.

Alexander the Great and the End of the Persian Empire

Archaeology has very recently shown, if not the civilization, at least the magnificence of the royal house of Macedon, in what may be the tomb of Philip II (359–336). Philip organized the Macedonian state and army with such brilliant success that his reputation as a ruler and general was outshone only by that of his even more brilliant son Alexander III, the Great, for whom (if evidence of being civilized is needed) he provided as tutor no less a person than the philosopher Aristotle. On his succession Alexander (336–323), building on the supremacy which his father had established over other Greek states, conceived the notion of liberating all Greek peoples from the Persian yoke. In 334 he

crossed the Hellespont and won the battle of the Granicus, perhaps from then onwards beginning to entertain the prospect of a
conquest of the Persian Empire itself. During the next ten years
he achieved this extraordinary aim, acquiring himself an empire
whose territory at its greatest extent stretched from Macedonia
through Asia Minor and Mesopotamia even further into India
than Cyrus had known was possible. The results of his conquests
are incalculable. After the battle of Issus (333) in southern Cilicia,
near the north-eastern corner of the Mediterranean, Alexander
forbore to be swept along by a sense of success and so to pursue
the Persian army eastwards; instead he turned south through
Syria–Phoenicia and Palestine into Egypt. The consequences of
this move for the hellenization of the area cannot be exaggerated.
For the Jewish people it meant the sharp and lasting challenge of
confrontation with an entirely different world-view from their
own, and the immeasurable results of both reaction and assimila-
tion. For this area, and in due course for the rest of what had been
the Persian Empire after Alexander had continued his advance
eastwards into it, it meant the fuller introduction of the Greek
language and the settlement of Greek people in countries hitherto
as remote from them as the beings of another planet. Alexander's
conquests meant in fact the building of many Greek cities, and
the increasing dominance of the Greek language in many places
throughout the Fertile Crescent, following on an army which
entered it from its western extension.

The Seleucid Empire (c. 320–140 BC)

Brief reference has already been made to the death of Alexander
in 323 and the division of his empire among the 'Diadochi'. We
are now concerned with the empire of the Seleucids, since Babylonia and Mesopotamia were part of their territory. For a list of
these kings and their dates, see p. 221. Seleucus I at one time
looked as if he might become the true successor to Alexander, but
his reign was marked by many changes of fortune, and during the
reign of Seleucus II (246–225), the third ruler after him, the strain
of keeping intact an empire which spread so far both east and
west began to show. In 245 civil war in the west gave
opportunity for the defection of the satrapies of Bactria and Parthia. Seleucus II was defeated by Celtic invaders at Ancyra in Asia
Minor, and this gave Arsaces, leader of the tribe called Parni from

the south-eastern side of the Caspian Sea, an opportunity to seize Parthia.

The event proved more important than the border raid which it seemed to be. The tribesmen became known by the name of the territory which they had seized, and have since always been called Parthians. Arsaces founded a dynasty, many of whose kings were known by his name as a title as well as by their own names (much as Roman emperors were called Caesar). It might be said that Parthia was therefore lost to the Seleucids under Seleucus II, but the satrapy was made tributary again by Antiochus III (the Great, 223–187). This king too came near to making the Seleucid dynasty the most powerful after Alexander. In 200, by his victory at Panion (later known as Caesarea Philippi) over Ptolemy V, he secured for Syria the whole of Judaea as far south as the Egyptian border. But the difficulties of maintaining such an extended empire at such a time proved insuperable. The main reason was the appearance of Roman power in the Middle East.

Rome had destroyed the power of Carthage in 202, its arch-enemy Hannibal escaping to the east and taking refuge with Antiochus. This was not the only cause of hostility between the Syrian king and Rome, for the Romans were seeking to bring Greece, then Asia Minor, and so the whole of the Middle East and Egypt under their influence. Antiochus was unsuccessful in his attempt to assist the free Greek cause in Asia Minor, and was forced to make a peace with Rome (at Apamea in Phrygia, 188 BC), by which he lost among other assets his possessions in that area. The positive side of the agreement was that he became a 'friend of Rome', that is a vassal king; as such he held consider-able territory, which included the enlarged Syria, extending to the Egyptian border. His son Antiochus (later Antiochus IV Epiphanes, 175–164) was among the hostages sent to Rome. (Hannibal escaped to Pontus but later took poison to avoid being handed over to the Romans, *c.* 183.)

Although Rome apparently took no steps to deprive Antiochus of his eastern territories, it is probable that in 187 he lost control of Parthia. He may have been intending to campaign for the return of this and other eastern lands, for in the same year his actions showed a desperate need for money. He in fact met his death while plundering a temple in Elymais, the satrapy east of Babylonia and south of Parthia, the ancient land of Elam (see map p. xvii).

The elder son and successor of Antiochus III was Seleucus IV, whose reign was uneventful until both he and his young son were murdered. He was succeeded by his energetic brother, Antiochus IV Epiphanes, until now a hostage in Rome, the king who was cast in the Jews' national consciousness for some time to come as the arch-enemy of their nation. In 166/165 he too made an expedition against Parthia, an enterprise which Tacitus (*Hist.* 5.8; cp. 1 Macc. 3:30–1 and 6:1–16) typically records with sympathy, accepting it as an excuse for the king's failure 'to reform this degraded nation', i.e. the Jews. He appears also to think that this was the occasion of Arsaces' insurrection and move for freedom. This may well be a natural mistake arising from the fact that Mithradates I (*c.* 171–138), king of Parthia, held the name Arsaces as a title. Although the evidence is not quite clear, 1 Maccabees appearing sometimes to confuse Antiochus III and IV, it seems that Antiochus Epiphanes failed to obtain possession of Parthia, Mithradates proving too efficient a warrior to conquer.

In 141 Demetrius II, nephew of Antiochus IV Epiphanes and rival claimant to the Syrian throne (p. 85), also attempted to obtain possession of Parthia (1 Macc. 14:1–2). The circumstances are interesting; according to Josephus, Demetrius had occupied Mesopotamia and while there received urgent deputations of 'Greeks and Macedonians' from Babylon to campaign against Parthia. Mithradates was still king and more than a match for Demetrius, whom he made prisoner, but he treated him as an honourable captive and gave him his daughter in marriage. The action may reflect the regard of a Parthian for a hellenistic nobleman, for there are signs (e.g. on coins) that the Parthians admired and imitated hellenistic culture. (Josephus *Ant.* XIII.5.11 (184–6).) In spite of this they were not prepared to accept the overlordship of the Seleucids, and indeed showed consistent favour towards the Hasmonaeans (see p. 97).

In contrast to Demetrius the Seleucid, Simon the Hasmonaean (p. 90) remained opposed to Hellenism. According to 1 Macc. 14:41, in the year of Demetrius' failure (141) his leadership in Judaea was ratified by the people. It is possible that Simon entertained ambassadors from Parthia, but such open friendship is more certainly reported of later years.

While Demetrius remained a prisoner, his brother Antiochus VII Sidetes (*c.* 139–129) succeeded him, establishing himself as king and reconquering Judaea; but he lost his life in a battle against the Parthians. This meant the end of Seleucid power in the east and justifies the date of *c.* 140 BC for the beginning of the period of Parthian supremacy in Jewish history. Demetrius was released from Parthia in 129, but he was quite unable to regain his throne and was no serious threat to Simon's successor, his son John Hyrcanus (135–104).

The Rise of Parthia (c. 140 BC)

The king who defeated and killed Antiochus VII was Phraates II (138–128), son of Mithradates I. The Seleucid enemy from the west was only one of his difficulties. Nomads from the east caused chaos in the realms where petty Greek states had been set up in the wake of Alexander, such as Bactria, and in north-western India. These states were finally to submit to the nomad raids by 50 BC; in the meantime Parthia, for her own safety, was unavoidably involved with their fortunes.

In 128 Phraates' Greek mercenaries turned against him and he was killed. He was succeeded by Artabanus I (*c.* 128–124), his uncle or great-uncle, who was killed in the fighting caused by the overrunning of Parthia and Hyrcania. At the same time an Arab prince Hyspaosines extended his small kingdom of Mesene at the head of the Persian Gulf to include part of Babylonia.

Parthia's fortunes were restored by Mithradates II (*c.* 124–87), son of Artabanus, who not only regained Babylonia but also attacked Armenia, taking prisoner Tigranes, the king's son. Such a venture towards the west has obvious significance for western history (he invaded Mesopotamia and by 113 had entered Dura-Europos on the Euphrates), but equally important were the conquests made by Mithradates in the east. He recovered Parthia and Aria and claimed Sacastene as a vassal state. The Chinese ambassador Ch'ang Ch'ien and ambassadors subsequently sent by the emperor Wu-ti all testify to Mithradates' greatness and to the extent of his conquests. These are recorded on a rock relief carved between 123 and 110 in Behistun; it shows the king with four vassals. The inscription is in Greek but the figures are reminiscent of the Persian Achaemenid dynasty (kings from Darius I to Darius III, 522–331); this feature harmonizes with the Persian royal title 'King of kings' found on the reverse side of a coin of Mithradates. The Behistun rock relief is placed just below the bas-relief of the triumph of Darius I (see p. 10).

The Rivalry of Parthia and Rome in the East (87 BC to AD 226)

The rule of Mithradates II serves as a pointer to the character and
the limitations of Parthian power. It had little capacity for political organization to match its military boldness and courage, and
seemed to be destined not to succeed for long in the west, just as
the Seleucid power had failed largely because it was too ambitious in extending eastwards. However, the main reason for the
failure both of hellenistic kingdoms and of Parthia was the
advance of Rome, no less unscrupulous than any eastern power
but better organized and equipped. Mithradates placed on the
throne of Armenia, on the death of its king, the hostage Tigranes,
and took some land as payment, but an invasion of Mesopotamia
brought him to the Euphrates at the time when the Roman Sulla
was approaching. Sulla arrived there in 92 but refused an embassy's request for an alliance. The event was symbolic: the great
river was the natural boundary between the two powers, although the Romans including Sulla did not realize that Parthia
was a power. For the time being indeed this was hardly revealed,
for Mithradates died in the midst of a period of rebellion and loss
of territory, including Babylonia and northern Mesopotamia, the
latter now seized by Tigranes who in his turn usurped the title
'King of kings'. There was also a struggle for the Parthian throne
itself and disturbance continued through the reign of Mithradates' son Phraates III (70–58). In his campaign against Pontus
and Armenia the Roman Pompey's lieutenant Gabinius significantly enough crossed the Euphrates, and pressed on as far as the
Tigris after Pompey himself had treated the Parthians with con-
tempt. Although in 64 Phraates and Tigranes accepted Pompey's
ruling over boundaries, this meant more as an alliance of the two
oriental kings than as an acceptance of the overlordship of Rome.
In 58 or 57 Phraates was murdered, and in the subsequent internecine struggle for the throne Orodes II (57–38) emerged as
undisputed king.

During the reign of Orodes the premature ambition of a Roman
to conquer Parthia was illustrated by a famous disaster: Crassus,
third member of a triumvirate whose other members were
Caesar and Pompey, and eager to establish a reputation as a
general equal to theirs, saw his opportunity in the proconsulship
of Syria which fell to him after his consulship in 55. He set out
deliberately to add Parthia to the Empire, but at the battle of

Carrhae (the Harran in Mesopotamia of the Old Testament, e.g.
Gen. 11:31f) in 53 he lost many dead, prisoners and Roman
standards, and finally his own life in one of the most famous
defeats in Roman history. After it the Euphrates was accepted as
the boundary between the two powers (effectively between the
east and west of those days) for more than a century. Both sides at
first threatened to ignore this natural boundary. Orodes' son
Pacorus made a raid into Syria in 51, but by the next year the
Parthians had withdrawn across the river. Caesar planned a great
campaign against Parthia but events were given a radically new
turn by his assassination in 44. In 40–39 Pacorus, Orodes' son,
campaigned with some success in Syria and Asia Minor, and this
led to the most dramatic intrusion by Parthia into the Middle
East. In 41 the last Hasmonaean to occupy the throne in Jerusalem, Antigonus Mattathias, obtained the support of Pacorus and
his general Barzapharnes, in the absence of Antony, the Roman
who by agreement with Octavian was nominally in charge of the
area. By this means Antigonus did in fact reign from 40 to 37,
albeit uneasily and in a capital besieged by Herod with Roman
assistance for the last five months. It was with Roman arms that
the Parthians were overcome and Pacorus killed, events which
led to the siege and conquest of Jerusalem, and to the execution of
the doomed Antigonus.

For a time it seemed that the fortunes of Rome and Parthia
were to be reversed, that the defeated Parthians might even be
further defeated on their own soil, as well as driven out of territory already claimed by Rome. Antony did indeed in 36 lead an
expedition into Parthia, but this led to even greater losses than
those suffered under Crassus. By 31 Antony, though he had pene-
trated as far as Media during his unsuccessful campaign, was dead.

During the next almost one hundred years Rome and Parthia
were often in disagreement over the rulership of Armenia, but no
warfare was waged between them. In 20 BC Augustus negotiated
the return of the famous standards and some of the prisoners lost
by Crassus and Antony. In AD 35 an event in the history of
Roman–Parthian affairs concerns a Jewish ruler, Herod Antipas.
In 35 and 36 Artabanus II of Parthia (12–38) opposed the
Roman-backed Vonones I (7–12), whom he had driven out in
11–12, and defeated him in battle. The emperor Tiberius next sent
Tiridates II (35–6), and bought Parthian support for this candidate so successfully that Artabanus fled to the eastern parts of the

Parthian Empire. At some point, whether before this or on his
return is not clear, Artabanus, in a time of relative success, had to
deal with the legate of Syria, Vitellius. The meeting was a success
in that peace was established between the two powers. Josephus in
Ant. XVIII.4.5 (101–5) reports of this meeting that Herod Antipas
acted as host, setting up a splendid tent on the bridge over the
Euphrates, where the two protagonists were to meet at the mid-
point of the crossing and were to be given a banquet. The terms
included Artabanus handing over hostages including his own son
Darius and, Josephus unbends enough to add, a Jew seven cubits
tall named Eleazar. Since this man (owing to his size, says the
historian unnecessarily, called 'Giant') was included among the
'many gifts' which accompanied the hostages, he may well have
been a slave; he remains a small (if we may be allowed the word)
illustration of the presence of Jews among the Parthians.

No direct clash occurred between Rome and Parthia after AD
35 until the year 60; in that year by the orders of Nero (emperor
54–68), Corbulo, legate of Syria, disputed the right of Tiridates
to the throne of Armenia, on which he had been placed by his
brother Vologeses I (51–76). Corbulo destroyed the Armenian
capital Artaxata and captured Tigranocerta, but he then retired to
Syria thinking there would be no more campaigning that year.
Paetus, legate of Cappadocia, now in charge of the front against
Parthia, was suddenly attacked by Vologeses and forced into a
disgraceful retreat. In 63 a peaceful compromise was found: Tiridates received the crown of Armenia but from the hands of Nero.
Monobazus II of Adiabene was a witness to the treaty which
included this settlement (see pp. 26f.).

The reign of Vologeses saw the emergence of interesting features in Parthian culture which suggest a reaction against the
hellenistic world. Aramaic lettering appears on the royal coinage
and a fire altar among the coin designs. A Zoroastrian tradition
attributes the collecting of manuscripts and traditions of the
Avesta to a king Valaksh who may well be Vologeses I. He
founded a new city in Babylonia near Seleucia, as a rival to the
hellenistic city; other cities begin at this time to be called by their
original names rather than those given them by the Greek Seleucids.

For a time there was apparently relative tranquillity, but from
about 70 onwards Parthia was torn by a mixture of internal strife
and invasions by barbarians from the north-east. In 113 Trajan

(emperor 98–117), once again using disagreement over Armenia as a pretext, made a further attempt to conquer Parthia. Osroes (89–127?) had deposed the king of Armenia without consulting Rome, and his embassy to meet the emperor at Athens was ignored. When Trajan arrived at Elegia in Armenia, he announced his intention to make Armenia a province of the Roman Empire; the Parthian nominee disappeared and Armenia was placed under a Roman governor. Trajan continued his progress and by the end of 116 his control extended over Mesopotamia and Babylonia and indeed as far as Spasinou Charax. Parthian counter-attacks robbed him of the territories which he had gained, and though he might have regained at least Mesopotamia in further campaigns, in 117 he died and Hadrian his successor handed back the newly-won territories, leaving a Parthian as ruler of Armenia. Parthian supremacy, not again seriously challenged by Rome, eventually succumbed to the new Persian Sassanid dynasty in about 226.

This date takes us out of the period with which this book is concerned, but it was the time of considerable rabbinic activity, moving towards the final form of those traditions which were to find their fixed expression in the Talmud. The Sassanid dynasty provided a strong government that was a match for the Roman Empire; the emperor Valerian was defeated and captured at Edessa in 260. The Jewish people, not always unmolested by the Persian government, supported it against the hated Rome, and were apparently not included in the opposition to the Christian church which was aroused by the radical change in favour of Christianity on the part of Constantine in 311. They remained loyal to the Persians, even though sometimes persecuted along with adherents of other non-Zoroastrian religions.

It was not until the fifth century that Babylonian Jewry was, for the first time, officially persecuted by the government, and the official leader of the Jewish community, the exilarch, became a rebel leader and maintained an independent state for seven years before being executed. The time of these troubles is associated in Jewish history with the 'sealing' of the Talmud (that is, the closing of its canon); they were followed by a more peaceful period, that of the Gaons or teachers of the Talmud. This final formation of the Talmud may therefore be dated about AD 500, and provides a tidy end to this historical survey.

We turn now to such review as is possible of religious and

social activity in the Jewish community in the Parthian Empire during the period of the Second Temple and the years immediately following (587 BC to AD 200).

The Jews in Babylonia and Mesopotamia

The traditional story in the Bible makes Hebrew and Babylonian history meet at three points. One is the departure of Abraham from Ur of the Chaldees (Gen. 11:31) or from Harran (Gen. 12:1, 4). The second is the visit of ambassadors from the wily Merodach-Baladan, seeking and foreshadowing the revival of Babylonian power during a period of Assyrian supremacy, and wooing the alliance of Hezekiah (2 Kings 20:12ff; Isa. 39:1ff) in *c.* 703 BC. The third is the destruction of Jerusalem in 597 and 587, and the associated taking into exile of the most important elements of the population. There is much literary evidence to suggest that these contacts are but the peaks appearing in history of much experience shared between the peoples of Mesopotamia (including Babylonia) and of Syria–Palestine.

Perhaps the most obvious, if often overlooked, link between Babylonia and Mesopotamia on the one hand and Judaea on the other was that of language. Hebrew belongs to the same broad Semitic language family as Akkadian (Assyrian/Babylonian) as do other languages such as Moabitic and Ugaritic (the Canaanite language of Ras Shamra (or Ugarit); see p. 81). Akkadian was the language of Babylon in the first millennium BC, and the diplomatic language whereby a Palestinian ruler of the fourteenth century BC wrote to his Egyptian overlord, as we can see from the Amarna letters, a diplomatic archive from Egypt (*Making*, pp. 20–4). By the eighth century BC another Semitic language had taken its place as the language of diplomacy. This was Aramaic, the language of the Aramaeans who had pressed into the lands of the Fertile Crescent from the Syrian desert as early as the second millennium BC. Some of these wanderers settled, after some time in the south, near the Persian Gulf. The Babylonians called them Chaldaeans. Their language was spread through the Crescent by Assyrian and Babylonian conquest, and by merchants; its use as a lingua franca among educated classes is illustrated by 2 Kings 18:26 (cp. Isa. 36:11) and by the Aramaic portions of Ezra and Daniel. It remained the means of communication throughout the Babylonian and Persian periods, but after the conquests of

Alexander, it was replaced in the west by Greek, though Aramaic remained the mother tongue of Jewish people both in Babylonia and Palestine.

The point in history which marks our starting-point for considering the Jews in Babylonia and Mesopotamia is the Exile, and some reaction to this experience can be clearly seen in the Old Testament. Psalm 137 reflects the sadness and bitterness of captives, but such live literature probably misleads us if we take it to be true of subsequent generations; their attitude conformed more to the spirit of Jer. 29:4–9, especially verse 7: 'Seek the welfare of any city to which I have carried you off, and pray to the LORD for it; on its welfare your welfare will depend.' Although the book of Jeremiah promises, as a reward for obedience to this injunction, an early return to the land of Israel, and later generations regarded it with reverence as the true home of the people, very few entertained any real intention of returning thither. As in the modern world, so then and at other periods and in other parts of the Diaspora, Jews included both those who were surprised when any of their number took seriously the idea of Return, and also a tiny minority who made not only the journey but also the immense mental effort involved in the necessary uprooting and new beginning. As in the twentieth century, so then there was an increasing number who spoke no word of the motherland's tongue, but only that of the country where they had been born or at least spent their youth. Thus, in the perhaps largely idealized scene of covenant renewal in Neh. 8:1–8, the necessary explanation of the Law may have involved use of Aramaic, the native tongue of by far the majority of the congregation, and the language which became the usual method of communication for the whole nation for centuries to come, the native tongue of Jesus and of Paul, as of the Christian churches which arose in a Jewish background.

The Cyrus Cylinder (*DOTT*, pp. 92–4; *Making*, pp. 17–18; C. M. Jones, CBC *Old Testament Illustrations*, pp. 94–5), using cuneiform Akkadian, describes the state of affairs in Babylonia at the time of Cyrus from the conqueror's point of view. The god Marduk was moved to compassion at habitations in ruins and the population of Sumer and Akkad 'like men dead', and 'he called Cyrus, king of Anshan ... to be ruler of all'. The god enabled Cyrus to take Babylon without a battle and end the power of Nabonidus, who did not revere Marduk. Cyrus 'sought daily to worship him'. He returned the gods of a number of cities and regions to 'their places and housed them in lasting abodes' and 'gathered their inhabitants and restored (to them) their dwellings'. Cyrus ends by expressing the hope that 'all the gods whom I have placed within their sanctuaries' will 'address a daily prayer in my favour before Bel and Nabu', and pray on his behalf and that of his house to Marduk.

The Jews are not mentioned, but the Cylinder is evidence for Cyrus' general policy which no doubt embraced them. Furthermore, some of the Aramaic material in Ezra 4:8 – 6:18 and 7:12–26 may preserve decrees promulgated under subsequent kings specifically for the Jewish people; the tone of this material is exemplified by Ezra 7:11–26, purporting to be a letter from Artaxerxes to Ezra. In it 'the God of heaven' is referred to with great respect, as the correct deity for Israelites to worship, but without any suggestion that he was the God for the Persians or their kings. The Cylinder suggests that Cyrus would have thought in the same way, and that it is unlikely that he would have proclaimed that 'the LORD the God of heaven has given me all the kingdoms of the earth' (2 Chron. 36:23; Ezra 1:2), since he attributed this action to Marduk, except perhaps, as a political gesture, in a document intended especially for Jews.

We have already seen (p. 2) that according to the biblical text just quoted the exiles were invited to volunteer to return, with the king's support, and that it is a fair inference that only a small party actually did so. This view is supported by evidence from Josephus. In *Ant.* XI.5.1–2 (121–38) he describes the letter to Ezra from the king (Xerxes in Josephus, Artaxerxes in Ezra 7:11–26 and 1 Esdras 8:8–24) which permitted and encouraged the Return, and he describes also the effect upon those to whom it was read. These latter were the Jews who were in the city of Babylon at the time, and a copy was sent to their fellow-countrymen 'in Media' (here a general term for the territory between the Caspian Sea and the Persian Gulf and central to the Persian Empire – see map p. xvii). It is clear that those who wished to return were given encouragement for what everyone knew would be a rough and dangerous journey, and Josephus expressly states that the people of the Israelites as a whole stayed in their places. He goes on to say that this is why there are two tribes in Asia and Europe subject to the Romans, and 'ten tribes beyond the Euphrates until now, countless myriads which cannot

be known by number'. A little later he expressly includes those
Israelites who remained in Babylon among those who contributed
to the expenses of the expedition. It is probably safe to assume that
in the course of time the lives and movements of these Babylonian
Jews took the forms which we know to be true of their descendants; and this included service in the armies of the countries to
which, in spite of ethnic difference, they did belong. It is not
surprising that as we approach nearer to Josephus' own day we find
Babylonian Jews figuring in his history with greater frequency,
raising in our minds the question how far travel between the two
areas had become less hazardous.

Travel in antiquity was always more of an adventure than it
has been for some decades in modern times. Even if now there are
still alarming hazards, the percentage of long uneventful journeys
successfully concluded in a short time must be immeasurably
greater than it was in any period even of the Roman Empire.
Besides the danger from bandits, who are often mentioned, there
were the added discomforts of extremes of temperature and
weariness to an extent unimaginable by the modern traveller. But
perhaps the greatest difference between travel in the period and
areas with which we are concerned and travel today is that between the time necessary then and now. Josephus in *Ant.* III.15.3
(318) refers to the journey of pilgrims from beyond the Euphrates
as involving great dangers and expense and taking four months.
Only the strong, well-armed and bold travelled in small numbers, and the usual method was to make up a caravan. There were
well-known routes: for a journey to or from the more northerly
parts of the Parthian dominions, Antioch in Syria was an obvious
post. The route lay across desert to Zeugma on the Euphrates and
thence to Nisibis or another nearby town. An extension of this
route would lead to Adiabene. Damascus was another much-used
post in the west, connected with a route across the desert by way
of Palmyra to Dura-Europos on the Euphrates, whence south-
east to Nehardea and Ctesiphon as well as places further east (see
map p. xvii).

Contact between Jews in Babylonia and Judaea was therefore
dangerous but possible; and it increased rather than diminished
with the passage of time, as political conditions made it feasible
and religious duty prompted pilgrimages for festivals. In spite of
the hopes expressed in Isa. 40–55, no dramatic improvement in
the lot of the Jewish people took place, but there can be little

doubt that a great many of the exiles made an acceptable life for themselves in the new country. 'The waters of Babylon' consisted not only in the great river Euphrates which ran through the city, but also of canals in the province, which were irrigated by human labour but were sufficient to render the land fertile. The country was able therefore to support a growing population and diligent agriculturists could flourish. It may be also that the skilled work-people mentioned in 2 Kings 24:16 and Jer. 24:1, 29:2, or their descendants and pupils, had won for themselves a place in society and in the economy. Certainly the evidence of later years is of a growing and able population; it was increased from outside from time to time, in spite of the hazards of travel, by additions from Judaea when its population heard of the prosperity of the Babylonian settlement while they were dissatisfied with economic, social or political conditions at home. Perhaps sometimes there was the attraction of a quite new opportunity, for Babylon was the only sector of Jewry outside the hellenistic–Roman world, while those from Babylon for their part included some whose piety led them to seek permission to return to the motherland where alone, they believed, true worship could be offered.

In the area which was from the Exile onwards regarded as first the Persian and then the Parthian Empire (Persian from 539 BC, Parthian from about 140 BC), the main body of the Jewish population were in Babylonia, but there were also many in Mesopotamia. The two provinces were closely connected; the map (p. xvii) shows that Mesopotamia is the northern, Babylonia the southern, part of the land between the two great rivers Tigris and Euphrates, Mesopotamia meaning 'Between the Rivers'. In the south the main centre for Jews was the city of Nehardea on the Euphrates, on almost the same latitude as, and less than fifty miles distant from, Ctesiphon on the Tigris, the Parthian winter capital. Here the half-shekel Temple tax was collected before being taken by organized pilgrims to Jerusalem. In the north Nisibis served the same purpose; the two towns feature frequently in the history of the Jews in Josephus, and very frequently in the Talmud.

During the period from 200 to about 100 BC the background of life in both Judaea and the lands beyond the Euphrates is the decline of the Seleucid power, that is of the greatest hellenistic power, which had reflected not only the might of Alexander but also a movement towards a Greek and largely urban culture and civilization. In spite of some evidence for their admiration of this culture the Parthians were not temperamentally fitted to it, and for reasons very different from those which influenced the Jews they were its political rivals. It is against this background that we must imagine (and we have material for little more) the life of Jewry in Babylonia and Mesopotamia at this time. One feature of which we can be sure is negative. There was no rising of patriotic or religious fervour against either Seleucid or Parthian by the Jews of these eastern lands. The probability is that Jews served in the armies conscripted from the localities in which they lived; they had opportunity for nothing else, and made no effort to assist any Hasmonaean leader. On the other hand, we discern no sign of appreciation or liking for any of the nations which held the supremacy in the lands where they lived. The prophet of the Exile known as the Second Isaiah could regard Cyrus as the servant of the Lord anointed for the task of delivering his people, but he shows no personal liking for him, nor inclination to give him political support. His theology is far from universalist; all that he hoped would happen would be the work of the God of heaven, the only real God, and for the sake of his people, that is the Jews, and only for them. No word of appreciation or thanks towards Cyrus appears in his writings or in the works of the Chronicler.

It was no particular love for the Jewish people, but rather opposition to Rome, which led to the Parthian support for the last Hasmonaean king Antigonus Mattathias, who reigned with their help from 40 to 37 BC. Antigonus was the son of Aristobulus II, brother and rival of Hyrcanus II, who was at this time in uneasy alliance with Herod. It was now that the Parthians captured Herod's brother Phasael along with Hyrcanus II (p. 97). Phasael committed suicide, but King Phraates IV (40–3 BC) treated Hyrcanus well, and the latter lived among the Babylonian Jews until Herod persuaded him to return to Judaea, secretly plotting to kill him. Herod had now become king and he appointed as high priest a Babylonian Jew named Hananel. Herod deposed him in favour of his own brother-in-law Aristobulus III in 36 BC, but reappointed him after contriving the murder of Aristobulus in 35 or 34 (*Ant.* xv.2.1–3.3 (11–56)). Hananel, like so many others, depended on Herod's favour for his position, and Josephus describes him as an obscure person, suggesting that Herod was reluctant to appoint anyone illustrious; but later Josephus describes him as of high-priestly rank. Since Herod was seeking the goodwill of the Jews at the time of the original appointment, it may be that Hananel was connected with the ancient high-priestly family. In the Mishnah, Par. 3:5, he is apparently mentioned as a high priest who had prepared a red heifer (for a brief explanation of the latter see J. Sturdy, CBC *Numbers*, p. 134), but in the Mishnah passage he is called Hanamel and 'the Egyptian'.

Herod was not unsuccessful in wooing the Babylonian Jews; some were in his army after immigration from Babylonia, and a specially interesting glimpse of this part of Herod's policy is afforded by Josephus when he tells the story of the men of Bathyra (*Ant.* XVII.2.1–2 (23–8)) who figure also in the Talmud. To secure his territory in the north-east on the boundary with Trachonitis, Herod gave 'a village not less in size than a city' to a Jew from Babylonia who commanded 500 horse-archers, in the adjoining Batanaea. These men were evidently intended to act as a kind of private army, since the gift of land was made free of tribute, and in accepting Herod's invitation they built a fortress, calling the village associated with it Bathyra. It is tempting to guess that these warlike Jews had received their training under the Parthians and had learnt their particular form of fighting from them. The community became important in a different sphere of history, for descendants of the original settlers supplied chiefs of the sanhedrin, and later representatives of them settled at Jamnia where they were sometimes opponents of Johanan b. Zakkai on points of halakhic interpretation (p. 120). It is possible but not certain that the famous Hillel was one of them, for he is known to have come from Babylon about this time (p. 190).

It was a little later that the Jewish people had, according to Josephus' story, some influence on the struggle between Parthia and Rome (*Ant.* XX.2.1–4.3 (17–96)). The exact chronology is impossible to establish but Josephus tells of the conversion of the ruling house of Adiabene to Judaism in the early years of the first century AD. Adiabene was a relatively small vassal kingdom within the Parthian Empire, on the eastern bank of the Tigris north of the Lesser Zab river, and containing the ancient Nineveh and Arbela within it, the latter city being its capital (see map p. xvii). Shorn of legendary and pious propagandist decoration, the main facts are these: the king Monobazus I had by his wife Helena two sons, the first his own namesake and the second Izates, who is the hero of the story along with his mother as the heroine. Izates was the favourite of his father and suffered from the jealousy of half-brothers, sons of the king by other wives. As Josephus tells the story Monobazus I and Izates were loyal and kindly to one another. The king sent Izates away from this jealousy to live at the court of the king of the territory round Spasinou Charax at the head of the Persian Gulf. There Izates grew up happily and was given lands on which to subsist, besides the king's daughter in marriage; in due course he returned home, and Monobazus I installed him in Harran. On his father's death, with the help of his mother and nobles at the court, he obtained the throne of Adiabene, temporarily ousting Monobazus II his elder brother.

During his time in Spasinou Charax a Jewish merchant named Ananias converted to Judaism some of the women in the king's entourage and then converted Izates. On his return home Izates took Ananias with him and found that his mother Helena had just been converted by a Jew in Adiabene. He appears to have acted with some skill in anticipating opposition to his kingship, sending some of his brothers as hostages to the Parthian court and some to Rome, thus securing their absence as rivals and the goodwill of the two powers which a small kingdom in that area had to fear. It was also perhaps a diplomatic caution which prevented him from taking the final step as a convert and accepting circumcision, his mother urging this caution in her fear that his subjects would not wish to have a Jew for a king. It is remarkable indeed how Josephus includes in his narrative features which have been characteristic of Jewish people throughout history: confidence in their own moral and spiritual superiority combined with a realistic assessment of their lack of popularity with other races. Ananias agreed with Izates' decision, assuring him that he could worship the true God without circumcision so long as he showed himself zealous for Judaism, for this was more important than being circumcised. Later however Izates submitted to circumcision on the insistence of a Jew from Galilee named Eleazar.

Helpfully for subsequent historians doing their best to supply these events with a chronology, no less a person than Artabanus II of Parthia now appears on the scene, in the somewhat unexpected guise of a suppliant, seeking the help of Izates after being driven from his throne by rebellious satraps. Izates received him and restored him to his throne (though it is not clear how). Artabanus rewarded him with some territory at the expense of Armenia, the territory known as Nisibis, previously a Macedonian city with the name of Antioch. 'Not long after this' Artabanus died and was succeeded by his son Vardanes; we have therefore apparently reached the year AD 38/39. Vardanes, unsuccessful in persuading Izates to join him in a war against Rome, declared war on him, but before any actual hostilities began was replaced through a popular uprising by his brother Gotarzes II (38/39–51). The latter was succeeded by another brother Vologeses I in 51, according to Josephus, but it may rather be that this Vologeses was the son of a short-lived usurper Vonones II (51). Vologeses delegated government to his brothers, placing Pacorus over Media and Tiridates over Armenia (*Ant.* xx.3.4 (74)).

Izates of Adiabene, in spite of Josephus' contention that his Judaistic piety ensured him success and happiness, endured two plots against him towards the end of his reign, when his nobles plotted first wih an Arabian king and then with Vologeses to overthrow him, wishing on the second occasion to replace him with a Parthian. But Vologeses, though he advanced on Adiabene, was forced to retire through hearing of raids on his kingdom by the Dacae and Sacae from the north. Soon after this Izates died and was succeeded by his brother Monobazus II. This apparently long-suffering elder brother showed his respect for Izates and their mother, who died soon after her son, by having their bones buried in Jerusalem under three pyramids which Helena had had built.

Josephus claims that God rewarded Izates for his conversion by preserving him and his sons from various dangers, and that it was delight at her son's success through piety that led Helena to make a pilgrimage to Jerusalem, where she found a famine which she and Izates did much to relieve. Later Josephus (xx.5.2 (101)) dates this famine specifically as that in the procuratorship of Tiberius Alexander, i.e. 46–8, the famine referred to in Acts 11:28. How far this chronology may be trusted is not clear, although no other dates which we know concerning Izates and Helena contradict it. His accession evidently occurred before the death of Artabanus II in 38 and he survived the threat of invasion by Vologeses I in 51. We know that he died before 61 when his brother Monobazus II suffered an invasion by Tigranes of Armenia. The goodwill and reverence shown by Izates and Helena towards Jerusalem were very genuine. According to Talmudic references Helena was an observant orthodox Jewess after her conversion, taking Nazirite vows and making many donations to religious buildings and their decorations. In Yoma 3:10 the king associated with her is Monobazus II (cp. MYom. 3:10; MNaz. 3:6; ySuk. 1:51d; bSuk. 2b).

The three pyramids mentioned by Josephus (see above) in connexion with the mausoleum may have been the form taken by the roof, like the single pyramid roofing the 'Tomb of Zechariah' in the Kidron valley. The identification of the tomb of Helena with that for years called 'The Tombs of the Kings' near the junction of the Nablus and Saleddin roads north of Jerusalem is not universally accepted, but seems to be assumed by Yadin in *Jerusalem Revealed* (p. 18).

One other episode of Babylonian Jewish history has been preserved by Josephus (*Ant.* XVIII.9.1–9 (310–79)). It is difficult to date but again it is one connected with Artabanus II (12–38) and has usually been placed in the twenties of the first century AD. Two Jewish brothers, weavers by trade, named Asinaeus and Anilaeus, who lived in Nehardea, driven to lawlessness by their employer-mother's nagging and blows, began to operate a 'protection racket', imposing taxes on local shepherds and gathering a considerable number of followers. They defeated the governor of Babylonia who attacked them on a sabbath, and Artabanus was compelled to make some arrangement with them which meant that they controlled large areas of Babylonia. How far their guerilla warfare would have developed into a politically stable situation is an idle guess, because they quarrelled with one another with fatal results.

The occasion of the brothers' quarrel was a Parthian wife taken by Anilaeus; this woman had been the wife of a Parthian killed in battle, and as a captive wife should according to Jewish law have undergone prescribed cleansing ceremonies and been thus received into the community (Deut. 21:10–14), but she continued with Anilaeus' connivance to worship her ancestral idols in their house. This scandalized his fellow-Jews, who prevailed upon Asinaeus to remonstrate with his brother. His pleas to Anilaeus to dismiss the erring wife were repulsed and followed by his own death, giving rise to the suspicion that his sister-in-law had poisoned him. Anilaeus added to his own troubles by making an enemy of Mithradates, son-in-law of the king, by humiliating him after capturing him. On his release Mithradates took his revenge by a successful attack in which many of Anilaeus' men were killed.

From this time the activities of this remaining brother, Anilaeus, were much more those of the brigandage which for Josephus had always characterized both brothers. Anilaeus was finally killed by gentile Babylonians in a surprise attack. According to the historian, these events gave a terrible impetus to the always potentially great animosity to the Jews of other nations in the area. A bitter persecution forced Jews from many different parts of Babylonia to take refuge in Seleucia, where their welcome from the local residents did not long survive attacks by the Greek element who, originally at enmity with the native population, brought them over to their side. Five years after their coming to Seleucia the Jewish refugees suffered another massacre and some of them escaped to Ctesiphon. Nehardea remained a bastion and a refuge, and archaeology has supplied evidence of persisting Jewish life in the west, as at Edessa and Dura-Europos.

The site of Dura-Europos, known since 1898 and excavated from 1920 onwards, was a frontier fortress (Dura means fortress), founded about 300 BC by Nicanor, probably the known General of Seleucus I, and settled by soldiers. The site is on a barren plateau 100 feet above the river plain, a position from which much territory could be patrolled, close to the centre of the caravan route from Antioch, western capital of the Seleucid Empire, to its eastern capital, Seleucia. The Parthians took Seleucia in 141 BC and established a new frontier along the Euphrates, capturing Dura-Europos in 113. From 50 BC to AD 100 there was much building, including temples of different religions. The Parthian rule was interrupted by Trajan's campaign in AD 115 but re-established about 121. The synagogue there, rich in decoration, is due to rebuilding in AD 243–4 and incorporates an older smaller building, whose original date is uncertain, but which witnesses to the presence of the Jews from the early years of the Christian era.

Babylonian Jewry and the Books of the Old Testament

The sparse narratives of the destruction of Jerusalem make it hard to imagine that the exiles took with them any rolls of leather or papyrus on which were written the material destined to become sacred scripture, but it is probable that a full record in some form of what so far ranked as authoritative was taken into Babylon by those with a scribal training. During and following the period of the Exile not only were records of recent experience made; there also took place a great process of editing older documents. A great deal was stored in men's memories and was now perhaps for the first time written down, beginning its double existence as both oral and written tradition. Much of this was interpreted in the light of the Exile, viewed as divine punishment. There is no absolute certainty about where this writing and editing took place, but many scholars regard Babylon as virtually certain for at least the final formation of many Old Testament books. Important examples include the Deuteronomic history, a highly composite and comprehensive but 'single history written in the style and from the theological perspective of Deuteronomy' and containing Deuteronomy, Joshua, Judges, 1 and 2 Samuel, and 1 and 2 Kings (see Miller and Tucker, CBC *Joshua*, pp. 2–6). The same is true of the book of Ezekiel and most of Isa. 34–5, 36–9, 40–66.

With regard to the Priestly recension of the Pentateuch, all would admit the difficulty of ruling out Palestine altogether, but many would be confident that it was carried out in Babylon. However, Porter (CBC *Leviticus*, pp. 4–6) argues attractively for the view 'that the priestly work was a result of the united priesthood, formed between the old Jerusalem priests when they returned from Babylonia and the priests from other Israelite shrines who had replaced them during the exile, and that its background is Jerusalem from the period of Haggai and Zechariah onwards'. Such cooperation would be a signal example of reciprocal influence between Babylon and Jerusalem, foreshadowing that which became an integral part of the development of Judaism within our period of 200 BC to AD 200.

Again it is probable, though not certain, that Babylon saw the final formation of the collections of records and memories of ancient and more recent prophets which gave us, for example, the books of Amos, Hosea, Isaiah and Micah.

The Persian period itself (with the Seleucid period, 539–140 BC) is reflected in stories afterwards written up in Esther and Daniel. The Parthian period (i.e. from *c.* 140 BC onwards) seems at first sight not to provide any very obvious examples; but the Persian story of Esther, current in various forms (see Fuerst in Dancy, CBC *Shorter Books of the Apocrypha*, pp. 132–8), seems to have received the form by which it is known to us some time after 180 BC, the date of Ben Sira, who does not know it; and Daniel virtually dates itself to 165 BC. Among shorter books, Tobit seems to have been written in Judaea but the scene of the story is laid in the Jewish colony in Media, although the author of the form of it which we have did not know the geography of Media. The tale may therefore have originated from somewhere in the Parthian Empire some time in the later third century BC or even later, and passed through many changes. Something similar may be said of the book of Judith, whose story was told in many versions and settings; that in our Apocrypha suits Maccabaean Judaea, but the villain Holophernes is an Assyrian not a Seleucid. Corresponding features in the Additions to Daniel are obvious; for example, the opening of Bel and the Snake proclaims its pro-Persian and anti-Babylonian outlook, while that of Daniel and Susanna firmly places its story in Babylon. (See Dancy, CBC *The Shorter Books of the Apocrypha*.) Variations and additions, often made to suit local needs, invite speculation about the exact milieux which produced this variety. Teaching was almost synonymous with the handing on of tradition. While this often took the form of repeating old material faithfully, it might receive a sort of commentary or *midrash*. This midrash could take a legalistic form (*halakah*) where this was appropriate, or a story-telling form (*haggadah*). (See further p. 196.) It is a reasonable guess that such teaching, including story-telling, often took place in the synagogue, a statement true whether here 'synagogue' means 'assembly' or the building provided for such assembly (p. 146).

ASIA MINOR

This large area of land, sometimes called by the general name of Anatolia and constituting Asiatic Turkey, indeed the larger part of that country, was in antiquity divided among a number of nations, some remaining remote from even their neighbours by reason of geographical boundaries and features such as difficult mountain ranges and waterless areas. To trace the history of these areas lies beyond our task; it must suffice to make a quick survey of the west to the east (see map p. xviii). The west coast, along with many islands associated with it, had received before 700 BC many Greek settlements and constituted the Ionian Greeks. They comprised the relatively small and yet scattered collection of cities and city-states which seemed to mainland Greeks to lie on the edge of the barbarian world to the east, and which provided the western world with the beginnings of its intellectual heritage. Such a flowering may have at least in some places benefited from partly unwilling fertilization by the oriental, including the Semitic, world. It is certain that here Greek and 'barbarian' lived close to one another, especially in the states of Mysia, Lydia, Asia (later to give its name to the whole land mass of Anatolia and afterwards to the whole eastern continent), Caria and Lycia – to name the western countries from north to south.

Herodotus of Halicarnassus in Caria (*c.* 484–424) was a Greek of this kind. His history opens with a short passage about the Trojan War, in which the legendary element swamps whatever there is of the rest, and passes on to describe the kingdom of Lydia in a manner which allows history to begin to predominate without leaving legend entirely behind. The kingdom of the Mermnad dynasty is the first empire to receive mention from a western historian, and its story comes to a climax with the episode concerning Croesus (*c.* 560–546), the king whose fabled wealth was even greater than the real. His true importance is that he lost his empire to Cyrus of Persia (pp. 9f.), that he is regarded by Herodotus as the first foreigner with whom the Greeks (i.e. properly civilized people) came into contact, and that his story leads into description of the at first remoter and much mightier empire of Persia. From this time onwards Persian history is interwoven with that of the Greeks.

Mysia is remarkable for embracing the Troad, the north-western corner of Asia Minor, which was the starting-point for travellers venturing like Paul from Asia into Europe; it contains also the ancient city of Pergamum, like Sardis a centre of culture. It attained the status of a kingdom when Attalus proclaimed himself king in 230 BC. He had inherited the leadership in 241 from his uncle Eumenes, who had gained independence from the Seleucid state in 263. It was annexed by Rome in 133, the last king Attalus III (138–133) having left it by will to the Romans.

Lydian territory extended in its heyday as far as the river Halys and thus embraced the Phrygians, whose territory was next to Lydia on the east. But the enduring importance of this rather short-lived empire is that its capital Sardis flourished as a centre of learning. Herodotus tells us credibly of the Greek wise men who visited it, including Solon the Athenian. Phrygia shared the central plateau of Asia Minor with Cappadocia to the east. Phrygia was once an extensive territory, from the time of its conquest by European Phryges at the end of the second millennium. Later it lost parts on the west to Lydia and on the north through the incursions of Mysians and Bithynians from Europe. After the Lydian conquest it was never again independent. In 116 BC most of its land became part of the Roman province of Asia, and in 25 BC the remainder was absorbed into the province of Galatia, but its peoples were influential through the persistent practice of a popular religion. Their language survived into the Byzantine period and Diocletian made Phrygia a separate province. On the north the warlike Bithynia and Pontus, made into a joint province by Pompey, bordered on the Black Sea. Pontus was closely associated with Cappadocia, which originally was regarded as including the Pontic territory, but after the rise of the Mithradatic kings of Pontus in the fourth century BC, it was reduced to a still large area to the south of it, consisting of an inaccessible plateau and volcanic ranges. Cappadocia contributed directly to Judaean history through its king Archelaus who as a vassal under the Romans from 36 BC to AD 17 provides a parallel with Herod the Great of Judaea. They were friends, Archelaus' daughter Glaphyra being married to Herod's son Alexander (whom Herod killed in 7 BC), and later to another son Archelaus, namesake of her father, who succeeded Herod. Alexander and Glaphyra had two sons, one of whom was Tigranes, one of those oriental nobles who through force of circumstances spent much time at Rome. It was he whom Nero sent to take possession of Armenia in AD 63 (Tacitus, *Ann.* 14.26; (see p. 18)).

South-west of Pontus and north-west of (southern) Cappadocia lay the land of Galatia, populated by Celts who had crossed the Hellespont in 278 BC and who had been confined at last to this territory in 230 by Attalus of Pergamum. This was the ancient Galatia. Amyntas, their last king, not unlike Herod in the way he survived changes of fortune among the rivals for Roman power after the murder of Julius Caesar, was killed in 25 BC. He left his kingdom to Rome, and Augustus, passing over his sons, made of it a province with the addition of Pisidia and Lycaonia to the south, part of Phrygia to the south-west and of Pontus to the north. South of Cappadocia lay Cilicia, in the south-east corner of Asia Minor and a natural partner for Syria (with which it makes as it were a rough right angle embracing the north-east corner of the Mediterranean Sea). From 44 BC Syria, from the Roman point of view, included at least the eastern part of Cilicia, and the two territories are closely associated in Acts 15:23, 41 and Gal. 1:21, in the latter by Paul who was born in Tarsus, the capital of Cilicia. To complete the link with the Fertile Crescent we have but to mention that the land of Cappadocia shared a frontier and much history with Armenia, which has figured in our sketch of Parthian history and especially in disputes between Parthia and Rome.

To this rapid survey, designed to tempt the reader to look at the map of this lesser known part of the world (p. xviii), we may add the unexpected kingdom of the Bosporus, a vassal of Rome after the fall in 63 BC of Pontus to which it had originally belonged. It consisted of territory on the north shore of the Black Sea, including the Crimea and a tract of country on the opposite side of the strait separating the Sea of Azov from the Black Sea (i.e., to give their ancient names, separating Lake Mareotis from the Euxine or Pontus Euxinus). This strait was the Cimmerian Bosporus, while the strait separating the Sea of Marmora (Propontis) from the Black Sea was the Thracian Bosporus. The word was explained by the Greeks themselves as derived from *boos poros* ('ox-ford'), though the explanation seems doubtful; it is used also of other straits, including the Hellespont. The ancient Greek name for the Crimea was Chersonesus which means peninsula and is therefore found applied to other places also. The Crimea was sometimes distinguished from them by the half-Latin name of Chersonesus Taurica.

There is ample evidence for the presence of Jews in these lands from the Seleucid period onwards. For the collection and onward transmission of the Temple tax four cities are known: Apamea in Phrygia, Laodicea in Asia, Pergamum and the port of Adramyttium in Mysia. Cicero (*Pro Flacco* 68) tells of Flaccus, proconsul of Asia 62–61, forbidding the export of the money from Asia, mentioning Laodicea, Adramyttium and Pergamum in this connexion. There appear to have been Jews in Sardis from an earlier time, as is implied by a grave inscription apparently belonging to the year 349 BC. Interesting for our purpose is the account in Josephus (*Ant.* XII.3.4 (147–53)) of Antiochus III's transportation from Babylon of a number of Jews with their families to settle in Phrygia in order to help the satrap of Lydia against unrest in his satrapy. The Jews are spoken of in glowing terms and their way of life and piety seems in the king's eyes to be matched only by their loyalty to himself. Their strict piety – even allowing for exaggeration – is perhaps a point in favour of the theory which suggests that the arrival of these Jews in Phrygia explains the existence at Colossae of the Essene heresy which was contested in the Letter to the Colossians (2:9–23). They are held to be evidence for a movement towards a stricter adherence to the Law among the exiles, a movement which later manifested itself in different times and localities as Essenes of various kinds, including those at Qumran (p. 172).

Various items of evidence (including those in the New Testament) testify therefore to the presence of Jews in virtually all of the lands mentioned in our rapid look at Asia Minor. As an interesting example of non-literary evidence we may cite from the kingdom of the Bosporus an inscription recording the manumission (i.e. setting free) of a slave which evidently took place in a synagogue. The manner of it suggests that the model for the procedure was that in a pagan temple, though the presiding deity to whom the inscription is formally addressed is 'the Highest, Almighty, Blessed'. Such chance evidence is supplemented by fragments of pottery, coins or weights discovered in Palestine which came from other lands including the Ionian islands, suggesting commerce which no doubt meant the passing to and fro of Jews as well as Gentiles. Philo (p. 140) offers evidence, hardly needed, for the presence of Jews in such large islands as not only Crete and Cyprus, but also Euboea nearer the Greek mainland. In the mainland of Greece the considerable number of cities in which Jews were living in our period is evidenced by the travels of Paul, and inscriptions show their presence there at least two centuries earlier than his visits. Although Herod was not a Jew, his patronage of and gifts to Athens (as to Pergamum and other cities) remind us once more of the constant and continuous operation of forces which brought peoples of very different characteristics and traditions into the same 'world' of discourse and commerce, the world which began with Alexander's conquests. Greeks can thereby see a successful Idumaean adventurer as a hellenistic prince, and Jerusalem as a city-state.

3. Italy: Rome and the Jews

The arm flung out westwards from our imaginary crescent has passed through Asia Minor into the Greek islands and mainland. If it is extended further westwards into Italy we still find that Jews are present among the different peoples. In Italy Rome stands out as supremely important and it could be argued that from about the middle of the second century BC the history of the Jews is inseparable from the history of Rome.

Our next task therefore is to outline the history of Rome during the four centuries with which we are concerned. It is convenient to begin the period from 264 BC, when Rome became master of all Italy, and to end it with a brief reference to the reorganization of the now widespread empire by the emperor Diocletian (AD 284–305), which marked the beginning of a new political era.

THE ROMAN CONSTITUTION

One of Rome's most distinctive, perhaps most valuable, bequests to posterity is her well articulated if rather complex constitution. In a past upon whose history a heavy accretion of legend had already adhered in classical times, Rome had been ruled by kings. In the later times, still those of classical Roman history, their overthrow was regarded as an essential, creative and archetypal liberation, so that even to seem to aspire to anything like kingly rule met with bitter and automatic hostility.

It was far otherwise with the ancient council of the kings, the senate, which survived the dismissal of the tyrants with honour. The origin of the distinction within this council of elders (which is the meaning of senate) between patricians (leading families) and plebeians (of the people) is as hard to explain as the idea is easy to understand. The patrician senators were called *patres* (fathers), the plebeian *conscripti* (enrolled ones), so that a speaker addressing them as *patres conscripti* originally meant 'fathers and enrolled members' rather than 'enrolled fathers'.

The senate put forward names for the *comitia* (assembled people) to elect two as *consuls* each year, it becoming quite early established as law that at least one must be a plebeian. The consuls were the supreme magistrates, originally military, and after holding office were qualified to govern a province as *legatus* (legate), *praefectus* (prefect) or *procurator*. They were the eponymous officers of Rome, that is, the year in which they held office was designated by their names. Legate was originally the general word for an ambassador or deputy, especially of a military supreme commander or of a provincial governor. Later, besides wider uses, it denoted especially the commander of a legion (who was also the governor of a province if it housed only one legion). In imperial times it was used for the governor (on behalf of the emperor) of a province.

There was a recognized series of steps to the consulship (the *cursus honorum* or, very literally, course of honours), the pattern of which varied only slightly down the ages. Generally it was from *quaestor* (whose duties were mainly financial administration) to *praetor* (administering justice in Rome or a province, often wielding great power, especially when taking sole charge of a situation in the absence or through the instructions of a superior such as consul or proconsul or legate); and from *praetor* to *consul*. At various periods it was necessary, and always possible, to include in the cursus the step of being an *aedilis* (aedile), either before or after being quaestor. An aedile originally looked after a temple but his scope was much widened under the Republic, so that a number of aediles supervised public buildings, water-supply and archives. From quaestor onwards the official was a senator.

Side by side with this structure, originally over against it, stood the ten tribunes of the people (*tribuni plebis*). Thus giving them their full title distinguishes them from the *tribuni militum*, tribunes who were important officers of the legions. The tribunes (of the people unless otherwise stated) were the constitutionally provided defenders of the people; their basic right was to veto any action by a magistrate. They also convened the *comitia* from whom they obtained decisions (often after suggesting actions which they left no doubt they would themselves recommend) and had absolute power to enforce them. Several crises led to attempts to curtail their powers, but from the first century BC tribunes became senators, and their great influence with the people made them always, and now more than ever, formidable.

In the troubled times which dissolved the Republic, aspirants to leadership showed their grasp of the importance of the tribunate, and it became one of the offices desirable to hold under the principate or Empire.

City-states usually show constitutional features which reflect their organization for war. The *equites* were originally the Roman cavalry but formed also part of the *comitia*, and, being by 200 BC less effective as cavalry, remained a distinctive element in the social and political structure. In the army their place was taken by auxiliary troops, the *auxilia*, or troops enlisted from outside Italy and supplying light infantry as well as cavalry. Socially and politically the *equites* remained a group from which officers and staff of governors were drawn, a stratum of society entered with increasing ease by qualifications of wealth or connexions with good families such as wealth often wins. With the enfranchisement of Italy their numbers were much increased. Their characteristic abilities were financial and administrative, allied only occasionally to political ambition. Usually *equites* were content to assist and to be rewarded by the ambitious, although they could enter the senate when they wished (though they could not easily become consuls), and they often intermarried with senatorial families.

The term *equites* has in the past frequently been translated as 'knights', which is accurate only in so far as that term means 'horsemen' and only for the earlier time when the *equites* were cavalry. Since it is otherwise misleading it is better to use the Latin word untranslated. The singular noun is *eques*.

During the period of the Republic the power of the senate, whose formal task was to advise magistrates, was in fact immense. It could for example in time of crisis appoint a *dictator*, a temporary office to ensure concentration of the national effort, lasting at the most six months. The senate also decided on war or peace (though formal declaration of war was the privilege of the *comitia*), received foreign ambassadors, decided the character and extent of the work of magistrates and officials, and could cancel legislation already formed by demonstrating its inconsistency with the constitution. Composed as it was of men who had acquired or were acquiring experience of government, the senate when true to its traditional constitutional role enjoyed immense prestige. Even in the time of the Empire there were prolonged periods when it could have continued to be the pivot of

government, as under part of the reign of Tiberius and under
Claudius, but it lost, understandably enough, the will to do so. At
other times it could only carry out the emperor's sometimes
capricious and selfish policies. Disagreement with the emperor
could mean death (as for example under Caius, Nero and Commodus). Its value as a meeting-place of minds, sometimes very
able, and as a repository of wisdom and experience, is witnessed
to by the fact that though as an instrument of government it
became at times a mere cipher it never ceased to exist.

The Triumph. It was one of the powers of the senate under the
Republic to grant to an individual victorious general a triumph.
This was a basically religious procession, by a prescribed route
through the city to the temple of Jupiter Capitolinus, of the
magistrates, the senate, the spoils of the war concerned which
included important captives, followed by sacrificial animals, the
triumphator (the victorious general) in a chariot with a slave holding a crown over him and murmuring 'apotropaic' words (i.e.
words to turn away the wrath of the gods at any apparent mortal
arrogance), and the general's army, necessary to show that the
war was won. Other necessities were a victory over a foreign
enemy (at least 5,000 killed) by a magistrate who had been given
an *imperium* (supreme authority of a particular office and over the
sphere attached to that office) and his own *auspicia* (i.e. right and
duty to take the auspices, that is to discover by prescribed divina-
tion the divine favour or warning). Rules concerning the qualifications of persons and circumstances for a triumph were in time
relaxed, and in the Empire became the monopoly of the emperor
and his family (with his permission).

The ideal Rome was therefore a structure in which both oligarchy and democracy featured and sometimes at least operated
together in harmony; ideally experience and superior intelligence
advised, people decided, both acted for the whole. Thus a decision of the state was a *senatus consultum* (decree of the senate),
often abbreviated, as on coins, to s.c.; and the famous standards of
the legions carried the initials S.P.Q.R. which stood for *senatus
populusque Romanus* ('senate and people of Rome', linking senate
and people with an idiomatically close 'and'). The Roman system
of government lent itself to its own self-destruction under the
blows which it endured at the end of the Republic, and much of
its operation was too often inhumane to the point of cruelty. But

there is a positive side to its story, that is, to its constant operation by a countless number of lesser officials, most of whose names have passed into oblivion and many of whom administered a civilization which, even its keen critics had to admit, secured for them more fully than any other the world had known before the possibilities of art, industry, commerce and development. Such minor officials often caused surprise by their benevolence towards their subject peoples which is implied in inscriptions or chance reminiscences in literature. Neither the benevolence nor the surprise it evoked are strange to us: the gospels record more than once the congenial character of centurions and the surprise of Jesus when he met it (e.g. Luke 7:1–10).

ROME: OUTLINE OF HISTORY 264 BC TO AD 284

I. *The Rise and Decline of the Roman Republic*

By 264 BC Rome had become an entity transcending by her power and widening outlook the city-state from which she had expanded. She had done so by conquest and by a genius for organization and road-building. She now faced the Carthaginians in her own sphere of the western Mediterranean and in the hellenistic world in the east. She was soon to come into contact with the Parthian Empire (pp. 16–19) further east. By 202 the power of Carthage had been destroyed, and Rome had gained Sicily, Sardinia and Spain. The great Carthaginian general Hannibal escaped to the east in 202 and took refuge with Antiochus III of Syria. Africa was added to the empire in 146. It was limited at first to part of Tunisia and never extended far to the south, where the desert offered a natural boundary; but it was to become under Augustus a large province stretching from Libya to Morocco.

A Gallic invasion had been broken in 225. The northern frontier was secure through this success and through the pacification of tribes in what we should now call northern Italy. The district then consisted of Cisalpine Gaul ('Gaul this side, i.e. south, of the Alps') and the peoples on its flanks, including Venetia and Istria at the head of the Adriatic, and even the Dalmatian coast (see map p. xx).

This extension to the east coast of the Adriatic reflects the conquest of Illyricum. Inevitably there followed confrontation with Philip V of Macedon (221–179) and Antiochus III of Syria

(223–187), both allies of Hannibal. Against these kings, Rhodes and Pergamum invited the intervention of the Romans, who were at first content to curb the might of Antiochus by the Peace of Apamea (p. 13) and to annex no territory. Macedonian restlessness, continuing under Philip's son and successor Perseus (179–168), led eventually in 146 to Macedonia becoming a province. By 146 Corinth was destroyed and the Achaean Confederacy had been defeated. Greece was from henceforth, under forms which changed only slightly and never significantly, entirely subject to Rome, whose authority was accepted also by such hellenistic kingdoms as Pergamum (bequeathed by King Attalus in 133 to Rome), Rhodes, Bithynia and Galatia. Thus by 133 Rome's domination of Asia Minor was well begun. Meanwhile in the west two-thirds of Spain had been organized into two provinces.

During this period old Roman virtues, largely those of a feudal aristocracy with a strong military tradition, were vigorous enough to survive the many new influences and developments which these conquests brought. Building, business (enhancing the position of the *equites*, corresponding perhaps to an upper middle class) and farming all flourished. With greater social freedom the position of women improved, but slavery increased, and the gap widened between the rich (some now luxuriously so) and the poor. Contact with Hellenism in southern Italy and in Greece itself was a truly civilizing influence on many for whom culture meant Hellenism, and the earliest Roman historians wrote in Greek, which became a much-used tongue in an increasingly cosmopolitan city. Even the most distinguished poets of the years which were to follow claimed originality because they had successfully adapted Latin words to Greek metres. (See pp. 210–19.)

Rome's engagement with Greece and Asia Minor was accompanied by a similar intervention in Egypt. In 168 C. Popillius Laenas ordered Antiochus IV Epiphanes out of the country which he was about to annex. Egypt remained in theory independent, but in fact subject to Rome, of whose empire it became a kind of province under Augustus' settlement in 27 BC.

In about fifty years Rome had passed half reluctantly from local, largely defensive, expansion to an incipient empire, some parts of which were provinces, others client kingdoms, others *de facto* subjects. The situation placed a strain upon the Republic. Provincial administration in now more distant countries was proportionately more difficult, but the standard of government fell largely for moral reasons, although corruption at the top was not always matched by corruption at the local level. No doubt tax farmers and collectors earned assiduously the hatred almost universal in mankind, but many of the less exalted officials of government were locally recruited and exercised an influence on military and civil officers from Rome which mitigated harshness. Necessary daily cooperation with the local population created by degrees something like mutual understanding; thus provincials became Roman for other reasons than mere self-interest, seeing the value of a system of government which maintained an order better than that of the native rule before its defeat.

We hear more of the corruption at the top. Governors too often saw in provinces an opportunity for riches, and especially for raising the money necessary to discharge a pressing debt. Power brought corruption; and both percolated down to local officials, so that government began to be synonymous with oppression. In addition, adventurous persons arose whose conquests were afterwards ratified as irreversible facts, rather than as the patriotic tasks which the senate had authorized and which had been exceeded or altered in their performance so that they bore little relation to what the senate intended. Moreover, once provinces were established in the public mind as sources of wealth, there was obvious temptation to add to their number. In such a situation all ranks in the armies looked less to Rome than to their general, whose survival depended on how profitable he could make their loyalty.

The glittering prizes of the expanding empire blinded many men to its realities and problems. The internal situation was no less troubled than the world outside. A struggle developed between the ruling landed classes and the people, who became increasingly discontented at being ruled by the senate. The growth of *latifundia*, large farms with a *villa* headquarters and a *familia* of slaves, replaced small farmers and labourers who pressed into the towns, including Rome, where they remained unemployed. Meanwhile owners of *latifundia* tended to become independent of national authority.

Sharp differences also arose between citizens and distant provinces and allies, especially since the manpower of the allies within Italy was essential to the growth and security of the fast-growing empire. These Italian allies included, north of Rome, Etruscans and Umbrians (whose independence jointly ceased in 290) and, south of Rome, Latins, Samnites, Apulians, Campanians, Lucanians and Bruttians. The last two oppressed the Greek cities of southern Italy, whose scattered sites extended from Cumae and Neapolis in the north to Rhegium and Sicilian Zancle-Messana in the south. By the end of 272 all of Greek Italy was Roman, since the attempt of Pyrrhus, king of Epirus, to seize former Carthaginian possessions had failed. Sicily was a Roman province from 211, after the failure of local tyrants and Carthaginian arms in the Second Punic War (218–201).

These problems were tackled by the brothers Tiberius and Caius Gracchus, who as tribunes carried out some agrarian reforms and urged the granting of the franchise to the allies. Opposition arising from the ruling classes and the senate was mistimed, for their ability was found wanting in the war of Jugurtha of Numidia in north Africa, a Numidian prince who claimed the throne. The war of succession became a revolt against Rome (112–104). It was brought to a successful conclusion by the ambitious *eques* C. Marius, who became consul in 107 (itself a rare distinction for one whose family could boast no previous consul), enjoyed a triumph in 104, and was consul several times afterwards. He was the first to use military power and prestige to flout political custom, and he showed some signs of recognizing the problems which an expanding Rome was facing. His reforms were most successful in the army, where he overcame a shortage of recruits by admitting to it all, even the poorest, classes of citizens. He was supplanted by Sulla, who had served under him in Numidia and advanced his reputation by moderate success in the east, even confronting Parthia (p. 16). In the Social War (91–87), when the Italian allies attempted to assert their equality with Rome, he fought successfully, but Rome 'won' finally by granting citizenship to the allies.

Sulla then began the kind of activity which in less than a century destroyed the Republic. He had received from the senate his command against Mithradates VI (the Great) of Pontus (120–63) who had occupied most of Asia Minor, the Aegean islands, except Rhodes, and much of Greece; but there had been strong opposition, so Sulla for the moment left the war in the east (though his safety must depend on success there) and marched on Rome (88). He thus inaugurated a dire period of civil war and bloodshed. He then took up his command against Mithradates who was defeated but left alive. Sulla then returned to further civil war, and by 82 was elected dictator. Sulla was in one sense a natural successor to Marius, but his instincts were in the direction of aristocratic authority. Somewhat ironically in view of his bloodthirsty career, he aimed now to restore the authority of the senate against the rising power of tribunes and military commanders, and retired voluntarily in 79.

The massive revolt of slaves in 73–71, led by Spartacus, for a time very successful, was at last put down by M. Licinius Crassus with ruthless cruelty. Pompey (Cnaeus Pompeius – with the addition of Magnus after his African successes in 81), returning from his victory over the rebellious Sertorius in Spain, crucified a number of stragglers and claimed the victory. Crassus swallowed the affront, and the two joined forces and became consuls in 70. These two former supporters of Sulla curiously swept away much of his legislation by the agency of the tribunate, now become a weapon of immeasurable strength in the ensuing struggles for power which engulfed the Mediterranean world for the next half-century.

The year 70 saw the first resounding success of M. Tullius Cicero, an able and cultured man of humble origin, who had been a student (79–77) in both Rhodes and Athens, and who was to become one of the most influential literary figures in the whole story of Rome, and indeed of the civilized world (p. 212). We are concerned here only with his political career; he began ardently to support Pompey, whom he saw as the great hope of an enlightened conservatism. In 63 Cicero became consul and unmasked the treasonable conspiracy of Catiline, putting to death the conspirators with a dispatch which he never wavered in insisting was essential for the safety of the state, and which has been the subject of debate ever since. He might have won even more admirers among posterity – both immediate and later – if he had not been his own most ardent advocate, writing in unsurpassed prose but unattractive verse. He was supported by Cato (95–46), the rigid die-hard who became like his great-grandfather (234–149; both were Marcus Porcius Cato) almost a synonym even in his lifetime for stern traditional morality. P. Clodius, of whom the exact opposite could be said, and who became a plebeian in order to be a tribune, had previously been antagonized by Cicero. In 58 he took revenge by enacting a law against any who had executed a citizen without trial. Cicero, thus threatened, fled to Macedonia.

Pompey's career in the east began, not with the command of a province (though he had been consul in 70), but with a commission to destroy the pirates in the Mediterranean, many of whom were based on Cilicia. He succeeded in six months, and went on to defeat Mithradates, who escaped to the Crimea where he committed suicide in 63.

Pompey's settlement in the east is outlined in the section on Judaean history (p. 94). On his return to Rome in 62 he wished to retire but asked first for settlement of the veterans in his army, and for senatorial ratification of his acts in the east which had perforce exceeded his brief. In all this he illustrated in bold outline and colour the situation which the bursting asunder of the Republic was creating. The significant deeds were done by individuals but they sought their legalization, and this could be granted only with the implication that such a programme of similar boldness, and fraught with similarly immeasurable consequences, might be undertaken by the next applicant. His opponents blocked the necessary measures and thus pushed him into alliance with C. Julius Caesar and Crassus, the so-called (but unofficial) First Triumvirate ('three-man board'). They worked, largely through tribune supporters, to obtain offices for themselves and made rough bargains about the measures which each would carry out when in office. Caesar as consul in 59 obtained measures all three wanted, including his own command in Gaul.

In the autumn of 57, Cicero returned from exile and was welcomed by the people. He was an ardent admirer of Pompey and tried to separate him from Caesar, but all intrigues designed to break up the triumvirate were resisted by its reaffirmation at a conference in Luca in 56. This arranged that the consuls in 55 should be Pompey and Crassus, an arrangement which obtained for Crassus his ill-fated command against Parthia which ended with his death at Carrhae in 53 (p. 17). Under a special law each received a five-year *imperium*, that is a supreme military and administrative power usually united with a special commission and sparingly granted by the senate. This *imperium* was only part of complicated legislative schemes, mostly put through by the tribunes, whose main object was to bestow effective power on the *triumviri*. Their continuous agreement could not be guaranteed but was essential if a constantly changing situation was to develop in ways favourable to the Republic, which certainly needed either a more representative and flexible constitution or the renunciation of that Empire which had, as it were, by unobserved degrees become over-extended. Continuous agreement was beyond possibility for two such men as Caesar and Pompey, closely bound though they were by some ties. The chief of these was loosed in 54 by the death of Julia, Pompey's wife and Caesar's daughter. With Crassus' death in 53 the two famous rivals stood at the head of affairs alone.

In 52 Caesar approved of Pompey's recent measures, as he had of his acts in the east, but there was a strong demand for Caesar's removal from his command in Gaul, and Pompey finally heeded the pressures of conservatives to acquiesce in the senate's demands for Caesar's recall from Gaul. Cicero, who had on more than one occasion been made to feel the power of the triumvirs and been frightened into supporting them, was absent from Rome as proconsul in Cilicia. On his return he was swept into the civil war; for in January 49 Caesar crossed the river Rubicon, the boundary between Cisalpine Gaul and Italy, without surrendering the command over the army with which he had made his famous conquests in Gaul. This virtual invasion of Italy was a further important advance from the true republican situation where all ultimate authority rested with the senate, and towards a much more fluid situation. In this changing state of affairs, extraordinary authority was at first accepted from the senate by men empowered to deal with a crisis, but who then arrogated to themselves this power, making it their own. In this way the armies which they commanded with the Republic's authority for the enlargement or defence of frontiers became in effect the generals' own armies and were tragically used in civil wars. Leaders in such positions might still cherish the intention to restore authority to the senate and thus to the Republic when the crisis was solved, but were likely to be overtaken by the impetus of events or by their own well-nourished ambition, or both. Pompey showed the face now of a would-be restorer of the Republic, now of an ambitious general. In Caesar it may be fair to see one who equated the fulfilment of his ambitions with the renaissance of the state, the constitution of which would certainly have to be changed. His conception of its character and of his own place in it are hard now to determine; but his career from 49 onwards certainly impelled him towards an autocracy, whether benevolent or not.

In 49, then, Caesar mastered Italy, but Pompey escaped to Greece where a number of republicans planned to resist the rise of

Caesar to sole power. Caesar invited Cicero to join what was left of the senate (i.e. the pro-Caesar element), but to his credit Cicero made the hard decision to leave Rome again and joined Pompey and his supporters in Greece. Caesar proceeded to secure his position by defeating Pompey's lieutenants in Spain, and in 48, with Marcus Antonius (Mark Antony) as his chief lieutenant, he crossed to Epirus where after one setback he decisively defeated Pompey at Pharsalus in Thessaly. He pursued him to Egypt where Pompey was murdered as he landed. Caesar now became involved in a war with Ptolemy XIII and the city of Alexandria. He supported Cleopatra VII who had been joint ruler with Ptolemy XIII since 51 but had been expelled by his party in 48. She accepted Ptolemy XIV as her new consort and Caesar left three legions to support them. Cleopatra subsequently bore a son who she claimed was Caesar's. She visited Rome at his invitation in 46.

Cicero took no part in the battle of Pharsalus and afterwards was allowed by Caesar to return to Rome, where he lived quietly but made one speech in Caesar's favour. In the meantime Caesar embarked on a series of important victories; at Zela in Pontus he defeated Pharnaces II, king of Bosporus (p. 35), a position which he had been granted by Pompey. Caesar's victory cut short the king's attempt to win back the Pontic kingdom, the main part of which had been ceded to Rome in 63. It was the occasion of Caesar's laconic dispatch to the senate 'veni, vidi, vici' ('I came, I saw, I conquered'). Asander, a rebel who had married Pharnaces' daughter and killed Mithradates of Pergamum to whom Bosporus was assigned, was later fortunate enough to win recognition from Antony and Octavian, and was thus able to rule until 17 BC.

Caesar's next campaign was in Roman Africa (a province administered by a praetor and consisting of part of northern Tunisia) where Pompeian forces under Scipio opposed him. Caesar won a decisive victory at Thapsus in 46, the die-hard Cato committing suicide to express his conviction that the Republic was doomed. This melancholy action was prophetic enough, but Caesar, even if he celebrated four triumphs in 46 (Gaul, Alexandria, Pontus and Africa), had still to subdue Pompey's sons and his lieutenant Labienus in Spain. He finally succeeded in this by fighting the hardest battle of his career at Munda in 45.

In 44 the various powers which Caesar assumed included those which made him dictator for life. The bestowal of the life dictatorship was an eloquent implicit admission that Rome faced a perpetual crisis. With hindsight the matter could be put more positively: with Julius Caesar the principate (in fact the Empire) really began, although his own tenure of it was cut short on the Ides of March when he was murdered on the Capitol.

Cicero, who was not one of the conspirators, expressed his delight at the death of Caesar without restraint or taste, and wished only that Antony also had been killed. For him Brutus and Cassius, the two chief assassins, were heroes, and he imagined that they, together with Octavian, Caesar's great-nephew and heir, could be his true friends. But Octavian was playing for time, and playing for a final win with dogged persistence. In 43 he formed a triumvirate with Antony and Lepidus, one of Caesar's former lieutenants, and allowed Cicero to be sacrificed to Antony's hostility, proscribed and put to death by Antony's soldiers in December 43.

In 42, while Lepidus was looking after Italy, Antony fought the battles of Philippi which led to the deaths of Brutus and Cassius. In this campaign Octavian was inactive through ill-health, but he was to emerge as victor from the complicated pattern of events which Caesar's death had set in train, and which were to establish him as the first emperor. (It was not until 27 BC that he received the title of Augustus, and he died in AD 14; he is therefore listed conventionally as the emperor Augustus 27 BC to AD 14, and for events from 27 BC onwards he is correctly referred to under that title.) Our outline may now justifiably follow events mainly from the point of view of his career.

II. *The Age of Augustus*

Octavian proceeded with caution, allying himself as far as possible with moderate republicans as well as with Caesar's supporters. For a time he was less prominent than Antony, though under a triumvirate arrangement after Philippi he held Spain, Sardinia and for a time Africa and he also settled legionary veterans on land allotments.

Through this latter task he came into opposition from L. Antonius, a brother of Mark Antony, who championed the cause of the dispossessed Italians in the north. Octavian had therefore to suppress a rebellion, his actions involving the siege and plundering of Perusia (on the Tiber and on the Etruscan side of the border of Etruria and Umbria) which sheltered L. Antonius. The campaign is therefore called the Perusine War; its successful outcome brought significant results for Octavian. His victory strengthened his hold on Italy and his lifelong friendship with Marcus Vipsanius Agrippa (a strong candidate for the title of the most useful 'right-hand man' of an important statesman in all history), and that with C. Maecenas, similarly indispensable to Augustus but always in an unofficial position. Maecenas was so great a patron of the arts as to lend his name to posterity as a synonym for such in more than one modern language. Both made their debut at this time as Augustus' faithful lieutenants.

In 40 Octavian and Antony renewed their alliance, Antony marrying his ally's sister Octavia. Octavian himself divorced his wife and married Livia, whose children by a former husband Tiberius Claudius Nero included the future emperor Tiberius. She bore none to Octavian and it was therefore her children rather than his who were to have such a large influence on future events. She was a very remarkable woman whose character has been variously assessed. It is certain that she had a great and daily influence on Octavian who for many years set great store by her advice.

For some time Pompey's son Sextus Pompeius had some success in rallying some of his father's former supporters, mainly in Spain and later in Sicily whence he blockaded Italy. Octavian and his supporters had considerable difficulty before finally defeating Sextus at sea. He escaped to Asia but was finally forced to surrender and was put to death in 36. In the same year Lepidus, who had acted independently against Sextus Pompeius and claimed Sicily as his province, was forced to retire into private life by the support Octavian won from his army.

This left Octavian and Antony who had renewed their partnership at Tarentum in 37, but Antony departed, without Octavia, for the east where he lived with Cleopatra. Thereby he obtained access to the resources of Egypt, and at the same time his friendship with Herod gave him an able ally in Palestine; but he had reached the zenith of his career. In 36 came the disaster in Parthia (p. 17) and in 35 his partnership with Octavian began to break up. He refused to receive Octavia when she came east and brought with her only a small number of the troops from Rome for which he had hoped. The personal break being made, Octavian had no difficulty in engineering indignant opposition to Antony in Rome by publishing Antony's will which revealed his submission to Cleopatra. Antony had in any case alienated much Roman support by promises of territory made to Cleopatra and her children. He now divorced Octavia, thus giving a public character to his break with Octavian. This made it easier for the latter soon afterwards to declare war on Cleopatra, the struggle being in fact against Antony's miscellaneous oriental forces assisted by the Egyptian fleet. The naval battle of Actium in September 31 was decisive. Antony's forces dissipated and he and Cleopatra committed suicide before Octavian entered Alexandria in 30. Octavian commemorated his victory by founding Nicopolis (see Titus 3:12) on the Actium peninsula at the extreme south of the coast of Epirus. He peopled it from the local Greek communities.

Octavian had now firmly established his position, which constitutionally might be presented as continuous with that of his great-uncle Julius Caesar, but it was shaped in ways that were significantly different. Octavian was never dictator but from 31 to 23 was consul. Marius had more than a century before given an example of flouting the republican rule and assuming a continuous consulship, and it was to become the precursor of a system which debased the ancient office even further. In 28, assisted by Agrippa, Octavian held a census and began the reduction of the numbers of the senate of which he was appointed *princeps* (a word denoting, with a useful mingling of apparent precision and actual vagueness, the same sort of position as is borne by the 'principal' of an institution in our own society where the head officer acts as sole director but appears at intervals as the executive of a board). By the census the senate gained in dignity but became more manageable. In these and many other ways (which included the revival of ancient religious ceremonies; he was himself a devotee of Apollo) Octavian restored to Rome its ancient constitution along with features which did not allow it to function except according to his wishes. His mastery of the system did not ignore the old constitutional machinery, but he worked diligently through it, controlling it by financial and military power.

In 27 Octavian gave back to senate and people the administration of the state, but obtained for himself an *imperium* which included not only the consulship but the rule of Spain, Gaul and Syria, while he continued to use Egypt as his private property. His superior position in an outward-seeming constitutional state was embodied in the title of Augustus which he now received and which history has accepted as his name ever since.

The great experiment in constitutional manipulation turned the Republic into a monarchical Empire, and the city which had built its hatred of kings into its constitution was now governed by as absolute a prince as ever occurred in history. The experiment could not have succeeded but for a real and widespread desire throughout Rome and the Empire for a period of peace after years of destructive civil war. Although in 29 after Augustus' triumph the gates of the temple of Janus had been closed to signify that the rare state of peace obtained, the need for military activity was by no means over, but increasingly the actions taken succeeded in contributing to peaceful development, so that from 31 onwards many nations and peoples ceased to be involved in continual wars. The boast of Augustus' supporters in literature that he had brought a kind of messianic peace to the world was not without foundation, though it could not be fully and literally maintained.

The final organization of Spain and Gaul was achieved largely by Augustus himself by 25. That of Egypt had already been settled by 26. The frontier between it and Ethiopia was established finally by the work of C. Petronius in 25, but the main work had been carried out in 29 by C. Cornelius Gallus, who for his successful mopping-up operations in Cyrenaica and Egypt was made the first *praefectus* of Egypt. He fell out of favour, partly because of a boastful inscription recording his diplomatic success with the king of Ethiopia, and for setting up, in the style of Rameses II, statues of himself all over Egypt, and partly for reasons unknown. He was recalled, and committed suicide in 26. It was an unexpected end for a man who appears to have been very popular, and a close friend of the poet Vergil (p. 218).

The settlement of Africa shows Rome at its best. Juba I of Numidia had joined Pompey in the civil war but after Thapsus in 46, having made a number of enemies, he committed suicide. Juba II, his son, was led as a child in Caesar's triumph in 46. Such a beginning might have led to a lifelong hatred of Rome, but Juba received Roman citizenship from Octavian and served in the army with him. In 25 he received the kingdom of Mauretania, the rugged country including the western half of the Atlas mountains, and in this apparently unpromising soil sought to plant Roman and Greek culture. His books are lost, but his two cities, Iol refounded as Caesarea (modern Cherchel) and Volubilis (Oubili), form some sort of monument to an intelligent and well-intentioned ruler, wise enough to accept the inevitability of Roman power and its advantages for his people.

If the measures of Augustus in the world at large bore fruit in the form of a large Empire, capable at its best of maintaining law and order and consequent prosperity for a great many people, his own life, both at home and in the government of Rome and Italy, presented him with a never-ending series of problems. The greatest and most vexing was that of finding an heir to the unique position in which he found himself and which he had done so much to create. He had no son, and from 23 when Marcellus, husband of his daughter Julia (by his first wife Scribonia) died, the problem of the succession occupied him and his advisers. In 21 Julia was married to Agrippa; she bore him two sons, Caius in 20, Lucius in 17, besides two daughters, and a further son born after his father's death in 12, Agrippa Postumus. (For genealogy bearing on the succession see p. 238.)

III. *The Empire*

In 23 Augustus resigned the consulship and accepted a lifelong *tribunicia potestas*, i.e. the perpetual authority of a tribune. Since this carried with it the tribune's absolute right of veto and thus was a vital element in his control of the senate, the measure incontrovertibly brought the Republic to an end, yet the pieces of the machinery of government were still called by ancient names.

The years which followed, 22–12, saw an enormous amount of activity, involving both much legislation in Rome and much travelling. Journeys in Sicily, Greece and Asia reorganized town and country. The threat from Parthia was neutralized by her recognition of Roman control of Armenia, Parthia handing back in 20 the standards captured at Carrhae, and an African expedition was also successful. In 16–15 Raetia and Noricum were annexed as provinces in an attempt to reduce the difficulties of the northern frontier, and in 15–13 Augustus lived for three years in Gaul, occupied with its reorganization, leaving for this period a prefect in charge of Rome.

In Rome in 22, Augustus accepted the *cura annonae*. The *annona* was the corn-supply and nothing was more important, for very large numbers of Romans depended upon its distribution, subsidized since C. Gracchus (123–122) and made entirely free by Clodius in 58. The cities and provinces had their own officials to ensure supplies, but the overall responsibility included that of importing from Egypt and Africa. The *annona* was therefore a burdensome task, and echoes of its difficulties are often met in literature, including rather faint echoes in the New Testament (e.g. Acts 11:28; Rev. 6:6).

Augustus' own legislation included moral and religious reforms; marriage became virtually compulsory and adultery a crime; luxury was discouraged; marriage of senatorial families with freedmen was forbidden.

In 18 Agrippa became a co-regent with Augustus and in 17 Caius and Lucius, sons of Agrippa and Julia, were adopted and thus designated heirs. In 13 the joint powers of Augustus and Agrippa were extended for another five years, but in 12 Agrippa died. His career was almost as distinguished as that of Augustus, to whom he gave such strong and constant support, both before the principate (for example, his was a decisive part in the battle of Actium) and as time went on in consolidating and administering it. When Augustus was ill in 23 he virtually entrusted the Empire to him. Certainly in that year and until 21 he administered the eastern half of the Empire energetically from his own headquarters, which were usually at Mytilene, the chief city of Lesbos. He was again in the east in 17–13, when he established Polemo of Pontus as king of Bosporus and visited Judaea at Herod's invitation (15 BC). The latter used his name for his grandson, the Agrippa I inaccurately called Herod in Acts 12. In Rome he is always remembered for his thorough overhaul of the water supply, and for his buildings which included two aqueducts.

Agrippa's death made the year 12 a turning-point, for his departure left a gap impossible for Augustus to fill. It saw also the death of Lepidus, who had retained since 36 only the office of *Pontifex Maximus* which Augustus now took over. For him it was no mere form, for he appears to have included the old gods among the patriarchal traditions which he strove to preserve or restore. His piety had a practical value: he was now head of the Empire in both politics and religion. In the provinces the names of Rome and Augustus, the genius of empire and emperor, were often coupled at one altar which therefore became a focus of loyalty. In a world accustomed to polytheism and syncretism, to object to making a god out of a man might be regarded as eccentric fanaticism, but more probably as political disloyalty.

The void left by Agrippa was filled not by his sons, for though adopted by Augustus they were still young boys, but by Augustus' stepsons Tiberius (who was thirty) and Drusus (who was twenty-six). Tiberius already had something of a career behind him, having for example received back the standards from Parthia on behalf of Augustus, and Drusus had early begun a senatorial career. It was inevitable that these two should over-shadow the two boys, and perhaps also that they should resent, as Tiberius seems to have done, Augustus' hesitation to adopt them officially as his heirs. For a time their influence was very con-siderable and this showed in military activity. The frontier of Illyricum was advanced to the Danube, and Moesia was made a province. The northern frontier was always a problem, exem-plified by Drusus' ill-advised though at first successful attempt to extend the Rhine frontier to the Elbe. His conquests had no lasting results although they earned him from the senate the title of Germanicus (it is however used normally to designate his son whose name it was). Drusus died in camp in 9 BC without being able to consolidate his successes. He had married Antonia (Minor), second daughter of Mark Antony and Octavia, who bore him Germanicus, Livilla, and the future emperor Claudius; after his death Antonia refused to marry again; she had been born in 36 BC and so at an early age became a 'queen mother' figure. In AD 31 she was to assist her brother-in-law Tiberius towards the discovery of Sejanus' conspiracy, and though held in honour during her son Claudius' reign, and even more by her grandson Caius, provoked the latter by no doubt well-justified criticisms, and was driven by him to suicide in AD 37. Her daughter Livilla married Drusus Minor, son of Tiberius and Vipsania, daughter of Agrippa. This Drusus' death in AD 23 was said to be caused by poison administered by Livilla, who was Sejanus' mistress.

In 6 BC Tiberius received the tribunal power but soon after-wards retired to Rhodes, jealous of the growing influence of Caius, who in 5 BC at the age of fifteen was proclaimed *princeps iuventutis* (youth leader) and who was married to Livilla as her first husband in 1 BC. Caius was now regarded as Augustus' heir, but after a mission to confer with the Parthian king in order to place a Roman nominee on the throne of Armenia, he was wounded in a revolt against this arrangement, and died in Lycia in AD 4. Lucius, who had been similarly advanced in honour, had died in AD 2.

These deaths greatly troubled Augustus, who felt forced to make Tiberius his heir by formally adopting him. Tiberius received again the *tribunicia potestas* and accepted the task of crushing the significant rebellion of Pannonia which took him from AD 6 to 9. In AD 9 we hear again of Varus who as legate of Syria from about 6 to 4 BC earned a reputation for ruthless severity in his suppression of the Judaean rebellion on the death of Herod. In AD 9 he was legate of the Rhine army, and lost three legions through an attack by the patriotic rebel Arminius, a disaster which led Varus to suicide and Augustus (who is said never to have recovered from the shock of the loss of the legions) to recognize the impracticability of conquering the tribes east of the Rhine.

Augustus died in AD 14, in so well-organized a manner as to present an oddly apt coda to his life. In 13 he deposited in the house of the Vestal Virgins his will, which included a summary of the military and financial resources of the Empire, and the Register of his Achievements, often called the *Monumentum Ancyranum* because the copy found on mosque walls in Ancyra in Galatia has enabled the reconstruction of most of the text. Suetonius calls it the *Index rerum a se gestarum*. It appears to be a second version of a previous *Res Gestae* (lit. 'Things done', so that 'Achievements' is a sensible translation).

The achievements were enormous. If it is possible to be 'great' by one's effect upon history without towering above the common run of men in the elusive area of 'personality', Augustus qualifies for the epithet. As a personality his great-uncle Julius Caesar, to whose fortunes he succeeded, was greater than Augustus; but the latter's achievements outshine his by their immense scope, their durable quality, by the perseverance which they demanded, and by the insight into what was both desirable and possible which ensured so great a measure of success. Such praise carries a faint echo of reserve, and many have felt it when paying tribute to this first of the Roman emperors. It is hard to crystallize the reasons for such hesitation, but they lie perhaps both in the circumstances and the genius of Augustus. His virtues and his actions were such as to bring peace rather than liberty to the civilized world, and many contemporaries greeted his achievement with the sigh of relief which ends a journey, rather than with the enthusiasm with which men set out to follow an inspiring leader.

Tiberius (AD 14–37), who succeeded Augustus, was the son of Livia by her former husband Tiberius Claudius Nero, and was tardily adopted by Augustus officially in AD 4 after the deaths of Caius and Lucius. He might have crowned a brilliant early career with a distinguished reign. In 20 BC he accompanied Augustus to the east and on his behalf received back the standards from Parthia. His military career continued but fell into relative dimness during the years 6 BC to AD 4 when he was mostly absent from Rome and when Caius and Lucius were being brought to the fore; but in AD 12 he completed the restoration of the situation on the Rhine after the disaster of Varus in AD 9, consolidating well the reputation won by his success in Pannonia between 12 and 9 BC and by his suppression of the revolts in Illyricum and Pannonia in AD 6–9. In the Roman social scene his star shone less brightly. In earlier years this was probably largely because he himself resented the advancement so eagerly granted to Caius and Lucius. Bitterness at his relatively lower status may well have been sharpened by personal grief; for in 12 BC he was forced to divorce Vipsania (Agrippa's daughter and mother of his son Drusus Minor) whom he loved deeply, to marry Agrippa's widow Julia, Augustus' daughter. The marriage was extremely unhappy.

We have seen that in 6 BC Tiberius retired to Rhodes. He returned to Rome in AD 2 and was adopted as successor in AD 4, himself being obliged to adopt his own nephew Germanicus.

Tiberius suffered much by being compared with the gifted and popular Germanicus, and it was unfortunate that as early in his reign as 17 a situation arose which closely concerned them both and demanded a decision by Tiberius. At the time of Tiberius' accession the legions in Pannonia and Lower Germany had been willing to name Germanicus emperor, and his high position in the succession was enhanced by further victorious campaigns. In 17 Tiberius, probably wisely, recalled him from his Rhine command. The action was as diplomatic as possible in the circumstances, since it was to celebrate a triumph, and he was in 18 to enter upon another phase of his career.

This did not go so well: Germanicus entered upon a second consulship in 18 at Nicopolis and began to be much occupied with eastern affairs, including Armenia. Then in 19 he offended Tiberius by travelling in Egypt, the semi-official subjection of which to the emperor had continued from the time of Augustus who had forbidden visits there to men of senatorial rank. Germanicus returned to Syria where he quarrelled with the governor Cn. Piso, whom Tiberius had appointed as a counsellor to him. Germanicus ordered Piso to leave the country, and falling ill soon afterwards, died convinced that Piso had poisoned him. His death caused great grief at Rome and could not fail to increase the unpopularity of Tiberius.

Some consolation of the Empire can be credited to the reign of Tiberius. Augustus' policy was followed, the boundaries of the Empire were defended but not extended, trouble with Parthia threatened but was met successfully by diplomacy. Tiberius lengthened the tenure of the office of a *legatus* of an imperial province. He was as economical in his appointments as he was in all matters of finance.

Much uncertainty surrounds the character of Tiberius; he has been accused (largely by Suetonius) of repulsive and decadent private actions – it may be without real evidence but with the credulity which attends hatred and ignorance combined. It is certainly hard to assess how far he was responsible for the many trials for treason which took place during his reign, mostly before the senate, many of whose members took no pains to disguise their constant hostility. In his reign the prefect of the Praetorian Guard, the select corps which provided the troops for protection of the person of the emperor, became a prominent figure. In this instance the prefect was L. Aelius Sejanus, the first of many such in the history of the Empire to wield decisive power. He encouraged in Tiberius an over-anxiety about his own safety, finding a victim who was perhaps easier to terrify since he had so often had real reason to fear the ambitions of others.

Whatever the exact reason or reasons, certainly partly through the persuasion of Sejanus, Tiberius retired in 26 to the island of Capri, whence he maintained aloof contact with Rome and the government of the Empire by letters to the senate. This bizarre state of affairs was maintained until his death. (Thus the years of the prefecture of Pontius Pilate, 26–36, during which Jesus was active in Palestine (Luke 3:1ff), coincided with those of the absence of Tiberius from the seat of government and of the dominance of Sejanus.) It is easy to understand how such a situation resulted in unlimited intrigue for power among those in high positions in Rome, so that many of the trials for treason may have been founded on well-grounded suspicion. Agrippina,

Germanicus' widow, and her son Nero (uncle of the future emperor of that name) were arrested in 29, her son Drusus in 30.
Their consequent deaths were followed by that of Sejanus and
many of his supporters in 31. Tiberius' last six years were a time
of obscurity for his story and his government. He died in 37.

In spite of the deaths in the family of Germanicus, who had
been Tiberius' nephew and appointed heir, one son of Germanicus,
Caius, remained and therefore succeeded as emperor. He reigned
from 37 to 41. As he grew up Caius had had considerable experience of military life, being with his parents on the Rhine as a
child of three- and four-years-old (the soldiers called him
'Caligula' – 'Little Boot' – after the military-style boots that he
wore), and later in the east. He was in Rome with his mother after
Germanicus' death in the east in 19 and was seventeen when she
was arrested in 29. He lived in turn with the ageing matriarchs
Livia (d. 29) and Antonia (d. 37). He was seriously ill in 38 and on
his recovery began a reign of terror through a kind of madness
which may have been a legacy of his illness or of the effect of the
insecure and terrible times in which he had grown up. He executed Macro, prefect of the Praetorian Guard, and Tiberius
Gemellus, son of Tiberius' son Drusus and joint heir with himself of
his grandfather's estate. It was the beginning of a reign of absolute
rule by a capricious tyrant, during which no one in political circles
could ever feel secure. Thus Caius forsook in effect, though not in its
official forms, the leadership of the Roman Republic for a hellenistic
monarchy, preserving its least attractive features.

Caius' campaign in Gaul and on the Rhine in 39–40 may have
been intended to lead to an invasion of Germany or Britain, but
he lacked the support of his army in which indeed there was
indiscipline. In any case, abandonment of a proposal needs no
further explanation than Caius' unstable character. On his return
to Rome his cruel conduct aroused sufficient danger to himself to
lead to his assassination in 41. Fortunately for the Jews his death
brought, as perhaps nothing else could, a definite end to his
project to set up a statue of himself in the Temple at Jerusalem
(p. 112). His anti-Jewish measures also occasioned unrest in
Alexandria, and thereby Philo's *Legatio ad Caium* (p. 140).

Caius was succeeded by his uncle Claudius (41–54), the dashing Germanicus' far from dashing brother. Hitherto the senate
had voted authority to the designated emperor. Its formal sanction was still necessary, but on this occasion we find extended to

Rome itself the now well-established practice of an army proclaiming its own leader as emperor, thus providing a (not always successful) candidate. Now it was no frontier or proconsul's army which acted with such decision. Two officers of the Praetorian Guard, according to Suetonius, murdered Caius. In the ensuing chaos Claudius was found by one of the soldiers of the guard hiding in fear of his life. He was then after some further horseplay adopted by the Praetorians as their own candidate, with what degree of seriousness is not clear, in the teeth of an attempt by the current consuls to declare a restoration of the Republic.

This inauspicious beginning was consistent with the whole life of Claudius hitherto, for he suffered from bad health, a timid disposition, and a grave sense of inferiority which was encouraged by all around him, including his mother Antonia and his grandmother Livia. He had once been nominally consul but was never allowed actually to carry out the duties of this or any office. Two apparently contradictory things may be said of the opposition to his rule: he ardently shared it and he overcame it. For one on whom sovereign power had been thrust he made a remarkably good ruler, by any standards as good as average and a great deal better than many.

So unwarlike a person was an unlikely friend of the army, but the circumstances of his accession and a hitherto hidden sagacity caused him to take a great interest in it, while at the same time he released the principate from the absolutism of Caius. He extended the Roman citizenship and constantly urged the senate to take its duties seriously. It was as though, while perceiving the necessity for a powerful director at the top, he wished the administrators of the state to administer and not merely to dance like puppets. In his reign there emerged a class of administrators uninhibited by a sense of past glories now dimmed, which must have made many senators feel that there was only a spurious honour in being an officer of the Empire. The new men were such as had never felt the honour of rank, and were more than content with actual power without its trappings. This is at least how they began, though they quickly grew to desire recognition. They originated among freedmen, a class of people who had won their civil liberty by the formal ceremony of manumission after serving a family as slaves, and continuing in its service naturally enough after manumission, since there they had familiar employment and had learnt how to gain their own and their masters' ends perhaps better than the masters themselves. Less fastidious than some members of the nobility, they were able therefore to achieve much more, holding positions as private secretaries and executive officers under those who held official power. These freedmen were often shrewd and able men with insight into the not always immaculate realities of politics, but their positions of influence without direct responsibility were inevitable temptations to corruption. Through their knowledge of backstairs gossip, intrigue and financial affairs, they often made themselves indispensable to their principals and hence to those who sought advancement. It may well be a sign of Claudius' 'innocence' that he became dependent on such people, e.g. Narcissus his private secretary and Pallas (a freedman of his mother) his financial secretary; both of these acquired enormous wealth, and eventually reluctant official recognition by the senate as servants of the state.

Claudius' care for the Empire was marked by the addition of some provinces, including Mauretania. Perhaps of greatest interest, Britain was invaded in 43, only two years after his accession, in a campaign possibly designed to obliterate his reputation for softness and incompetence. He managed to be with the army personally at the capture of Camulodunum (Colchester), which was destined to be in turn the springboard for the conquest of the rest of Britain and in 60 the scene of the violent sacking by the rebellious Boudicca.

Claudius was married four times. His third wife Valeria Messalina, his second cousin and granddaughter of Octavia, Augustus' sister, was a wanton whose excesses Claudius was scarcely able to believe when finally Narcissus, who had been a party to some of them, revealed them to her husband, and encompassed her death before the unhappy man could recover his senses. The fourth wife was his own niece Agrippina, daughter of Agrippina and Germanicus; she brought with her a stepson for Claudius, a son of Cn. Domitius Ahenobarbus. His name was Nero and in 50 his mother persuaded Claudius (who was also his great-uncle) to adopt him, thus supplanting Britannicus, son of Claudius and Messalina, who was the natural heir and who died, probably poisoned, in 55.

When Claudius died in 54, his successor was therefore the famous Nero (54–68), whose name has passed into history as a synonym for tyrannical and unnatural cruelty. Wicked though many of his deeds were, it would be easy to find other rulers whose actions rivalled their enormity and surpassed their nastiness. (His uncle Caius would be a likely candidate.) Indeed at the beginning of his reign he showed fair promise, reassuring in one whose accession was clouded by rumours that his ambitious mother had hastened Claudius' end. Stress was laid on his descent (on the female side) from Augustus, his mother being the granddaughter of Julia, Augustus' daughter. To complicate the genealogy of the Julian and Claudian houses, he married in 53 Octavia, daughter of Claudius and Messalina; but he divorced her in 62 to marry Poppaea, whose previous husband was M. Salvius Otho.

At the beginning of Nero's reign Otho had encouraged him to assert his own will against the overwhelming Agrippina. Although he wished rather to enter the world of art and artist, and to achieve recognition as a performer in more than one branch of it, he can be credited for following sound political advice at the outset of his reign. He initiated good legislation and appointed some good governors, e.g. Suetonius Paulinus, governor of Britain 58–60, and Corbulo, legate of Cappadocia and in command against Parthia 58–66. The advice came largely from the scholarly philosopher Seneca (p. 217) and Burrus, a favourite of Agrippina who had secured his appointment under Claudius as prefect of the Praetorian Guard. Burrus was one of the first to hold such a position and at the same time to take a part in political affairs continuously, as he did until his death in 62.

Before this, in 59, Nero had taken the drastic step of securing the murder of his mother as part of his throwing off the yoke of too much tutelage. In 62 Burrus died and Seneca retired. Octavia was divorced and then murdered. Nero married Poppaea.

Freedom won by such terrible acts was not at first used only for bad ends. It was used to promote games and musical contests (which Nero had a happy knack of winning without more than mediocre skill or voice), to write verse and to dabble in painting and sculpture. But in conjunction with his power it was also used for extravagant self-indulgence. Thus it degenerated – inevitably after such a beginning – into licence and terror; avarice and luxury created a situation carrying the constant temptation to accuse rich men of treason. After their execution confiscation of their goods went some way towards replenishing the selfishly plundered treasury, brought low also by wars in Britain and in Armenia.

In 64 a great fire destroyed half of the city of Rome. Nero was delighted with the opportunity to rebuild it with greater magnificence, including the Domus Aurea (Golden House) for his own residence. He was suspected by some (including Suetonius), and still is, of having instigated the fire himself and of having made a spectacle of it at a party which included recital of his own poems (this antic has led somewhat anachronistically to the charge of 'fiddling while Rome burned' – the 'fiddle' would have been a lyre or similar instrument). Suetonius does not record the choosing of the Christians in Rome as scapegoats for the fire. For him their faith was 'a new and malicious superstition' and measures against them were thus a part of the general policy of Nero's reign of which the historian would approve (Suetonius, *Nero* 16.2).

It is Tacitus who, reflecting the same popular dislike of Christians, tells of Nero blaming the fire on them, so that within the city a bitter persecution raged, claiming according to Christian tradition both Peter and Paul among its victims (Tacitus, *Ann.* 15.44; (see p. 218)).

A conspiracy in 65 to assassinate Nero and to replace him with C. Calpurnius Piso, a popular but ineffectual celebrity, failed. It involved among others, whether justly or not, Nero's old tutor Seneca who was forced to commit suicide. Poppaea died in the same year, and in 66 Nero married Statilia Messalina, who survived him.

The reign of terror increased; it did not diminish through being mixed with some political activity and enterprise. At first there was success in Armenia, where Tiridates received his crown at Nero's hands in 66. This year saw also the outbreak of the Jewish revolt, caused in part at least by a series of corrupt and oppressive procurators (pp. 113ff.), probably reflecting a general decline in standards and quality natural in such a reign. Nero left Rome for a tour of Greece, which he declared 'free', and sent Mucianus as legate of Syria with Vespasian to pacify Judaea. Corbulo was recalled to meet Nero at Cenchreae and to commit suicide, probably because of his many connexions of kinship with families involved in the assassination attempt, but perhaps also because he had been too successful in his final arrangement with Parthia.

Nero's presence at Cenchreae, Corinth's port on the Saronic Gulf, was due to his ambitious but potentially useful proposal to have a canal constructed across the Isthmus of Corinth. The project failed, in sharp contrast with Nero's games and concert tour, in which he won many honours. Digging started on the canal, but in the winter of 67–8 Nero's freedman Helius, left in charge at Rome, came to urge the emperor to return to the capital. He was the forerunner of the end: Nero's crimes had lost him many former friends; they now began to raise up effective enemies. One was C. Julius Vindex, governor of Gallia Lugdunensis. Another was Galba in Spain, and a third Clodius Macer in Africa. Once more the decisive step was taken by the prefect of the Praetorian Guard, Nymphidius Sabinus, who bribed his men to declare for Galba. Nero fled from Rome and committed suicide in June 68.

Galba, whom Vindex supported, had declared himself a legate of the senate and people, and for a brief time his star was in the ascendant. Vindex indeed was defeated and killed at the battle of Vesantio by Rufus at the head of the army of Germania Superior, but on the other side of the balance were Nero's death and the support of the Praetorian Guard and of Otho, now governor of Lusitania. Galba and Otho entered Rome in October. Now Galba's luck began to ebb. Nymphidius was killed by his own men and Macer refused to support Galba. Macer was executed, but Galba made a serious mistake by a massacre of marines whom he might have won over by diplomacy. Thus he lost his judgement and thereby his grip on events.

In the meantime Galba had sent Aulus Vitellius to command the legions in Lower Germany but in January 69 they hailed their new commander as emperor. Galba's most obvious mistake was in passing over Otho as his designated successor. Otho organized a revolt among the Praetorians and Galba was assassinated a few days after Vitellius was proclaimed on the Rhine.

Thus January 69 ushered in the 'year of the four emperors'. Galba counts as the first. Otho was destined to be a short-lived second; he had the support of the legions on the Danube and the Euphrates, and of Egypt and Africa, but Vitellius' cause was acquiring a momentum which, though it was halted for a time, was soon strong enough to overcome Otho in a decisive battle at Bedriacum (between Mantua and Cremona in northern Italy). Otho committed suicide in April.

Vitellius was still in Germany when he heard of the victory for his cause in Italy and he accordingly marched on Rome as though a conqueror. In July he claimed to be Nero's successor and *consul perpetuus*. It was now his turn to commit errors of tact, humiliating rather than conciliating the defeated army. Moreover in his case too a rival was already making progress, for Vespasian had left the siege of Jerusalem to his son Titus and was making a bid for the principate, having by the time of Nero's death already subdued Judaea.

Titus Flavius Vespasianus (he and his two sons Titus and Domitian make up the 'Flavian' emperors, breaking the Julio-Claudian line) was a very competent and successful soldier, with a lifetime's experience of campaign and administration. He was the legate (i.e. officer commanding) of the Second Legion in the invasion of Britain in 43/44, leading the advance to the west. Later he was consul, and proconsul of Africa in (probably) 63. In 66 he was with Nero in Greece (where he endeared himself to history though not to Nero by sleeping during the emperor's singing) on his way to his command in Judaea. He and Mucianus, legate of Syria, acted together after the death of Galba, whom Vespasian had at first supported. They transferred their support to Otho, but after his suicide collected their own forces, Mucianus being apparently happy to assist another to the throne rather than aim at occupying it himself. Vespasian, whose regal destiny Josephus had confidently forecast for him on the basis of a dream, probably began to feel confident of success when auguries and portents seemed to be indicated by his acclamation as emperor by the two Egyptian legions under the Jewish-born prefect Tiberius Alexander, nephew of Philo, and by those in Judaea and Syria. The decisive declaration in his favour was that of M. Antonius Primus, commander in Pannonia. Persuading the other Danubian legions, he marched on Rome by way of northern Italy, defeating the army of Vitellius at the second battle of Bedriacum. Mucianus arrived with his legions soon afterwards.

Such support and events were no doubt decisive, but Vitellius' support was in any case fading, and those still loyal to him failed to rally further recruits to his cause. The fleet at Misenum also deserted him. Rome was once more the scene of the final catastrophe: Vespasian's brother Sabinus tried to make him abdicate, but the mob compelled him to remain in charge; a fight against Sabinus' followers caused the destruction by fire of the temple of Jupiter; then Primus arrived and defeated the pro-Vitellius party, entering Rome one day after Vitellius had been murdered.

Primus did not remain in control, for very soon Mucianus arrived and took over the government on behalf of Vespasian.

The senate recognized Vespasian (69–79) immediately and he was formally granted explicit powers. These were the more necessary because he could claim no connexion with the hitherto ruling house and represented the new men. His mother had belonged to an equestrian family, her brother having entered the senate. His father, also equestrian, had been a tax gatherer. Vespasian publicized a number of omens which pointed to his accession, and thus added to the *auctoritas* which the senate formally acknowledged. He and his sons frequently held the consulship. Since Augustus a consul no longer necessarily held office for a year but as *consul suffectus* for two or four months. Two consuls gave their names to the year only if they entered upon their office on 1 January. (*Suffectus* means 'substitute', the term under the Republic being used for officials appointed to take the place of those who died in office, sometimes exercising power as substitutes for very short periods, even only hours.) Thus the consulship retained administrative duties and power, but very little of the honour which had clung to it in the Republic. Vespasian indeed made plain his intention to pass on his *imperium* – the real power – to his sons. Whether on this issue or on others, he met some opposition in the senate, for there were still men (such as the Stoic Helvidius Priscus) who had the courage to express support for republican principles, and eventually to pay for it with their lives.

From 70 onwards Vespasian was much occupied with raising money. After Nero and the turbulent year of 69 the state was in dire need of funds; it is absurd to accuse the emperor of greed simply on the grounds that he raised new taxes. On the other hand, he may be accused of extravagance in his restoration of the Capitol, the building of the Forum which bears his name, and the temple of Peace, and beginning work on the famous building which is always known by its mediaeval name of the Colosseum. It was in fact the Flavian amphitheatre, and its construction at this time emphasizes the need for more adequate plant and apparatus for the entertainment of the large number of people in Rome whose dependence on 'bread and circuses' was part – for some virtually the whole – of their way of life. (The word 'amphitheatre' is contemporarily and frequently misused, being applied to an outdoor theatre (roughly semicircular); an amphitheatre is a 'double' theatre, i.e. almost or entirely circular.)

Discipline was restored in the army, building on Mucianus' work which had reduced the size of the Praetorian Guard. Vespasian commanded respect as a soldier, and the army everywhere became more effective. Agricola, the famous governor of Britain from 78 to 84, was the agent of extended frontiers and development of civilization in that country, and in the east Vespasian recognized the importance of Rome's strength by establishing three armies, each of two legions, one army in each of Judaea, Syria and Cappadocia. It is not surprising that Vespasian is described by Tacitus as the first emperor who changed for the better. By the standards of his time and circumstances he is distinguished by his sincere care for the state, industry and lack of self-glorification; relatively rough and uncultured, he was honest and efficient. His successors were not an improvement.

Vespasian's reputation might have been less good in the eyes of posterity if he had been able to stay in Judaea and see the war there to its end. As it was, it fell to his son Titus to preside over the horrors of the siege and fall of Jerusalem (p. 119).

Titus (79–81) was associated with his father in government both before and after the latter became emperor, and shared with him a triumph to celebrate the conquest of Judaea; the sack of Jerusalem is graphically commemorated on the Arch of Titus in the Roman Forum. Titus was in love with Berenice, daughter of Agrippa I, who lived for a time with her brother Agrippa II (Acts 25:13, 23), both brother and sister having favoured the Roman cause during the Jewish War. Drusilla, another sister, was the third wife of Felix (Acts 24:24). Berenice visited Titus in Rome, but he eventually reluctantly dismissed her. His reign was beneficent and generous; under it, says Gibbon, 'the Roman world enjoyed a transient felicity'. There was great popular grief at his early death in 81.

Titus' brother Domitian (81–96) was the third and last Flavian emperor. His unbalanced character is illustrated alike by his cynical self-glorification and by his fear of opposition. He used the title *Dominus et Deus noster* (Our Lord and God). His reign was marked by deterioration of relations with the senate, and in 89 and 95 by an expulsion of philosophers (thought to be subversive) from Italy. The last years 93–6 saw a large number of tyrannical prosecutions ending in executions. It is a feasible interpretation of Rev. 17:9–14 that the eighth who is one of the seven means the hated and dreaded *Nero redivivus* – 'Nero come-back-to-life' – in the person of Domitian. There may have been local persecutions

of Christians as well as Domitian's known harshness to Jews;
from the latter he extracted the half-shekel Temple tax in spite of
the Temple's destruction, as a condition of a Jew being allowed to
practise his religion. Certainly Tacitus and Pliny the Younger
look back on his reign as one of terror.

The conspirators who murdered Domitian in 96 chose M.
Cocceius Nerva (96–8), of an old senatorial family, to succeed
him. The divisions and the financial difficulties left behind by
Domitian could not be cured in Nerva's short reign, even though
it was conducted with a deliberate policy of reconciliation, and
faithfulness to the constitution. Nerva was too old to take the
necessary steps to unite under his authority either the provincially
based armies or the factions in the capital, but his choice of
successor was a happy one. This was M. Ulpius Traianus – Trajan
(98–117) – the governor of Germany and thus the commander of
the nearest sizeable force to Rome. His family came from the
town of Italica in Spain, so that he was the first emperor of
provincial origin. He restored good relations with the senate and
seems to have excited the genuine admiration of Pliny. His military exploits brought a new acquisition in Dacia, and for a time it
seemed as if he might conquer Parthia, but his hold upon it was
clearly precarious when he died in Cilicia in 117.

His successor Hadrian (117–38) – his full name was Publius
Aelius Hadrianus – was Trajan's nephew and ward. At the time
of his uncle's death he was governor of Syria. The announcement
that he had been adopted as heir and successor was followed by
the execution of four prominent senators for 'conspiracy' before
he had reached Rome. This aroused disbelief and suspicion,
shared by the historian Cassius Dio (*fl. c.* AD 200) who tells the
story of a coup. Hadrian's reign aimed at grandeur, but he was
genuinely interested in the classical culture (literature, architecture and art) which he ostentatiously patronized. On one of his
many extensive tours he passed through the western provinces
including Britain, where in 122 he established the definitive frontier known as Hadrian's Wall. These tours had administrative and
military value, and included Syria, Asia Minor, Pannonia, Greece
and Sicily in 123–5 (with a winter in Athens 124–5); Africa in
128; Greece, Asia Minor and Syria again in 128–32, this time
including Judaea and Egypt. (On the Jewish revolt 132–5 see
pp.122–5.) Hadrian founded cities when on tour. His organization of the Empire was able and his relinquishment of Parthia

shows wisdom. His character was many-sided, marred by an excessive egoism which bred distrust of himself and those about him. The end of his reign was sullied by a number of executions, the result of suspected plots on his life.

Hadrian's final choice of successor was Antoninus Pius (138–61) who had himself to adopt two prospective successors: one was his nephew by marriage, Marcus Antonius Aurelius (emperor 161–80); the other Lucius Verus (joint emperor 161–9). Antoninus Pius with Marcus Aurelius (as he is always known) and the latter's son Commodus make up the 'Antonine' emperors. Little is known of the reign of Antoninus Pius who never left Italy and maintained excellent relations with the senate. An eloquent testimony to his character has been left by M. Aurelius whom we know from his own writings, especially his *Meditations*, which express his Stoic convictions. Ironically, the reign of this other-worldly philosopher was dominated by wars; he campaigned against barbarians across the Danube, L. Verus against the Parthians, and finally M. Aurelius and his son Commodus (joint ruler 177–80) again across the Danube. M. Aurelius died on his last campaign in 180 and Commodus (180–92) made peace with the barbarians and returned to Rome to begin at the age of eighteen a reign as sole emperor, a reign of self-indulgence in which features of Nero's reign were reproduced. Conspiracies and intrigues by favourites matched his own self-glorification and self-exhibition as a gladiator. In 192 he was strangled in his bath.

A period of confusion followed. The murderers of Commodus turned to an elderly senator Publius Helvius Pertinax (193), whose creditable attempts at reform lost him the support of the Praetorian Guard and thereby his life after a reign of only three months. The winner of the ensuing struggle of some senators with the Praetorians was swept aside by L. Septimius Severus (193–211), governor of Upper Pannonia, who was proclaimed emperor at Carnuntum on the Danube, in Noricum and close to the Pannonian border. His rivals were also provincial governors, Pescennius Niger in Syria and Clodius Albinus in Britain. Severus fought a four-year civil war with them, finally defeating both at Lugdunum in 197. He then fought the Parthians, who had supported Niger, and annexed Osroene and Mesopotamia. After years in Syria, Egypt, Rome and Africa he began a campaign in Britain, hoping to subdue the Caledonians. In this he was unsuccessful and died in York in 211.

Severus left two sons, of whom the younger, Geta, had been governor of Britain during the Caledonian campaign. The elder brother was M. Aurelius Antoninus but is always known by his nickname Caracalla. Their bitter rivalry ended with the murder of Geta, contrived by Caracalla, in 212. The next year he campaigned with some success in Germany. His chief strength was in his military career, although it is his civil administration which marks him out in history for having in 212 granted Roman citizenship to all communities within the Empire (to obtain increased revenue from inheritance tax). He was in the east and preparing a new and thorough assault on Parthian territory in 217 when he reaped the reward of many cruel and arrogant acts by being assassinated at Carrhae. The assassin Macrinus (217–18) was again the prefect of the Praetorian Guard, the first *eques* to be proclaimed emperor. His reign was short, for he was killed by conspirators who supported an exotic figure Elagabalus (218–22), great-nephew of Severus' Syrian widow and hereditary priest of Elagabal, god of Emesa. His reign, which inspired Gibbon's eloquent indignation, has been justly described as 'a mere catalogue of immoralities and follies'. A court intrigue replaced him by his cousin Severus Alexander (222–35), who was dominated by his mother Mammaea and for a time by Ulpian, an unusually sober and legally-minded Praetorian prefect. With the latter's help Alexander attempted to govern sensibly, but they were frustrated by the all-powerful army, especially the Praetorians, who would not tolerate reform or strictness.

Elagabalus and Alexander, the first representatives of the Greek east to occupy the throne, were both only fourteen when made emperor. The contrast between them in manner of life and purpose makes all the more striking their oneness in being ineffective rulers; this was the result of circumstances, which no emperor could change without outstanding abilities such as few possess. Alexander campaigned successfully enough to recover Mesopotamia from Persia in 232, and after a triumph in 233 had to attend to unrest on the Rhine frontier. Here he tried to buy peace, and the legions interpreted his action as cowardice. They chose as leader Maximinus, a Thracian soldier who had risen from the ranks, and Alexander was murdered in 235. The rise of Maximinus (235–8) emphasizes the character of a new era now beginning. With the fatal division and frequent change of loyalties on the part of the legions, the emperor, to secure tranquillity, would have to be an outstanding war leader devoted to peace. No such conveniently paradoxical person emerged at this time, and a period of wars and civil wars followed.

Confused as the period (roughly 238–84) was, it is also ill-reported. Dio Cassius' *History* (which opened with the beginning of Rome but is preserved, with gaps, only from 68 BC) ends at AD 229. Herodian, a minor official of the early part of the century, wrote an account of the years 180–238, ending with the death in civil war of Maximinus. Lack of contemporary sources is hardly made good by the *Historia Augusta*, a fourth-century collection of biographies of emperors which is accorded little respect by modern scholars, and has no information on AD 244–60. (See pp. 210ff. for historical writers.)

The shifting of authority from senate to military commanders was part cause, part result of the varied complex of changes which had earlier turned the Republic into a despotism and were still active. They were changes due to the growth of the Empire, which made control by the mixture of democracy and oligarchy in the Roman constitution impossible, and allowed that control to pass into the hands of able commanders who were themselves limited by the degree of contentment enjoyed by their soldiers. Often that contentment took the form rather of hopes, which all knew could be fulfilled only by success in battle. The battle was often against a rival commander, in itself therefore destructive, but if it was against the barbarian on the frontier, success meant a further addition to an Empire whose size many intelligent observers saw already to be a radical problem. By 238 the situation was critical; the senate tried to appoint the emperor, the army chose him. It was increasingly common for him to come from lands bordering the Danube, since it was in these frontier regions that the most powerful forces were stationed.

At the beginning of the period the senate made itself felt by proclaiming as emperor the 79-year-old proconsul of Africa. This was Gordian I who associated with himself his son Gordian II. Their opposition to Maximinus led swiftly to their deaths, but Gordian III (238–44; son of a daughter of Gordian I) maintained rule for six years even though he was only thirteen when he succeeded. On his murder in 244 the Arabian Praetorian prefect, Julius Philippus – Philip the Arab (244–9) – took the throne and headed in 248 the celebrations of the thousandth anniversary of the foundation of Rome. He established good relations with the senate but pressures from the Goths in Moesia and the rise of rivals in the Danubian provinces led to his replacement by the Pannonian C. Messius Quintus Decius (249–51). In his reign the first general persecution of Christians was officially proclaimed, part of the policy of returning to the ideals of ancient Rome, including its religion. He was killed at Abrittus in Moesia in a battle with the Goths, whose raids were part of the many disasters which now befell the Empire, and filled the joint father-and-son reign of Gallus and Volusianus, that of Aemilianus (253), and that of Valerian (253–60) with his son Gallienus (253–68). Valerian has the melancholy distinction of having been captured and humiliated by Shapur, the Persian king of Palmyra, and ending his life in obscurity, presumably in captivity. Valerian had instituted a persecution of Christians which was ended by his son Gallienus, who sought to encourage intellectual rather than physical opposition to the Church and favoured the Neoplatonist philosopher Plotinus.

Gallienus was killed in civil unrest in 268 and was followed by a series of emperors who strove to discharge the task of repelling barbarian invasions while holding together a divided Empire. They were Claudius II (268–70) from Dalmatia, Aurelian (270–5) and Probus (276–82), both from Pannonia. Aurelian restored Roman prestige in the east, among other successes capturing Zenobia, queen of Palmyra. When he was murdered in 275 the senate was actually invited by the army to nominate his successor. They chose Tacitus, an aged Italian senator who achieved a victory over the Goths in Pontus but was murdered while on campaign in the east. Florianus, his Praetorian prefect, claimed the Empire and was recognized except in Egypt and Syria, where Probus was supported. Florianus failed to defeat him and was murdered by his own disappointed troops. Probus' considerable successes were ended by death, again at the hands of his own troops who deserted to Carus (282–3), another Praetorian prefect and another victim of treachery. His sons and successors, Numerianus (283–4) and Carinus (283–5) also soon lost their lives, the first probably by treachery, the second in battle. He was succeeded by a soldier from Dalmatia named Diocles. He appears first as the avenger of Numerianus, but went on to become the famous emperor known as Diocletian (284–305). His success, which contrasts so strongly with previous misfortunes and failures, was possible no doubt partly because his predecessors had

had to hold barbarian invasions at bay, but he had his own serious difficulties both within and on the borders of the Empire. He overcame them largely because he possessed in some measure the necessary outstanding qualities for which the Empire had been waiting. He shows something like genius as an organizer, and immense energy as both civil and military administrator, delegating with insight and good fortune.

His persecution of Christians was part of another example of enthusiastic 'Roman' reform. His successors Galerius (305–11) and Constantine (312–37) reversed this measure, Galerius only partially and on his deathbed, Constantine – with whatever motives – more wholeheartedly. The latter's far-reaching reforms and innovations followed on the completion of the reorganization by Diocletian, whose work abides as a landmark in the history of the Roman Empire. Its details lie well outside the term of our period (AD 200) and must therefore be left aside.

JEWS IN ROME

The earliest point at which Jews and their relation to others in Rome comes to light is 139 BC, when an attempt to set up Jewish places of worship within the *pomerium* (the ancient boundary of Rome proper, whose sacredness was occasionally invoked in a somewhat legalistic manner) caused an expulsion of Jews from Rome. This was part of a long and intermittent struggle to keep Rome free from foreign religions and ideas. It is doubtful if all Jews were expelled, and probably many returned soon afterwards from the other places in Italy to which they had fled.

Numbers of Jews in Rome were increased by the prisoners of war taken by Pompey in 63 BC, and there is little doubt that many purchased their freedom in a comparatively short time. Cicero in his *Pro Flacco* (59 BC) – his defence of Flaccus, governor of Asia 62–61 – speaks of gold being exported 'from Italy and from all our provinces'. This reference is to the Jewish collection and sending to Jerusalem of the Temple tax. He also speaks of the vigorous activity of Jews in Rome at this time. When Caesar was dictator (from 49 BC) he met the threat to state security of the *collegia* (clubs ostensibly for religious observances) by banning them; but he made exceptions for some, including the Jews, who were allowed by him to meet for worship and common meals, to observe the sabbath and festivals, to hold funds and to build synagogues. Jews would dislike Cicero for his support of Flaccus. In the rivalry between Pompey and Caesar they were divided, since Hyrcanus II and Antipater supported Pompey, while Caesar sought to help Aristobulus II escape from Rome to claim the Judaean throne. After Caesar's favourable treatment of them in 47 BC (p. 96) they were more united in support of him, and their gratitude for his wide-ranging legislation carried out in many places in the Diaspora is often mentioned.

In understanding the attitude of Romans to Jews in the years which followed, it is necessary to avoid making judgements of a too general kind. Writers such as Horace and Juvenal betray the dislike of the Jewish nation often found in any age in which Gentiles misconceive altogether the character of Judaism, and concentrate their criticism on such externals as circumcision and food taboos. A minority looked further and perceived that what had appeared a stubborn and fanatical monotheism was linked with a superior moral earnestness and a genuine personal piety; they were drawn to learn more, and often to attend Jewish worship as 'godfearers'. This minority knew that Judaism was falsely represented in the popular mind and that the official attitude was usually nearer to that of the unthinking multitude than that of the thoughtful scholar or soldier.

Augustus (27 BC to AD 14) ought not to surprise us therefore when he includes Jews and their religion in his general distaste for foreign cults. Nevertheless he represents the best side of the fair-minded but ignorant administrator, since he showed himself willing to have a synagogue called after him, and avoided the sabbath when arranging distribution of largesse to the Roman people. Tiberius (AD 14–37) is hard to judge, since historians differ so much in their assessment of his character. He was certainly much under the influence of his favourite Sejanus, who seems to have been specially anti-Jewish, although the measures in AD 19 were taken against Egyptian priests and Jews alike. The failure to distinguish between rites of Isis and Jewish missionary teaching probably owes more to ignorance or indifference on the part of the authorities concerned than to any resemblance whatever between the two. The two rival 'religions' would seem to Romans to be equally reprehensible because foreign. It is probable that the fall of Sejanus in AD 31 reflected a change in the official attitude towards the Jews, although the personal offence of Caius (37–41) against them was 'religious', since he regarded himself, or pretended to regard himself, as a god, and as such entitled to be worshipped in association with the Olympians. He tried to enforce this notion upon the people of Jerusalem and Judaea by having his statue set up in the Temple at Jerusalem (p. 111). His own death saved the lives of more than those closely concerned with this affair, and it was perhaps a reaction against his manic behaviour that led Claudius (41–54) to revoke the measures against the Jews, when he succeeded to the throne. However, Suetonius says that because the Jews made disturbances at the instigation of Chrestus, Claudius expelled them from Rome (cp. Acts 18:2). This has too often been taken as dating to the year of Claudius' accession (41), but F. F. Bruce in his commentary on Acts is surely right to prefer the later date of 49–50 provided by Orosius, since Josephus records measures favourable to the Jews in Alexandria for the year 41. 'Chrestus' may be an alternative for 'Christus' (since the pronunciation would be very nearly the same) and the statement may therefore conceal some ill-understood record of Jewish anti-Christian disturbance, especially as Suetonius introduces it among a miscellany of acts by Claudius. But the connexion with Christianity is uncertain, and the Letter of Paul to the Romans remains the earliest sure testimony (about 55) to the presence of Christians in Rome (on which Acts itself strangely says so little). It should be noted that Suetonius does not say that Claudius expelled Jews from Italy, but from Rome, and many may have moved both under Tiberius and under Claudius to other towns, including Campagna, Puteoli, Naples, Capua and Pompeii, where it is known that Jews lived. Such removal may have been temporary for some and permanent for others. Certainly the Jewish population in Rome continued, and they were not included in Nero's persecution of the Christians in AD 64.

In 71 many Jewish prisoners were brought to Rome as slaves, and some, though not so many, in 135, when no triumph was held. Many of these in time obtained their freedom and thus their citizenship, especially after 212. The oldest and largest Jewish catacomb in Rome was in use from the late Republic to the time of Diocletian, but the greatest number of burials date from the reigns of Hadrian (117–38) and Septimius Severus (193–211). They are evidence of a free population, and its growth is shown also by others elsewhere in Rome, especially in the south of the city.

During the second century a rabbinic academy was set up in Rome. The rabbi associated with its establishment was Mattithiah ben Heresh (bSanh. 32b).

JOSEPHUS (AD 37 TO *c.* 100)

Josephus ben Matthias was born of a priestly family, and profited through his considerable ability from a wide-ranging education. He savoured the various Jewish 'philosophies', as he calls them, of Pharisaism, Sadduceeism and Essenism, and was prominent at different times as politician, military commander and historian. In 64 he was a member of a mission to the government in Rome and in 66 at the beginning of the revolt was made governor of Galilee. He was ambiguous as a patriot, some energetic measures contrasting with recurrent defeatism. He became the prisoner of Vespasian in circumstances of doubtful credit to himself, but he made a gradually deepening impression on the future emperor, and became the protégé of his family, calling himself Flavius Josephus. After the war he lived in the emperor's house in Rome, received Roman citizenship and became an imperial pensioner. His main defence against the charge of treason was his strong religious conviction that God's plan for his own nation involved the supremacy of Rome and that for this reason he had consistently advocated submission.

Josephus' Writings. His first work was the *De Bello Judaico* (often abbreviated to *BJ*) or *The Jewish War* (*War*), written in Aramaic about 73–4 and afterwards translated into Greek *c.* 75. It begins with the capture of Jerusalem by Antiochus Epiphanes (169 BC) and the Maccabaean revolt (166) and ends with the 'mopping-up' operations after the defeat of Judaea (*c.* AD 75).

The Antiquities of the Jews (*Ant.*), published *c.* 94, is a long work beginning with the Creation and following the Old Testament history, interesting for its later hellenistic Jewish additions and outlook. Of its twenty books, XIV–XX cover the Roman era of Jewish history (from 67 BC). Josephus ends book XX at AD 66 and refers the reader to the *War* for subsequent events.

The *Life* is not really an autobiography but a defence of his conduct in Galilee. It was published with the *Antiquities*, so that the two together constitute a defence of his nation and of himself.

The *Contra Apionem* or *Against Apion* (*Apion*). It is doubtful if this was the original title. Apion (p. 210) according to Eusebius (*Eccl. Hist.* III.9.2) wrote against the Jews, and it has been assumed that this book, which is certainly a reply to his charges, was always called by this title. In book 1 Josephus defends the claim of his nation to antiquity and the truth of its historical traditions, and in book 2 answers Apion's attacks on the Jewish religion, making some of his own on Greek religious beliefs.

4. Syria, Phoenicia, Judaea, Egypt, Cyrene

We have seen something of the life of Jews both in the east and in the west during the period with which we are concerned. We have now to follow the Fertile Crescent southwards in order to include the first three countries in Philo's list (p. 5); but we take them in their north–south order – Syria, Phoenicia, Egypt – and before the last of these we must pause to include the all-important Judaea.

SYRIA AND PHOENICIA

Syria

As a recent writer has summarized, 'In the last quarter of the second millennium BC a west-Semitic people, speaking various Aramaic dialects, spread out from the fringes of the Syro-Arabian desert ... fanning out over the Fertile Crescent, from the Persian Gulf to the Amanus mountains, the Lebanon, and Transjordan.' (A. Malamat, 'The Aramaeans' in D. J. Wiseman (ed.), *Peoples of Old Testament Times*.)

The westward expansion was into the country which constitutes the eastern boundary of the Mediterranean and stretches from Cilicia and Mesopotamia in the north to the Sinai Desert and Egypt in the south. It is the land often called Palestine and includes the ancient lands of Israel and Judah. It is the country which many ancient writers, Herodotus among them, called Syria; the word was often replaced by Coele-Syria to distinguish this country from the Syria of Mesopotamia (Coele-, 'hollow', refers to its being the country between mountains, Lebanon and Anti-Lebanon). Mesopotamian Syria was for many centuries the land dominated by the Assyrians and this name the Greeks shortened to Syrians, themselves using it for the Assyrian subjects nearest to them, that is those who occupied the strip of country at the east of the Mediterranean just described. (The name Palestine is derived from Philistine, an adjective applied originally only to the southern coastal plain occupied by the Philistines. It is found in Herodotus but came into general use only with later Latin

78

authors.) Under the Seleucids the term Coele-Syria became restricted to the northern land round Antioch and Damascus, and was used for the northern province of the Roman Empire under Septimius Severus (AD 193–211). This general area is often called Syria, especially to designate the kingdom called in the Bible Aram or Damascus, after the city which Rezon, its founder in the days of Solomon, made his capital. The Old Testament story in the books of Kings, from the division after the death of Solomon to the final engulfment of Aram-Damascus and Israel, has as its constant background the shifting pattern of alliances of these two states and Judah, only when united sometimes able to resist the power of Assyria, and doomed by their disunity, which led often to war among themselves and even to alliance with the common enemy. The Assyrian Tiglath-Pileser III (745–727) decisively crippled Aram-Damascus in 732 by conquest and shifting of populations, breaking up its territory into Assyrian provinces, including some parts of Israel. The unsuccessful rebellion of a few weak states in the area in 721 brought the same fate to Samaria. Henceforth these smaller entities (from 597 including Judah) were parts of the Assyrian and later the Babylonian Empire. When under Cyrus Persia succeeded to the leadership of the Orient (from 539), the whole of Syria was the 'satrapy beyond the river' (i.e. Euphrates) of the Persian Empire, until the latter was conquered by Alexander. On his death in 323 it became a bone of contention between Ptolemy and Antigonus, but in 301 it was divided (at the river Eleutherus, just north of Tripolis) between Seleucus I in the north and Ptolemy I (of Egypt) in the south. The arrangement brought no peace between the two rival Diadochi; their constant wars meant that the inhabitants of Syria frequently had to change their loyalties, until in 200 Antiochus III's victory at Panion secured Syria finally to the Seleucids.

Jerusalem, in the middle of the Seleucid and Ptolemaic strife, was captured by Ptolemy in 312 and thus became at the outset of the struggle in the eyes and minds of a growing number a hellenistic city. It made considerable progress in this direction for nearly a century until Antiochus III made his expedition against Egypt in 219–217 and was welcomed into Jerusalem by the joyful inhabitants, to whom he remitted taxes for three years and made provision for the repair and upkeep of the Temple. From this time onwards Jews who accepted Hellenism were of course supporters of the Seleucids and wished at times to be known as Antiochenes, thus even conniving at an attempt to change the status of their city to that of a Greek city. In 217 Ptolemy IV defeated Antiochus at Raphia, and Judaea passed again under Egyptian control until in 200 at Panion Antiochus won back all southern Syria. It then remained part of the Seleucid Empire until the Maccabaean revolt. In the Maccabaean struggle against Antiochus IV the city changed hands several times, and afterwards suffered a cruel siege at the hands of Pompey in 63 BC. His intervention came by way of his defeat of Tigranes of Armenia who had occupied Syria in 83, a time when the Seleucids had become hopelessly weak. Pompey's settlement in 67 BC turned Syria into a province of the Roman Empire.

Phoenicia

It is almost impossible to define Phoenicia geographically, since it consists of a number of towns on the coast of the eastern Mediterranean with a small hinterland affording some agricultural support for each city. The best known, listing from north to south, are Aradus (Arvad), Simyra (Zemara), Tripolis, Gebal (Byblos), Beeroth (Berytus or Beirut), Sidon, Zarephath and Tyre. Tripolis appears first in records in the Persian period, but all the others occur in Egyptian and other early records.

The very term Phoenicia being so little used in antiquity shows how little the cities were thought of collectively. Phoenicia did not then form a country such as we usually mean now, i.e. in the political sense. The cities are mentioned individually, and what we now call Phoenicia would be referred to by using the name of the great city that was being discussed at the moment, and by thinking of the whole country as belonging to it. Sidon was often used in this way and Phoenicians were often called Sidonians even when they belonged to other cities. The term Phoenicians does not occur in the Hebrew Old Testament, and hardly in the Septuagint. They belong to the amalgam of nations which the Bible calls Canaanites, and they have to be considered as part of the latter. They shared the general Canaanite culture. The first Phoenician cities seem to date back to about 3000 BC. Their position suggests their peoples would be familiar with the sea, and early Phoenicians may have used it as a way of travelling more than most early peoples, but their reputation as sailors comes much later, perhaps beginning with the fall of Minoan Crete and Mycenae, i.e. about 1200 onwards.

This maritime commerce developed from the position of the cities. One might think at first that an important part of this trade would have been the supply and transport of timber from the hinterland, e.g. to Egypt, or Israel as in Solomon's time (1 Kings 5, especially verse 9). Byblos was active in this trade, and the sea-snail which provided the famous purple dye was of course very much a local product, as it was not found except along this coast. But in fact these people were far more middlemen than producers. They learnt from others and industriously pursued ivory carving, carving of seals and metalwork, as well as pottery. But in addition they imported and exported, as well as working on imported materials.

Besides Byblos, there was another city-state which flourished as a metropolitan trading-centre. This was the city of Ras Shamra or Ugarit, which has yielded to archaeologists a large and varied library of clay tablets inscribed with cuneiform signs. These provide a wealth of information concerning the religion of pre-conquest Canaan, enabling much of the earliest material of the Old Testament to be better understood (see p. 20; *Making*, pp. 25ff). The language of the tablets is basically that of the Semites of the Levant, Aramaic and Hebrew both being cognate forms. As this Phoenician form of it exemplifies the earliest use of alphabetic writing signs (letters) as distinct from syllabic signs, it may well be, as tradition has it, that Phoenicians were the inventors of alphabetic writing; certainly all alphabets stem from theirs. Scholars have long regretted that little Phoenician literature other than the Ras Shamra tablets has survived, and have deplored this the more since references in classical and ecclesiastical authors (including Josephus and Eusebius) make clear that there was interesting and valuable material for both historian and theologian (e.g. records of the city of Tyre and a 'Phoenician Genesis'). The recent discoveries at Ebla (Tel Mardikh) in Syria belong in the main to a much earlier period than those at Ras Shamra. They may prove to enrich our knowledge of both history and literature, but it is too early to assess their significance and importance.

From about 1200 BC the Phoenicians ventured more on the sea. The Mediterranean was naturally their first sphere of adventure, and Phoenician sites are found all round its coasts; Carthage was founded from Tyre *c.* 814 BC. They also circumnavigated Africa, at the command of the Pharaoh Necho in *c.* 600. In *c.* 450

Hamilco of Carthage sailed to Britain. In the Mediterranean they were attracted to Cyprus by its copper (the word is derived from the Latin *Cyprium aes*, and the name of the island seems to be earlier than the word for the metal), and they founded Kition on the south coast *c.* 1000 BC, perhaps their first colony on the island. In the Old Testament the Kittim are Cypriots, and the word is extended to include the inhabitants of other islands. In later Hebrew literature, e.g. that of Qumran, the term is used for 'islanders', i.e. people from the west across the sea, and so even for Romans.

In the gospels, Jesus visits the territory north of Galilee round Tyre and famous Phoenician cities, places which were at the time part of the province of Syria. According to Mark 7:26 he meets there a woman who was 'a Phoenician of Syria', whom Matt. 15:22 calls 'Canaanite'.

Jews in Syria and Phoenicia

A glance at the map (p. xviii) shows at once that Syria and Phoenicia were natural overflow territories for Judaea; hence Jews who lived in such an area were regarded as in many respects belonging to the homeland. Josephus (*War* VII.3.3 (43–4)) says that Jews were spread in great numbers all over the world, 'especially in Syria, where the two nations are neighbours'. Many maintained links with Babylonian Jewry, which vied with Palestine as a chief source of additions to their numbers. For brief periods at the end of the fourth century BC, during the Ptolemaic–Seleucid struggle for supremacy in Syria, when the Seleucid ruler was successful the Jews of Babylonia and Syria were under the same government, though many probably remained scarcely aware of the fact.

Josephus says that the largest Jewish population in Syria was at Antioch itself, the capital. It became an important centre for Jews, giving them a prestige ranking with those at other famous cities, especially Alexandria and Rome. They enjoyed specially defined community privileges and, after the Seleucid triumph of Antiochus III in 200, the easy contact between Antioch and Jerusalem lent force to the desire of hellenizing Jews in Jerusalem to change the status of the city and to be known as Antiochenes. Such a movement does not imply a wish to abandon their faith, but to live according to it in a way adapted to the new civilization which they saw around them. Damascus also held a large number of Jews, and the action of Saul (i.e. Paul) in Acts 9 in seeking introduction to them in order to root out devotion to the risen Jesus reflects the importance of their community to a Jerusalem Jew about two hundred years later. Damascus was not the capital but was an older city and much nearer to Jerusalem.

JUDAEA

The Jews of Judaea 200–168 BC

Antiochus III was defeated by Ptolemy IV at Raphia in 217 but in 200 won the decisive victory of Panion which placed all Syria–Palestine under his rule. Besides Syrians, Phoenicians, Samaritans and Idumaeans his people included Judaeans, and it is to their history within the Seleucid Empire that we now turn.

In the absence of a king of their own, the person who repre-sented them, in the popular mind, was the high priest. It was an office filled by members of the Zadokite family, who according to an established dogma derived their origin from the priest Zadok of the time of David. This family had long been provided with a pedigree which brought them within the tribe of Levi as descendants of Aaron (e.g. Exod. 6:16ff and 1 Chron. 6:1–15) but the descent from Zadok was their primary source of prestige. The holder of the office was important in a national and political sense, since he was the natural guardian of the Temple, its sacri-fices, and all its associations. He would therefore be a natural bastion against change and especially against hellenistic influence which tended to universalize God and to diminish the exclusive-ness of the Jewish people. But holders of the office were no more immune from such influence than other men, and it was often held by men for whom it had political and social importance more than merely religious prestige. Even when this was the case, the office itself bestowed upon its holder, in the eyes of many, an indelible aura, and they felt its misuse or degradation as a profan-ation.

The high-priesthood was a very important issue in the changes which took place under hellenistic influence during the struggle of the two hellenistic empires for supremacy in the area, and continued to be so under the Seleucids. To make these issues and changes intelligible it is necessary to go back a little earlier than 200 BC. During the struggle between the empires it was inevitable that a people in the centre of it should be divided in their loyalties. There is little information about such divisions but Josephus cites Hecataeus of Abdera (historian of Egypt *c.* 300 BC) concerning a certain Hezekiah, a man of some substance and authority, and the high priest according to Josephus, though it is conjectured that he may rather have been an aristocrat of priestly family. In 312–311 he followed Ptolemy I on his retreat into Egypt and took with him a number of followers (*Apion* 1.22 (187)). In the reign of Ptolemy II (285–246) an official named Zenon (known from the Zenon papyri, CPJ 1, 4f) visited the estate in Transjordan of Tobias, head of a family who were to prove important in the intrigues which followed. The ultimate purpose of the visit was evidently to improve further relations and trade between the pro-Ptolemaic Tobiads and men in high positions in Egypt, including the king himself.

In contrast Onias II, the high priest from *c.* 245 to 220 in the reign of Ptolemy III (246–221), refused to pay tribute, which was naturally taken by the king to be an act of rebellion. The action probably reflects pro-Seleucid convictions, no doubt under the belief that Seleucid rule would be more favourable to the practice of Judaism. In the ensuing moves and counter-moves a nephew of Onias, Joseph son of Tobias, boldly ingratiated himself with Ptolemy and became chief taxgatherer for Syria–Palestine with troops at his disposal. Indeed the Tobiad family were the virtual vice-regents of Judaea through the reigns of Ptolemy III and Ptolemy IV (221–205). About 210 BC a split seems to have occurred in the Tobiad family, for Joseph's youngest son Hyrcanus, on a visit to Egypt, bought favour with Ptolemy. On his return there was open enmity between him and Joseph with his other sons. Hyrcanus had to retire to a family estate over the Jordan at Araq-el-Emir. He remained a supporter of the Ptolemies, and it seems probable that the rest of the family had become pro-Seleucid. It is indeed conjectured that Onias II's act of defiance had been a shrewd gamble on the coming success of the Seleucid king (Josephus *Ant.* xii.4.2–11 (160–236)).

The high priest at the time of Antiochus III's conquest in 200 was Simon II, son of Onias II. Simon, high priest *c.* 220–200, appears to have won from the king a number of pro-Jewish measures, and his lasting memorial is Ecclus. 50. In the Hebrew original of Ecclus. 50:24 the hope is expressed that the covenant of Phinehas (i.e. the high-priesthood − see Ecclus. 45:23f) will continue for ever in his family. We shall see that this hope was disappointed very soon after his death in 200.

An inscription discovered near Scythopolis and a letter from the king to his general Ptolemaeus preserved in Josephus *Ant.* XII.3.3 (138−44) show that the Jews were granted important rights and privileges in return for their substantial support for Antiochus in his victorious campaign. These included financial and material aid for the restoration of Jerusalem and the Temple, supplies for sacrifices, very generous exemptions from taxes (including permanent exemption from all taxes for members of the sanhedrin and priests), and express encouragement to live 'according to their ancestral laws', i.e. the Torah. To the letter Josephus adds mention of a decree excluding all non-Jews from the Temple court. Pro-Seleucid enthusiasm did not last long. Antiochus unwisely challenged Roman power (p. 13) and was forced to abandon his territories in Europe and Asia Minor. The loss of lands was accompanied by shortage of money, and it was this latter which precipitated the downfall of the king, who was killed when plundering the temple of Bel in Susa in 187 BC.

Antiochus was succeeded by his son Seleucus IV, whose brother Antiochus was a hostage in Rome until Seleucus effected his release by providing his son Demetrius as a substitute. This Demetrius was the true heir; but when Seleucus IV was murdered with Demetrius away in Rome, Antiochus IV (Epiphanes) − Seleucus' brother and Demetrius' uncle − seized the throne (Dan. 11:21; 1 Macc. 1:1−10). This is how the internal split in the Seleucid dynasty began; it was destined to lead the dynasty to powerlessness and to it there was added growing hostility from the Jews.

Simon was succeeded as high priest by his son Onias III who favoured latent pro-Ptolemaic tendencies which revived with the decline in the Seleucid power. This decline was for a time arrested by Antiochus IV (Epiphanes), who was supported by the Tobiads. Before he was secure on the throne they exacted from him the deposition of Onias, a deposition which was followed in 171 by Onias' murder. While he was still alive he was replaced by his brother Jason, pro-Seleucid and favouring the new ways. These new ways were those which resulted from the exposure of the pastoral, theocratic and conservative religion of the Jewish people to the urban, humanistic and progressive culture of Hellenism. Since most of our evidence comes from the hostile literature of the Jews, it is important to remember the positive values of Hellenism even when imposed and spread by conquest. The Seleucid kings, for example, were not only warriors. As Greeks they believed in the necessity of cities, a more natural sentiment than it seems to us. For cities, and only cities, could provide effective protection against barbarian destruction – in its simplest form the constant menace of the desert robbers' raids on cultivators of the soil – as well as the possibility of leisure founded on the centralization of industry and pursuit of the arts, athletics and philosophical dialogue. Not only did the Seleucids believe in cities, they worked extremely hard to found, build and provide a viable economy for them. They were not alone among the hellenistic empires in this activity; Alexandria, whose very name betrays its origin (p. 128), was cherished and fostered by the Ptolemies.

Whether such or similar benevolent motives influenced Jason cannot be known. Among the forms which pro-Hellenism took one was bound to be political; Jason illustrates the fact, for his attempt to make Jerusalem another Antioch, a Greek-style city-state, involved the support of Antiochus IV and the consequent abrogation of the pro-Torah edicts of Antiochus III. Moreover, Jason and his party controlled the citizen lists, favouring the richer elements of the population; the poorer elements, who were so often religiously conservative, in any case would not wish to take part in the activities, such as the athletics of the all-important gymnasium, which were to characterize the new *polis* (city-state). Although the 'reforms' were gradual and not meant to abrogate the Torah as a way of life for those who wished to follow it, the manners which they favoured were in many ways incompatible with the life of a faithful Jew as he understood Judaism. For example, nakedness, unthinkable in public for a Jew, was inseparable from Greek athletics, as the word gymnasium implies (*gymnos* is Greek for 'naked'). We know from 1 Macc. 1:11–15 that many Jews entered on gymnastic exercises, and in order to escape the censure or mockery of non-Jews, or perhaps simply to be in fashion, made themselves appear uncircumcised. The same passage implies constant mingling with Gentiles, whom we may imagine would provide the first instructors in athletics and gymnastics. Whatever the easily understood reasons for Jews wishing to appear in every way as up-to-date as their 'progressive' gentile friends, the action was a symbolic way of departing from the covenant and so of immeasurable importance. In this way we can understand the strict Jew's antagonism to wearing the Greek hat (2 Macc. 4:12), otherwise apparently such a detail, for it was the badge of one who had accepted the contemporary 'alternative' culture, and who had therefore presumably abandoned his Judaism. We have also to remember that the widespread tolerance in most parts of our civilization would have been unintelligible to a Jew of the time we are considering. Especially in a situation where the right to practise one's religion was either newly-won or threatened, and often both, it was difficult to regard one who abandoned any part of it as other than a traitor.

Jason was at least a Zadokite; it was a further shock for the orthodox when he and thus the Oniads were swept aside by the usurpation of the high-priesthood by Menelaus, supported by the Tobiads. Thus the office passed for a time out of the Zadokite family. Menelaus was cynical enough about the office he held to embezzle part of the Temple treasure, and thereby to cause a revolt in Jerusalem. From the safety of Antioch he encompassed the murder of Onias III (2 Macc. 4:32–4). Antiochus met the demand of the sanhedrin for justice by condemning the murderer, but Menelaus escaped punishment by bribery.

On the wider stage, Antiochus exploited the weakness of the government of Ptolemy VI Philometor (181–145) and was so far successful by winning the battle of Pelusium as to gain the twin crowns of Upper and Lower Egypt. The exact sequence of events is not certain, but at about the time of Antiochus' Egyptian campaign, the deposed Jason attempted a return to office and had enough support to drive the Seleucids from Jerusalem. The imminent return of Antiochus however forced Jason to flee the city, and in 169 Antiochus began his hostile acts against the people by plundering the Temple in revenge, assisted by Menelaus. It seems that Antiochus returned to Egypt in 168, but the Roman representative Popillius Laenas ordered him on the senate's authority to leave at once. Whether or not the humiliated king went straight to Jerusalem, his orders against it were savage. Executions were followed by the establishment of a garrison on what was called the Akra in the City of David (the site is uncertain but it must have been close to the Temple area and probably south of it). A pagan altar dedicated to Zeus Olympios was erected on the altar of sacrifice. This is the biblical 'Abomination of Desolation' (Dan. 11:31; 12:11; 1 Macc. 1:54; Mark 13:14 etc.). These outrages came hard upon the deposition and murder of a legitimate high priest, and with that constitute a composite trauma from which it might be said the Jewish people have never recovered. The statement may seem to be contradicted by the restoration effected by the Maccabaean revolt and the magnificence of Herod's Temple, but the destruction of that Temple in AD 70 is linked in their memory with the earlier atrocities. The ideological basis for the outrages is articulated in 1 Macc. 1:41ff: it begins with the principle of 'all to become one people and abandon their own laws and religion'. It was ostensibly applied to all the peoples of the Empire, but the actual measures indicate that it was really directed against the Jews as victims, forbidding sacrifices in the sanctuary and the keeping of sabbaths or feasts, abolishing circumcision and enjoining pagan sacrifices, including sacrifices of unclean animals. The penalty for disobedience was death.

Such extreme measures as had now transformed a struggle into a persecution met with the inevitable responses both of collaboration and of resistance even to death. The resistance was begun by a priest from Modin named Mattathias, whose pedigree is briefly given by Josephus in *Ant.* XII.6.1 (265), including his great-grandfather Asamonaeus, after whom the family is often called Hasmonaean, but alternatively Maccabaean, which derives from a nickname of Judas, Mattathias' energetic son, viz. Maccabi, which may mean 'Hammer'. This rebellion gives us another natural division.

The Seleucid–Hasmonaean Period (168–67 BC)

The Maccabaean or Hasmonaean revolt began in 168, and quite early the conduct of guerilla warfare was entrusted by Mattathias to his third son (out of five), Judas (c. 166–160). It is doubtful if even his wise and adroit tactics (which may fairly be called 'hit-and-run') would have prevailed but for division among the Seleucids themselves. Antiochus was absent on a campaign against Parthia, and Judas won victories over Lysias, Seleucid general and self-appointed regent, and three other generals, Ptolemy, Nicanor and Gorgias. Antiochus died on the campaign against Parthia and his successor Antiochus V (164–162) was only eight years old. Lysias thought it prudent to make peace with Judas because of the threat constituted by Demetrius' claim to the throne (see above p. 85). It was short-lived and in 164 Lysias was victorious at Beth Zur and would probably have been so against Jerusalem but for a rebellion by Philip, whom Antiochus IV had left as official regent. But there was peace for a while in 163. It seems that some effort was made by moderate hellenizers to pacify the orthodox Jews who had been scandalized by the profanation of the high-priesthood, and who had lent some support, more in the moral than the military sphere, to the Maccabees. Menelaus was dismissed and a Zadokite high priest appointed, named Alcimus. But the new high priest disappointed any hopes placed in him by the strict Jews. He was probably a hellenizer, for all the influence of his ancestry, and he asked Demetrius for help against Judas. The latter achieved considerable success, defeating and killing Nicanor at Adasa in 161 or 160. Demetrius was not stopped by this setback and called in Bacchides as a general, who defeated and killed Judas at Elasa in 160.

Judas' place was taken by his brother Jonathan (160–142) who achieved some minor successes in the field, claiming to rule from Michmash. Bacchides ceased hostilities but in 153 another claimant to the throne appeared in Alexander Balas, saying that he was Antiochus IV's son. He sought to win over Jonathan and appointed him high priest in Jerusalem. He was successful for a time, killing Demetrius in 150. However, in 147 Demetrius' son, Demetrius II, took arms against Alexander, and by defeating him in 145 was able to proclaim himself king.

Demetrius II attacked Parthia in 141. In 139 he was captured by Mithradates I (p. 14) and was not released until 129; during his imprisonment his brother Antiochus VII (Sidetes) took over the kingdom. He had to put down yet another pretender (Trypho) in Antioch in 138, and afterwards made the Judaean territory his in campaigns in 135–134, but in 130 he turned against Parthia. At first successful, he was finally defeated and killed by the Parthians in 129, and thus lost Parthia for ever from the Seleucid Empire.

Demetrius II's release from captivity in 129 did not guarantee him his Syrian kingdom. Jonathan the Hasmonaean had much earlier changed sides, supporting for a time the pretender Trypho. Jonathan had wanted to get the Akra evacuated but died in 142 without having achieved this aim.

Jonathan is important in the history of the high-priesthood. No doubt to obtain his support, Alexander Balas bestowed on him the title of high priest and in 153 or 152 Jonathan was duly installed. Since an alien was king, the high-priesthood was the only office an ambitious individual could aspire to, but to accept it at the hands of an alien was in itself an offence. More serious still was the fact that the Hasmonaeans were not Zadokites, although Levites. In the section on Qumran (p. 178) we shall see that Jonathan apparently succeeded no one, but rather filled a vacancy left after the death of Alcimus, and that he may be the person intended by the phrase 'Wicked Priest' in the Qumran literature.

On the death of Jonathan in 142 his brother Simon (142–135) took the leadership of the patriotic cause; such it still was, even if it was to become rather the Maccabaean or Hasmonaean cause. I Macc. 14 records the high esteem in which Simon was held by the people. He supported Demetrius II and enjoyed considerable independence, even forcing the garrison in the Akra to surrender, and expanding the territory which Demetrius had perforce to allow him to regard as his own. In any case Demetrius could not prevent him, for in 139 he was imprisoned in Parthia, allowing Antiochus VII to seize the throne in Antioch. The latter opposed his enemies vigorously and the pretender Trypho committed suicide. But Simon continued to hold his own, acting like a king. This was in fact not one of his titles, although he was given several by the people in a special proclamation, including that of high priest. His career was cut short unexpectedly by murder at the hands of his ambitious son-in-law, a wealthy landowner named Ptolemy, in 135. Some of his sons perished with him but one survivor, John Hyrcanus, who was in the newly conquered Gaza at the time, was able to take over without succumbing to Ptolemy's plot, which perhaps had been instigated by Antiochus. The latter had some success in the field against John Hyrcanus but he died in 129. In this year Demetrius II reappeared after his liberation and reigned as Seleucid king. But he had to contend with another pretender who was supported by Ptolemy VII (Physcon) of Egypt, and was murdered in 125. Antiochus VIII succeeded but family divisions later resulted in Antiochus VIII and Antiochus IX sharing the rule from 111.

Owing to the internal strife among the Seleucids, the reign of John Hyrcanus (135–104) was for all practical purposes that of an independent sovereign over a sovereign state. He ruthlessly acquired significant additions to his territory, showing no respect

for ancient traditions, except those of strict Jews, forcing circumcision on the Idumaeans and plundering the tomb of David. He
conquered Samaria and Shechem, which involved the destruction
of the temple on Mount Gerizim as well as the town of Samaria.
In the south he seized cities including Hebron and Marisa. In the
north he extended his control to the borders with Galilee.

Rome made for the time being little effort to interfere in the
affairs of Palestine. The evidence for an 'alliance' with Judas,
apparently preserved in 1 Maccabees, is less certain than that the
Romans encouraged him and his successors as 'friends' in order to
harass the Seleucids, whom no doubt well-informed Romans saw
as the main enemies in the Middle East.

Internally the Jewish state was not as strong as it might have
been if Hyrcanus had been a more sincere upholder of the Torah.
It was during his reign that the Pharisees first emerged as a recognizable group out of the strict supporters of the covenant, the
hasidim or 'pious ones', who had to some extent welcomed the
leadership of Judas and even of Jonathan and Simon, but who
were increasingly uneasy at the profanation of the high-
priesthood which seemed to mar the glory of the leaders since
Jonathan. The Pharisees would have been glad to see the leader
John Hyrcanus drop the title of high priest, but he retained it and
relied for support on the wealthy aristocratic families, who were
to become known later as the Sadducees. Hyrcanus died in 104.

Aristobulus I (104–103) did well to reign even for one year,
since his brothers and even his mother, whom John Hyrcanus had
made regent, were against his succeeding, although he was the
elder son. He extended his territory even further north, probably
to the northern border of Galilee. It is often said that he was the
first Maccabaean to call himself king, since Josephus reports this
in two passages, but another tradition preserved by Strabo
ascribes this step to his brother who ousted him.

This brother was Alexander Jannaeus (103–76), a violent man,
possibly the cruellest known ruler in Jewish history. With his
certain use of the title king and the epithet Philhellenos, the
leadership of the Jewish people became firmly a hellenistic monarchy. His campaigns were many but met with such varying
success that in the end they left him no better off than at the
beginning of his reign. Opposed by the Nabataean Arabs and
latterly by his own people, especially by the Pharisees, he used
foreign mercenaries and relied on the support at home of the

future Sadducees, the high-born, many of whom were related to the high priest and upheld a narrow and literal interpretation of the Torah. The Pharisees disliked Alexander for being an aggressive warrior, abusing the office of high priest. Their hostility was also due to religious scruples, for at this time the Pharisees further emerged into prominence and their characteristics became clearer than they were under John Hyrcanus. They owed their influence with the people to their loyal obedience to the Torah and their upholding it against opposition from authority. The king did not always obey the law and the Pharisees were sufficiently many and enjoyed such wide support that they wielded their power politically, contrasting with the more quietist piety which seems to mark them in the New Testament and later Judaism. (See p. 184.) Dissatisfied with Alexander, the Pharisees called on the Seleucid king Demetrius III (Eucaerus) to assist them in a revolt. He won a battle at Shechem, but was deserted by the Pharisees afterwards, and failed to take Jerusalem (88 BC).

The change of loyalty by the Pharisees, hard to explain, reversed Alexander Jannaeus' fortunes and did no good to the Pharisees. Regaining power in Jerusalem, Alexander committed the atrocity for which he has become famous in Jewish tradition: he slaughtered the families of eight hundred Pharisees before their eyes and then crucified them while he and his guests feasted as they watched them die. This was the first time a Jewish ruler used the barbarous and cruel method of execution by crucifixion, a practice which the civilized world owes to the Romans. We shall see that this event involving Demetrius III seems to be referred to in the fragmentary commentary on Nahum among the Qumran scrolls.

Fate was kinder to Alexander than he deserved, for he died a natural death. On his deathbed he advised his wife Salome Alexandra (76–67) to make peace with the Pharisees and to rule according to their advice. She obeyed, and for the majority of the people her reign was peaceful. That a queen should reign as the successor of a line of warriors, who had usurped the title of high priest and had been called king for less than thirty years, was remarkable. Paradoxically it was a successful reign partly by virtue of adherence to those religious principles which the reign of a woman might seem to contradict. For during her reign the Pharisees were strong enough to wage a struggle against their enemies, the aristocratic landowners and merchants who had supported Alexander and his predecessors and they brought about the death of many of them. Yet Salome did not rule entirely because of their support, being a character, Josephus tells us, without the weakness of a woman.

Salome did not of course aspire to be high priest and so appointed her elder son Hyrcanus II as high priest during her reign. When she died his position was challenged by his younger brother, for their temperaments were contrasted, in that Hyrcanus preferred a quiet life while Aristobulus was ready for adventure. He had supported the men who had supported his father, and thus opposed the Pharisees when they demanded vengeance on those who had approved Alexander's ghastly massacre of the eight hundred. Hyrcanus' high-priesthood is traditionally dated from the year of his mother's death so that it counts as a 'reign'. Since Aristobulus' activities and those of Pompey caused changes in their fortunes, the dates are conventionally given as Hyrcanus II 67, 63–40 and Aristobulus II 67–63.

The events of 67 onwards make a somewhat confused transition from the Seleucid–Hasmonaean to the Roman period. In addition to the three elements thus implied, the Idumaean house of Antipater took an active part in the transition, and so for a short time did Aretas king of the Nabataeans. In 67 on the death of Salome actual war broke out between her two sons, and Aristobulus defeated his brother in a battle at Jericho. At this point Antipater the Idumaean intervened. His father, of the same name, had been an administrator (and probably general) under Alexander Jannaeus, but he supported the son who was committed rather to the peaceful policies of Salome, persuading Hyrcanus to take refuge with Aretas in Petra, and to seek help against Aristobulus, offering the return to Aretas of some cities which his father had taken. The move was successful and Aretas and Hyrcanus were soon besieging Aristobulus in Jerusalem.

Pompey was at this time in the Middle East. His main task there was to defeat Mithradates of Pontus, which he accomplished in 66. He had then to turn his attention to Syria; the Seleucid power there, under the two rivals Antiochus XII and XIII, had been reduced to very small areas round Antioch and round Damascus. In 83 the country fell to Mithradates' ally, Tigranes I of Armenia, who held it from 83 to 69, ending the Seleucid power for ever. Tigranes became involved in the Mithradatic war with Rome, but in 66 Pompey separated the

allies and Tigranes fled. The country then fell victim to roaming
brigands, and Pompey had first to restore order. This task in the
years 64–63 did not hinder his intervention, through his lieutenants Gabinius and Scaurus, in Judaean affairs. They had in 64
favoured Aristobulus, but in 63 Pompey received delegations at
Damascus which represented not only Aristobulus and Hyrcanus,
but also what Josephus significantly calls 'the nation'. The last-
mentioned received apparently little sympathy, and Pompey decided for Hyrcanus, although Aristobulus was asked only to 'keep
quiet' while Pompey moved on to attack the Nabataeans.

JUDAEA UNDER ROME

I. *The End of the Hasmonaeans (67–37 BC)*

It was not in Aristobulus' nature to 'keep quiet', and during
Pompey's absence against the Nabataeans it seems that he began
further moves for rebellion against the incipient power of Rome,
now felt directly in Judaea. Whatever the exact course of events,
they led to the siege of Jerusalem and the capture of Aristobulus.
Pompey entered the Temple, including the Holy of Holies, an act
of profanation whose effect on the minds of many pious Jews he
probably did not understand. But he refrained from plunder and
restored worship in the Temple. It was thus that the year 63 BC
saw the arrival of Roman power in Jerusalem.

The territorial settlement of Pompey enlarged Bithynia and
Cilicia and added Crete and Syria (including Judaea) to the
Empire. Syria had become a Hasmonaean kingdom only recently,
beginning with the enlargement of territory by John Hyrcanus
and his sons, and at no time did it appear to be firmly established.
Under Rome it retained Idumaea, Peraea and Galilee, and lost the
coastal strip from Gaza to Carmel, Samaria and the cities of the
Decapolis, a loose federation of Greek city-states, some dating
from the time of Alexander the Great. All of them were on the
east side of Jordan except the important Scythopolis. They were
ten in number as the term implies, but lists are not always identical. Pompey left Syria to the government of Scaurus and took the
captive Aristobulus to adorn his triumph in Rome. His further
'settlement' was in the main the work of his lieutenant Gabinius
who became governor of Syria in 57, third in succession after
Scaurus. The authority of Hyrcanus was confined strictly to the

high-priesthood, that is the supervision of the Temple and its worship; politically Jerusalem was entrusted to an aristocratic council, and the country was divided into five districts, one centred upon Jerusalem, one on Jericho, one on Sepphoris in Galilee, one in Amathus (east of the Jordan), and one in 'Gadara', which must be an error in Josephus, since Gadara was one of the cities of the Decapolis. Gazara, on the site of the ancient Gezer, or Adora in the south, are possible corrections.

The arrangement returned Judaea, along with other territories, to the position of being part of Syria, now a Roman province under a legate rather than a hellenistic kingdom. It was not really accepted by the Jewish people. Although Aristobulus had been taken off to Rome with three of his children, one son Alexander escaped, and for a short time gave trouble to Gabinius. He was obliged to submit after a desperate campaign, but that he resisted and found supporters is the significant fact. Patriotic elements did not have to wait long for further opportunities; in 56 Aristobulus escaped from his Roman prison, but it is unknown whether or not through help from pro-Caesar and anti-Pompey politicians. His return to Judaea and renewal of hostilities, like those of Alexander after his failure and return to Rome, are once again more important to demonstrate popular feeling than for any measure of success they achieved. They illustrate also the use of ancient hill-top fortresses by resisters, Alexandrium and Machaerus being used at different times in these abortive risings.

In 55 Crassus, one of the *triumviri* (p. 46), began his governorship of Syria. He wished to establish a reputation as a general equal to that of his rivals Caesar and Pompey and had few scruples in attempting to accomplish this ambition; thus he plundered the Temple in Jerusalem of all its wealth as part of his preparations for an attack on Parthia. He was attended by bad luck, and at Carrhae in 53 suffered a severe defeat by the Parthians, and lost his own life. His quaestor was C. Cassius Longinus who took over command for the years 53–51, crushing a rebellion in 52 in Judaea, where a leader named Peitholaus had succeeded Aristobulus. Antipater shows his influence at this point, persuading Cassius to put Peitholaus to death. Antipater was shortly to turn to his advantage the civil war which Caesar had inaugurated by crossing the Rubicon in 49 (for the civil war and the death of Pompey see pp. 47–9). At first he and Hyrcanus II profited incidentally from the actions of the Pompeians. Caesar had again procured the release from prison of Aristobulus and was providing him with two legions with which to fight against Pompey in Syria; this plot was crushed by Pompeians who obtained the death of Aristobulus by poison. His son Alexander also was put to death in Antioch by Pompey's order. Subsequently however it was as Caesar's supporters that Antipater and Hyrcanus found advancement. This was the first change in the series of events in Syria–Palestine in the fateful years 49–30 BC (the crossing of the Rubicon to the death of Antony, Caesar's great supporter) which reflect the changes in Roman history. Antipater and Hyrcanus together accepted the result of Caesar's defeat of Pompey at Pharsalus and Pompey's murder in Egypt, and set out to render service to Caesar in his war with Ptolemy XIII (p. 48). Mithradates of Pergamum was going to aid Caesar with auxiliary troops in 47 when he was stopped by the non-cooperation of Jews in Pelusium. Hyrcanus was able to provide Antipater with 3,000 Jewish troops with which he went to Mithradates' aid, supporting him also in the rest of the campaign, in which Hyrcanus assisted by procuring the favour for Caesar of Jews throughout Egypt.

In the summer of 47 Caesar was in Syria and making dispositions to reward his friends and to provide for the future of the region. Hyrcanus was appointed ethnarch of Judaea, thus receiving back the political authority which had been taken from him by Gabinius. Antipater became procurator of Judaea, having previously been invested with Roman citizenship and immunity from tribute. Caesar gave permission also to rebuild the walls of Jerusalem. In addition territorial restitution was made of much, if not the whole, of what Gabinius had taken from the Judaean kingdom. What would impress Jews even more, they obtained privileges both in Judaea and outside it which protected them from molestation in practising their religion.

Their satisfaction was short-lived. Sextus Caesar, governing Syria for his ambitious relative, was assassinated and succeeded by the Pompeian Caecilius Bassus in 46. There ensued a struggle between the factions which was still undecided in 44 BC when Caesar was murdered in Rome. At the end of the year Cassius, who had been one of the chief conspirators in the murder, returned to Syria and was able to take over forces both of Pompeians and of those hitherto favourable to Caesar. Antipater and his son Herod took advantage of the turn in events to change sides also. Their aid to Cassius consisted in helping to gather and extort taxes needed for the upkeep of an enlarged army. Herod had been appointed governor of Syria by Sextus Caesar, and Cassius made the same appointment. In about 43 Antipater was removed from the scene through a plot by a would-be popular leader named Malichus. Herod avenged his father by securing the death of Malichus with the assistance of Cassius, who left Syria in 42, destined to lose his life in the autumn of that year at Philippi.

The two battles of Philippi reversed the fortunes of the Roman parties, which had been Pompeian, and the former supporters of Caesar. The latter, recovering from their great loss of Caesar himself, now seemed to be in the ascendant, for all Asia was in the hands of Antony. Octavian (p. 49), his fellow victor, had yet to establish himself. Parallel with the reversal of the Roman fortunes, those of Herod and of his brother Phasael, his companion and assistant, were also changed. Aristobulus' son Antigonus had pleaded in vain before Caesar against Antipater and Hyrcanus. Now some members of the Jewish aristocracy appeared before Antony in Bithynia to complain against Herod and Phasael, and renewed their efforts in 41 in Antioch after Antony had agreed to the liberation of those Jews sold into slavery by Cassius in his tax drive. But they were no more successful than Antigonus had been. Antony had served under Gabinius in 57–55 and had then made friends with Antipater. This friendship was now extended to the next generation; Herod and Phasael were made tetrarchs of the Judaeans. Hyrcanus was stripped of his political power, which to him was no loss since he had no political ambitions.

Adroit as Herod was in advancing himself, it cannot be said that he studied the love or welfare of the people over whom he wished to rule. His friendship with Antony, whose presence in Syria led to constant tax demands on top of the oppressive acts he had himself already committed, meant all the more popular, if usually hidden, support for the Hasmonaean Antigonus. A further element in the situation was the activity of the Parthian army which supported Antigonus and with whose support he was able to reign for three years. During the battle between Antigonus with his Parthian allies and the two Idumaeans, the Parthian general Pacorus lured Phasael and Hyrcanus to their camp on the pretence of making peace. Here they were made prisoner, and while Herod, who had foreseen the treachery, made his escape with his family to the Dead Sea fortress of Masada, they were put at the disposal of Antigonus. He and his allies were no more civilized than Herod was to prove to be; Hyrcanus had his ears cut off to render him unfit for the high-priesthood, Phasael committed suicide to escape his enemies, and the Parthians plundered the neighbourhood and finally took Hyrcanus away prisoner to Parthia.

The reign of Antigonus was precarious and short, but he entered upon it with high hopes and the pugnacious tenacity which had marked so many of his ancestors. His coins take up the fashion established by them from Aristobulus I; his title appeared in Greek as 'King Antigonus' accompanied by his Hebrew name and title, 'Mattathias High Priest'. He was king because of Parthian support. Herod's only hope of becoming king lay in Roman support, and this he set about obtaining. He set out by way of Alexandria to Rome where he sought the help of Antony and bribed his way into the good opinion of others, including Octavian. He thus obtained a declaration from the senate which recognized him as king. This took place in 40, the year of Antigonus' accession.

The Parthians were in 39 driven out of Syria by Ventidius, a lieutenant of Antony, who left Antigonus in possession though exacting tribute from him. In the same year Herod landed at Ptolemais and collected an army, with which he was able to regain possession of Masada which had been under siege. In 38 the Romans, slow to support Herod, were busy repelling a renewed Parthian attack, and Herod applied himself to the task of subduing the entire country, which was continually ravaged by bands of brigands, especially in the high ground and caves of Galilee. Here especially he was successful, and it should be noted that the 'brigands' almost certainly included patriotic fighters such as might support the Hasmonaean cause or the perhaps impracticable ideal of those later called 'Zealots', a restored theocracy whose leaders would be such as could be approved from the Torah. But nothing succeeds like success, and as Herod progressed he gained adherents from the majority whose sense of their own advantage precluded strict religious scruples. In the meantime Ventidius had conquered the Parthians and was besieging Samosata, the capital of Commagene, from where Antony came before the siege's successful end. Herod took the opportunity to visit the camp and was well received by Antony who ordered Sosius, who succeeded Ventidius in the Roman command, to give Herod all assistance possible.

Antigonus had been active during this time against Herod's brother Joseph, who was protecting Herod's family, and had conquered and killed him in battle. Herod returned to Palestine and presently fought a pitched battle with Antigonus' general Pappus, who was killed and his army utterly defeated. The country was now in Herod's hands and in the spring of the next year 37 he laid siege to Jerusalem. He was joined by Sosius with a great force, and a terrible destruction followed, which included carnage among the inhabitants such as Herod did not desire, since he planned for them to be his subjects. Antigonus was taken prisoner to Antioch by Sosius and beheaded at the request of Herod. Thus ended the life of a considerable personality and with him the Hasmonaean rule. It is therefore reasonable to regard the Seleucid–Hasmonaean period as ended with this year 37 BC which indeed opens a new period with the reign of Herod.

II. *The Reign of Herod the Great (37–4 BC)*

The reign of Herod may conveniently be divided into three periods, though this inevitably means some oversimplification: 37–25 consolidation of power; 25–13 prosperity, in high favour with the Romans; 13–4 domestic trouble causing marked decline.

(a) 37–25 BC. Consolidation. At the beginning of his reign in 37 Herod had to reckon with formidable enemies, and it is a clue to understanding his actions to remember that he only occasionally enjoyed anything like popular support. The people at large knew too much of his ruthless actions to find in him any compensation for his being an Idumaean, thus a hereditary enemy of Judaea, or for his pitiless demand for the execution of Antigonus. The aristocratic families might have been won if he had acted with respect for their religious scruples and to their worldly advantage. He took the opposite course, executing the supporters of Antigonus and confiscating their property. He needed the money not only for his army and other obvious expenses, but also for bribing Roman rulers, on whose favour his very existence depended. The Hasmonaean family represented another focus of opposition, and towards them Herod showed an interestingly ambivalent attitude. He had, even before the siege of Jerusalem was truly started, married Mariamme, his second wife and one for whom he had a passionate attachment. She was, significantly enough, a staunch

Hasmonaean, the daughter of the formidable Alexandra, herself the daughter of Hyrcanus II, and Alexander, the elder son of Aristobulus II. Such a marriage may be put down to strong natural attraction, but presumably Herod reflected on the importance of marrying so definite a Hasmonaean. In 35 he found it politic to listen to the criticism of his appointment of Hananel from Babylon as high priest (p. 26); this was voiced loudly by Alexandra, who championed the right to the office of Aristobulus, her own son and thus Herod's brother-in-law. He was only seventeen but Herod accepted him, and Hananel was forced to cede to Aristobulus III. The latter was shown too much favour by the people, and Herod exhibited the other side of his ambivalent attitude, no doubt a mixture of jealousy and fear, by arranging for the young man to be drowned at Jericho at the end of the same year (35). There were still forces able to protest against Herod's atrocities, and he was summoned to Laodicea to answer for this one to Antony. The issue was hardly in doubt, and he was dismissed by Antony with his favour.

The domestic trouble which gives a title to the third period of Herod's reign was in fact present during the whole of it; this is illustrated by the fate of Joseph, Herod's uncle and brother-in-law (his wife was Herod's sister Salome). While absent at Laodicea Herod left the elderly man in charge of his household, with a special command to guard the honour of Mariamme, whom Herod loved and suspected with equal passion. Joseph had secret orders to kill Mariamme if Herod did not return, since he could not endure the thought of her belonging to another. On his return Salome accused her husband to Herod of adultery with Mariamme, and Herod, disbelieving at first, discovered that Joseph had revealed his secret orders. Herod then believed the accusation and had Joseph executed.

If Herod's foes were often at least in his own fears 'those of his own household', he had yet another external enemy. This was Cleopatra, who coveted territory in Palestine, which she pestered Antony into giving her (p. 50). She was a great ally of Alexandra, but even more trouble by reason of her influence over Antony. Herod's compliance with the necessity to cede the oasis of Jericho and lease it back from her illustrates his surprising ability to bow to the more powerful even when it meant humiliation. Cleopatra came near to being his ruin. She prevailed on Antony to order Herod to fight against the Nabataeans, who were defaulting in paying her tribute. Herod was winning a battle against them when he was attacked by Athenion, one of Cleopatra's generals, and had to break off the battle. Then in 31 a severe earthquake hit Judaea causing a great loss of life and disheartening the soldiers. It was a turning-point for Herod; he rallied his troops and won a decisive victory. But 31 was a turning-point in another way for him; at the battle of Actium Octavian's success meant the end of Antony's fortunes and the foundation of lasting superiority for Octavian himself.

Herod rightly judged the situation, and had no scruples in abandoning his friend Antony; the latter had by his own infatuation with Cleopatra proved his own worst enemy, and with her committed suicide in 30. In the meantime Herod took opportunities to show goodwill towards Octavian, assisting Didius in hindering some gladiators of Antony from going to Egypt to support him, and then going to meet Octavian in Rhodes early in 30. Before setting out he thought it prudent to remove his only possible rival for the throne, the aged Hyrcanus, who had indeed a better right to it than he but no ambition for it. The octogenarian former high priest, who had always tried to avoid political entanglement, was put to death on a charge of plotting with the king of the Nabataeans; his execution illustrates well that mere existence in Herod's world could be a danger, however innocent the disposition. Octavian received Herod favourably though without enthusiasm in Rhodes. After the end of the Egyptian campaign, however, he signally confirmed his goodwill, returning to Herod besides Jericho, Gadara and Hippos (two cities of the Decapolis), Samaria, Gaza, Anthedon, Joppa, and Straton's Tower (to become famous as Caesarea).

Home life provided a contrast; for his absence in Rhodes Herod had arranged for Mariamme's protection as before, with a certain Soemus in place of Joseph. This time Salome acted out of direct jealousy against Mariamme and her plot resulted in the execution of both Soemus and Mariamme (29). Herod's rage was poisoned with doubt as to their guilt, and his remorse made him ill, so that Alexandra began to plot with the commanders of fortified places in Jerusalem, in the hope that future change would give her opportunity for power. She was reported to Herod and was executed in 28. Not long after, Salome caused the death of her new husband Costobar. The date (27–25) closes the first period of Herod's reign, for with this last event Herod was apparently secure at last on his throne. It also illustrates the weakness in the too simple division of the reign, for the period had been one of domestic unrest and cast its shadow over the remainder of the reign, perhaps most of all because of Herod's own temperament, the greatest enemy to his happiness. As a victim of his guilt-engendered suspicion he was to endure the pangs, as he was to enjoy the ambitions, of a Macbeth.

(b) 25–13 BC. *Prosperity.* A great feature of the second period was his building activity; that he could afford it meant that even in Herod's reign there must have been some prosperity, since even the extortioner must have something to extort. Indeed during the long period of peace in the Empire, 31–4 BC, inducing some real relaxation of tension after 20 when Augustus made an arrangement with Parthia, agricultural prosperity by its very nature induced wealth and so higher taxation. Herod's building was typical of a hellenistic prince, but with a marked tendency to flatter Rome. He can be seen as one of those kings ranked as friends or allies of Rome who built cities named after Caesar in their lands, as reported by Suetonius. From another point of view his actions are those of a governor of a province instituting games in the emperor's honour, Caesar temples, theatres, amphitheatres and stadia. While Judaea was not the only country which boasted of buildings due to him, for he benefited other cities such as Athens, it is still a witness to his widespread building, in Jerusalem, Hebron, Masada, Jericho, rebuilt Samaria now called Sebaste (the Greek for Augusta), and many other places which he desired to fortify or to make more comfortable when the court was there. Above all he built on the site of Straton's Tower what was to serve as the Roman administrative capital in the form of a great city called Caesarea (Maritima), the centre of much important history in centuries to come.

In addition to these evidences of a successful hellenistic monarch in alliance with Rome, the Temple at Jerusalem bore witness to Herod's desire to be regarded as a benefactor of the Jews. The setting with which it was provided made it the most striking of his monuments, and it is ironical that it was undertaken as a rebuilding of an already existing Temple, yet it is now lost without trace of its magnificence, other than some massive masonry in the remains of the retaining wall of the Temple Mount and the remarkable substructures of its extension to the south. It was this

Temple which was so savagely destroyed in AD 70. One of the features of popular resistance to foreign rule was the use of remote and hardly accessible fortresses, several not far from Jerusalem but in mountainous regions. They had been used by Hasmonaeans, including those of latter times such as Aristobulus and his family, and it is indicative of Herod's basic sense of insecurity that he repaired their fortifications. Such were Alexandrium and Hyrcania, Herodium, Machaerus and Masada. The last three were also well-appointed residences.

Herod's provision of a glorious Temple is no sign of adherence to Judaism. He was generous also towards Greek cities and their temples. He respected the Pharisees and especially the Essenes, but did not follow their *halakah*, or way. He usually tried to avoid offending the susceptibilities of Jews by confining decorations in his palaces to non-representational motifs, or those of plants; but archaeological discoveries in his palace in Jerusalem show animals represented in mosaics. It is probable that these elements would occur in rooms where he entertained non-Jewish guests, but it may appear that there were some Jewish-born people who had been influenced enough by Hellenism to accept without offence such decorations in the house of a non-Jew. Herod was not altogether consistent, for he had erected over the gate of the rebuilt Temple a representation of an eagle; this was to lead to the martyrdom of two men, Judas and Matthias, who appear to have had a following of their own, near the time of Herod's death. Some of their pupils tried to cut down the eagle and were along with the two teachers burnt to death by Herod's order. There is difficulty about the dates of the beginning and end of the building of the Temple. It was begun according to Josephus in 20 BC and it has been customary to accept the tradition of John 2:20 as indicating that it was complete in AD 26, but Josephus in a later passage says that cessation of work on the Temple owing to its being complete caused unemployment in the procuratorship of Albinus in AD 64. No doubt the Temple as such was ready for use early in the period but the extensive system of porticoes, walks and stairways connecting the site with the rest of the city, now revealed by excavation, would require work for many more years, and may have been often interrupted.

This second period of Herod's reign was marked by increase in contact and favour with the emperor and other powerful Romans. Octavian had become Augustus from 27. He was in

the east deciding on boundaries and appointing or confirming
rulers in the years 22–20, and he paid Herod the compliment of
adding to his territory the difficult regions of Batanaea and
Trachonitis and Hauran. He knew Herod would be able to do
something to reduce the banditry in these regions, a phenomenon
with which a local chief named Zenodorus had come to dubious
terms. On the latter's death in 20 Herod received his territory
also, which included the famous Panias (or Panion), in the north
at the source of the Jordan, and thus his territory reached its
fullest extent. Herod visited Augustus in Syria on the occasion of
the first granting of these wild lands, and saw him again in 18 or
17 BC, when he went to Rome to bring home his two sons
Alexander and Aristobulus who had been educated there. But
Herod's main contact with Roman men of power was with
Marcus Vipsanius Agrippa (p. 50), who returned Herod's visit to
him in Mytilene (23–21) by visiting Jerusalem in 15; Herod again
visited Agrippa in the Crimea in 14. This friendship is the reason
for the adoption in Herod's family of the name Agrippa.

(c) 13–4 BC. Domestic Trouble. Clearly, in view of the fate of
Mariamme, Alexandra and others, the beginning of this third
period could be dated much earlier, but it is from 13 onwards that
domestic troubles were continuous as well as intense. It was to
counter the ambitions of the two sons of the once loved and so
cruelly executed Mariamme that Herod brought back from exile
to the court Antipater, his oldest son born of his first wife Doris,
an Idumaean. He made it known that Antipater was to succeed
him. Whatever the rights or wrongs of the complex story which
ensued, there was certainly strong rivalry between Antipater and
his two half-brothers, and in order to strengthen Antipater's position Herod asked Agrippa, about to return to Rome in 13, to
take his son and designated heir with him and present him to
Augustus. While Antipater was in Rome, the two sons of Mariamme showed increased hostility towards their father, and the
danger of their existence to Herod was impressed on him by his
sister Salome. In 12 Herod took the two sons to Aquileia to meet
the emperor in order to denounce them to him. Augustus succeeded for a short time in reconciling the family and even Antipater joined in the new attitude. It did not last. Suspicion grew
again when all were back home, and Alexander was put in
prison. His father-in-law was Archelaus king of Cappadocia who,

fearing for his daughter, came to Jerusalem and pretended to agree with Herod's indignation at Alexander's conduct and made as though to take his daughter home. Herod was impressed and defended his son against Archelaus, and thus for a time reconciliation came about.

About this time the difficult country of Trachonitis caused Herod trouble; dissidents from there found a champion in Syllaeus of Nabataea who had taken power through the weakness of the king Obodas. Syllaeus made the affair a means of denouncing Herod in Rome, and for a time Herod was out of favour with Augustus. To present his own case he sent one of the Greeks who were prominent at his court, the historian and diplomat Nicolaus of Damascus, after a previous embassy had failed in its purpose. In the meantime the family situation was worsening, largely through fomentation by another Greek courtier, Eurycles of Sparta. Herod committed Alexander and Aristobulus to prison and sent their accusers to Rome. Nicolaus had by now won over Augustus who therefore received the accusers well, but he counselled Herod to proceed on his own authority and to hold a council for the purpose at Berytus.

At the council it is doubtful whether justice could have been done. It was a matter of political intrigue and sycophancy. The few who supported the two sons were swept aside by the execution of an army officer who with three hundred others pleaded for them. They were put to death in Sebaste, about 7 BC. The event brought no peace; Antipater was too ambitious to be satisfied with this, and apparently began to intrigue with Pheroras, Herod's brother and tetrarch of Peraea. Whatever the truth, Antipater went to Rome to avoid conflict with his father and during his absence Pheroras died. It was then whispered that he had died of poison. Some said that Antipater had given it, others that it had been intended for Herod. Antipater was recalled from Rome and to his surprise found that this was to put him on trial. He was unable to produce a defence and Herod sent to Rome for permission to execute him. This permission arrived five days before his own death, for he had been ill for some time. During this illness he had made two new wills; the original one had made Antipater his heir. In the latest of them all he named Archelaus as King, his son by Malthace of Samaria; Malthace's other son Antipas was to be tetrarch of Galilee and Peraea. Philip, his son by Cleopatra of Jerusalem, was to be tetrarch of Gaulanitis, Trachonitis, Batanaea and Panias (cp. Luke 3:1 where Antipas is called 'Herod' as always in the gospels). The year was 4 BC.

III. *Palestine under the Herodians (4 BC to AD 39)*

Although it was Herod's last will which was eventually ratified and implemented, the transition of power from Herod to his sons did not go smoothly. There was serious and widespread popular revolt on the death of Herod, partly to demand the punishment of those who had advised Herod to execute so savagely the heroes of the 'eagle affair' which had occurred during his last illness, and partly due to a desire to be rid of alien oppressive rule and to replace it with that of a Jewish ruler. Failing this, as most realized must be the case, they would rather have Rome than an Idumaean, and especially than a Herodian. They were right; only Philip, ruling the most difficult of the areas administered by Herod's sons after his death, ruled with justice and an efficiency which won him support.

Archelaus succeeded in quelling the revolt for the time being, and made his way to Rome as his father had done, to obtain the necessary support for his rule. Archelaus had to argue his case, and was supported by Nicolaus, but opposed by another Antipater (son of Salome) who was supported by Antipas; others rallied to this side in the conviction that Archelaus was the worse of two evils. Augustus waited for further news from Judaea, which was serious when it came. He sent a procurator named Sabinus, who found it necessary to call for the help of Varus, the legate of Syria. An armed rebellion was then put down with ruthless cruelty and the war of Varus is marked in Jewish history as one of the worst of its disasters. It swiftly accounted for three popular leaders, of whom only one, named Simon, is mentioned by Tacitus, though the most important is probably Judas of Sepphoris, son of the bandit leader Hezekiah whom Herod had killed in Galilee in about 48 BC. While the war of Varus was still going on Augustus decided that the last will of Herod and its territorial provisions, as detailed above, should be implemented.

Archelaus ruled until AD 6; he displayed his father's cruelty, but lacked his ability. He was bad enough to unite Jews and Samaritans in a joint complaint to the emperor in that year and was banished to Vienne in Gallia Narbonensis.

Antipas had married a daughter of Aretas IV of Nabataea and

abandoned her for Herodias, daughter of Aristobulus IV the half-brother of Antipas. She was married to another half-brother, Herod Philip son of Mariamme II, and Antipas' taking her was the unlawful act for which he was rebuked by John the Baptist, whom he beheaded (Mark 6:17–28). Antipas' marriage with the daughter of Aretas had been part of an attempt to bring peace between Judaea and Nabataea, and its breakdown later brought renewed hostilities in which Antipas was defeated. This was during the reign of Tiberius (AD 14–37), who ordered Vitellius, legate of Syria, to act against the Nabataeans. Antipas seems to have gained a high status with Rome for a time at least, for he acted as host to Vitellius and king Artabanus of Parthia in an important conference which brought peace between Rome and Parthia. Antipas has a place in history as a builder. He restored Sepphoris after the war of Varus, and rebuilt Beth ha-Ramtah as Livia, later Julia. Desiring a winter capital warmer than Sepphoris, he chose a site towards the southern end of the lake of Galilee where hot springs were available and enabled him to make a city with Roman features such as baths. He called it Tiberias after the emperor, and the lake began early to be called by the same name, as the gospel of John (6:1, 23; 21:1) illustrates. At first taboo, owing to the proximity of an ancient burial-ground, Tiberias later became a very important city in the history of Judaism. It was the home of R. Meir (*fl.* AD 140–65), pupil of Akiba (d. 135) and teacher of Judah ha-Nasi (135–219), editor of the Mishnah. In later times still it was a centre of Jewish scholarship and was visited by Maimonides (1135–1204), who died there.

When Philip died in AD 34 his territory was attached temporarily to Syria, and Antipas hoped to have it added to his own, and to receive the title of king; but his brother-in-law Agrippa was in favour with the new emperor Caius (37–41), who on succeeding gave him the countries and the royal title. Antipas applied to Rome for the same title, but charges were brought against him and he was banished to Gaul. He had reigned from 4 BC to AD 39.

Of Philip there is relatively little to report, largely because he ruled well. His policy was a wise one – to rule diligently as a contented vassal of Rome. As such he issued coinage whose obverse held the inscription *Tiberius Augustus Caesar* and the reverse *Philip Tetrarch*. Moreover, the obverse included a head of the emperor with an olive wreath. Probably Philip could escape censure or even political disturbance through offence at such designs because his regions were largely non-Jewish, but he seems to have set an example which was soon to be followed in Judaea. He rebuilt the ancient Panias (or Panion or Banias) and named it Caesarea. As this name usually signified Caesarea Maritima, the great city on the coast serving as the Roman administrative capital and built by Herod the Great, Philip distinguished his capital by adding his name, so that the place was the famous Caesarea Philippi of the synoptic gospels (Mark 8:27). He married Salome daughter of Herodias, who according to the gospels of Mark and Matthew (though they do not give her name) danced so well as to obtain a boon from Antipas, and at Herodias' prompting asked for the head of John the Baptist (Mark 6:17–28). Neither she nor any other bore children to Philip, and the most creditable of the Herodians died without heir. As we have already seen his territory went to Agrippa I. His reign was from 4 BC to AD 34. (For details of territories held by Herodians, see map 3, p. xix.)

We have now sketched the reigns of Antipas, Philip and Archelaus. In the case of the last, and therefore for the history of Judaea in the exact sense, this brings us only to AD 6, and it is necessary now to resume that history.

IV. Judaea under Procurators (AD 6–41)

The official representing the emperor who was entrusted with government of Judaea as a Roman province was called sometimes *procurator*, sometimes prefect (*praefectus*). A stone found at Caesarea shows that Pontius Pilate was called *praefectus*, and it is generally stated that this was the term used until the reign of Claudius, when procurator was substituted. It seems rather that the terms were used fairly loosely, and sometimes thought of as synonymous. In general it would be safe to say that a procurator was an agent of the emperor and often sent to look after his interests, while *praefectus* implied some military authority. At the banishment of Archelaus, Augustus sent P. Sulpicius Quirinius as a civil legate, i.e. a governor with full civil powers and as *assessor* of property for taxation in Syria, to which Judaea now became an addition. At the same time came the first procurator of Judaea, Coponius, who was certainly the personal agent of the emperor subordinate to Quirinius, but as certainly had life and death powers in Judaea. The census carried out by Quirinius with the assistance of Coponius for Judaea thus took place in AD 6, and is no doubt that to which Luke refers in his gospel (2:1–5), being mistaken in thinking that it was a census of the whole Roman world and that it coincided with the birth of Jesus. It was the occasion of armed protest by Judas of Galilee and his followers, perhaps the same who led a rising at Herod the Great's death in 4 BC. In AD 6 Judas lost his life. The protest is interesting because it has a strong religious as well as nationalistic foundation: making a census was in itself an offence against God (cp. 2 Sam. 24); it was one to resist fanatically when it was carried out by an alien power. Judas was supported by a Pharisee named Saddok but received no help from the high priest. This office still offered an opportunity for political influence, and right of appointment to it was regarded as a politically significant privilege. In 4 BC Matthias was deposed by Herod as having been involved with the 'eagle affair', and succeeded by his brother-in-law Joazar, whom Archelaus dismissed under suspicion of helping the rebels and appointed Joazar's brother Eleazar, who was in turn deposed in favour of one named Jesus son of Sie. After Archelaus' banishment from AD 6 to 41 appointment was in the hands of the Roman governor. It seems that Joazar was reappointed by Quirinius, and on this occasion used his influence to quieten the people. By another unexplained twist of policy Quirinius subsequently deposed him in favour of Ananus, the Annas of the New Testament (Luke 3:2; John 18:13, 24; Acts 4:6).

We have no information about the next two procurators, M. Ambibulus and Annius Rufus. The next was Valerius Gratus, appointed by Tiberius after his own accession in AD 14. He deposed Ananus and three more high priests, and may therefore be suspected of receiving bribes, as well as inflicting severe taxation on Judaea. In AD 17 Judaea appealed to Tiberius for some mitigation of their burdens, but the result is not known.

Pontius Pilatus succeeded Gratus in AD 26. It comes as a surprise to those who know him only from the gospels that he was specially detested by the Jewish people. Philo, quoting a letter from Agrippa I to the emperor Caius, says Pilate was 'by nature inflexible and stubbornly relentless'. He accuses him of 'corruption, insults, rapine, outrages on the people, arrogance, repeated murders of innocent victims, and constant and most galling savagery'. Josephus says nothing of his character but narrates two incidents which are perhaps meant to speak for themselves. Near the begin-

ning of his period of government Pilate 'led his army from Caesarea and established it for winter quarters in Jerusalem, for the
purpose of destroying the laws of the Jews'. As this would have
been against previous policy it may have been inspired by higher
authority; if so, this may well have been Sejanus, the influential
praetorian prefect of Tiberius (p. 58) who seems to have been
anti-Jewish. It is possible that, in contrast to Josephus' views,
Pilate intended only to insist on his being obeyed, and that the
imperial insignia (mainly the legionary standards), whose
bringing into the capital were the main offence to Jewish scruples,
must be accepted as symbols of Roman authority. In the end he
smuggled them in. Pilate apparently returned to Caesarea and
Jews went there to protest, which they did for six days, until
Pilate gave way and ordered the standards to be withdrawn. In
Philo's *Legatio ad Caium* a different but similar incident is narrated
concerning some gilded shields to be set up in Herod's palace at
Jerusalem. Again Pilate gave way initially, on the threat of appeal
to the emperor, but it was reported to Tiberius, who rebuked
Pilate and ordered restoration of the old policy towards the city,
which guaranteed the people freedom from interference with
their religion. It is not known why the shields were offensive.
The second matter illustrates at once the exasperating and the
intelligible sides of Jewish attitudes to proposed new enterprises
which would benefit themselves. It concerns the building of an
aqueduct to bring water into Jerusalem, in itself beneficent – but
at the expense of the Temple treasury. It was not entirely because
the money had been given for other purposes; those purposes
were religious and the money was part of the sacred Korban, i.e.
treasury reserved for specific religious expenses. Again the action
of Pilate was discreditably secret. His use of soldiers should have
been official and open, but he sent some disguised among the
crowd in order to attack them clandestinely.

Both incidents occurred in the lifetime of Jesus. It has been
suggested that Luke 13:4 refers to disorder connected with the
aqueduct, but the incident in the gospel remains without positive
identification. Pilate has achieved a certain fame because Jesus was
brought before him as a disturber of the peace and a rebel against
Rome. There is no evidence other than that in the gospels to
explain his attitude on this occasion, but we have seen that there
were times when he did not stand well with Caesar. At the time
of the crucifixion Tiberius was in retirement at Capri and Roman

rule was virtually in the hands of Sejanus. Ironically, Pilate's character owes the considerable whitewashing which he has received to the gospel account. Josephus and Philo condemn him. He was finally brought to ruin by the affair of the Samaritans; a charlatan prophet offered to reveal to them the sacred vessels said to have been hidden by Moses on Mount Gerizim. Pilate massacred the crowd which assembled. The resulting complaint, in which Jews joined, moved Vitellius, legate of Syria, to order Pilate to Rome, but he escaped judgement through Tiberius dying before he arrived at the capital. This was in 37.

The next two governors, Marcellus, 36–7, and Marullus, 37–41, are obscure. They may have been the same person. During this period there was an improvement in relations with Rome. Vitellius restored to the people the custody of the high priest's robes and remitted some taxes.

V. *The Reign of Agrippa I* (AD 41–4)

We do not fully know the circumstances in which, after the departure of Pilate, the country of Judaea and other adjacent territories were once again entrusted to a native king under the suzerainty of Rome. Agrippa I was a grandson of Herod, the son of the Aristobulus who had with his brother Alexander been put to death in 7 BC, and brother of Herodias. He was one of the numerous high-born Judaeans who were sent to Rome for education, being therefore a kind of hostage. From the age of six he grew up attached to the imperial family as a close friend of Drusus, son of Tiberius. On Drusus' death in AD 23 Agrippa, having got into debt, sought better fortune in his old home. Antipas his brother-in-law gave him an administrative post in Tiberias, but this did not prove a success, and he set out for Rome again after raising a loan from Alexander the brother of Philo. There he became a close friend of Caius the future emperor (often referred to by his nickname Caligula), and was imprisoned for treasonable talk by Tiberius. On accession Caius released him and gave him the lands which had been Philip's as a kingdom. In 39 he received the tetrarchy of Antipas and was made king of Judaea and Samaria in 41. Thus he reigned over the entire territory ruled by his grandfather.

The year 41 was a fateful one; Caius, to punish the Jews for an attack on a Greek altar in Jamnia, ordered Petronius the legate of

Syria to prepare a statue of the emperor and to take it when ready
to the Temple in Jerusalem. Although the full details of what
followed are in dispute (Josephus and Philo differ in relating
them) the main outline is clear. Petronius held back the making
of the statue in Sidon, and deputations of Jews convinced him of
their sincere readiness to die rather than submit to the erection of
the statue in Jerusalem. Petronius reported the facts to Caius with
such firmness as was consistent with correctness, and showed
some courage considering the man with whom he had to deal. It
was Agrippa who saved the situation. Arriving in Rome and
hearing of what had been going on in his homeland, he fell ill
with shock and recovered enough to write to Caius to beg him to
desist. Strangely enough Caius gave in, and Agrippa must take
the credit for averting a tragedy.

Some of Agrippa's activities are puzzling, for they do not
accord with his apparent acquiescence in Roman overlordship.
Thus he began the work of constructing a wall to the north of the
city of Jerusalem which Marsus, governor of Syria, prevented
from being completed. Marsus also intervened personally to
break up a conference which Agrippa called at Tiberias of five
vassal kings: Antiochus of Commagene, Sampsigeram of Emesa,
Cotys of Lesser Armenia, Polemon of Pontus and Herod of Chalcis. Similar in apparent design and early failure were Agrippa's
attempts at dynastic alliances. Perhaps it is best to renounce the
search for consistency in the policy of a king distinguished by
volatility and change, and incapable of a single sustained grand
design.

It seems doubtful whether Agrippa paid much attention to the
day-to-day work of ruling a country, but he was popular with
the Jews. The Mishnah tells of his tears when reading the passage
in Deut. 17:15 at the feast of Tabernacles which enjoins that the
ruler must be of the Jewish race, and how the crowd assured him
with shouts that he was their brother (Soṭ. 7:8). He was careful to
observe the Torah, and some of his apparent anti-Roman adven-
tures may have been inspired by a desire to stand well with the
Pharisees. His hostility to the small band of followers of Jesus,
which caused the first martyrdom among the Twelve and the
imprisonment of Peter (Acts 12:1–19), is consistent with a strict
pro-Torah attitude, but was probably not popular with the
people. It is possible therefore that his good reputation in Jewish
literature is due to a somewhat external and official Judaism.

Accounts of his death are curious but he appears to have died suddenly at the games in honour of the emperor at Caesarea in 44 (Acts 12:23).

VI. *Roman Procurators (AD 44–66)*

The new emperor Claudius (41–54) was a reluctant head of state; he believed that Romans of senatorial rank should govern the Roman Empire. He was consistent therefore in returning Judaea to rule as a Roman province under procurators, but he deferred enough to local feeling to confer the right of making the high priest upon Herod of Chalcis, Agrippa I's brother, who had been given this obscure small kingdom by Claudius in 41 and who now made request for this honour. (This Herod, of whom little is known, died in 48.)

The first procurator was Cuspius Fadus (44–6), who ruthlessly suppressed a rising under Theudas (Acts 5:36f, which probably has Theudas and Judas in the wrong order). It is chiefly in relation to putting down bandits, who may well have been considered heroes by many Judaeans, that procurators of the time are prominent. The next procurator, Tiberius Julius Alexander (46–8), crucified the sons of Judas, Jacob and Simon, who had apparently inherited their father's position as a popular leader. He is remarkable for acting with Roman severity against his own people, for he was a renegade Jew, a nephew of Philo. Ventidius Cumanus (48–52) might have pleaded ignorance of Jewish susceptibilities, but in any case his skill in governing (if he possessed any) had no chance to show itself since he was ill-served by soldiers in his ranks, one of whom made an insulting gesture to the people at the Passover in 49 and caused a riot in which according to Josephus 20,000 people were killed. Another tore up a copy of the Torah in the course of a looting attack on some villages near Jerusalem in reprisal for an assault on an imperial slave. Cumanus was forced to order the execution of this soldier. Further trouble was stirred up by Samaritans who murdered some Galilaeans on their way to a festival in Jerusalem, and who bribed Cumanus into complicity; this was stayed by military action and pleas from Jerusalem Jews. Cumanus' career was ended by his being sent into exile by Claudius to whom Ummidius Quadratus the legate of Syria sent him for judgement.

Cumanus was succeeded by Felix (52–60), another Roman

known from the New Testament (Acts 23–24) and another whose character received mild treatment compared with his reputation in other sources, in this case Roman included. His initial successes in capturing a number of 'bandits' was due largely to the use of bribes, which he employed also to procure the murder of the high priest Jonathan. (Josephus narrates this in *Ant.* xx.8.5 (162) but does not mention anywhere Jonathan's appointment, unless he is to be identified with the Jonathan son of Ananus who was high priest early in AD 37, and to be understood at this point as 'former high priest'.) Jonathan had tried to remain apart from strife. This was difficult for many otherwise peaceable people, for the rebels in Jerusalem adopted a clandestine method of terrorism against neutrals by mingling with the crowds while concealing daggers under their clothes. These men were called *sicarii*, since their short concealed weapon was a *sica*. A cognate phenomenon of the times was the appearance of a number of religious fanatics, for one of whom Paul was mistaken (Acts 21:38).

Paul's arrest was the end of his freedom, and led eventually to his going to Rome as a prisoner. The date of his appearance before Felix seems to be 53 or 54, a time when Felix had recently married Drusilla, daughter of Agrippa I, who is mentioned in Acts 24:24 as Jewish. Paul's serious warning to them of judgement to come and Felix's hope of receiving a bribe from Paul are both true to the persons and the times. Felix seems to have been recalled to Rome in 60, where the influence of his brother Pallas may have been a strong factor in his acquittal, perhaps one of the least deserved in history. Some however argue that as Pallas fell from favour in 55, this is the latest date for Felix's trial in Rome, and that the little reported of Festus, his successor, is due to the latter's beneficent and therefore uneventful rule, not to its shortness.

If however we assume that the usual dating is correct, the procuratorship of Festus was confined to the year 60, in which he died while still in office. Festus was not corrupt but was unable to bring peace to the country still so much troubled by unrest. Paul was left to be his prisoner when Felix left, and according to Acts Festus was puzzled as to what he should do with Paul (Acts 25–26, esp. 25:17–20). When Paul claimed to be standing before Caesar, meaning Romans must judge the case and not Jews, Festus took the claim literally and sent him to Rome. Whether Paul ever appeared before Caesar or anyone there remains very obscure.

In Caesarea Festus staged a hearing largely to entertain his guests Agrippa II and his sister Berenice. Agrippa had been educated in Rome and stood well with Claudius and afterwards with Nero (54–68). We have seen that he obtained the kingdom of Chalcis in about 50 after the death of his uncle Herod of Chalcis, but he does not appear to have resided there. In 53 he had received the lands formerly governed by Philip, with Abila and some land in Lebanon. Nero added the cities of Tiberias, Tarichaeae and Julias. Agrippa thus acquired a status, but cannot be called a diligent ruler, since he lived mostly in Jerusalem which was never part of his territory. He was careful to avoid offending the Jews, but accepted completely the necessity of Rome's overlordship, and his coins bear the images of reigning Roman emperors.

After the death of Festus there was a gap of two years when there was no effective government. The high priest Ananus pursued private policies, including bringing about the death of James the brother of Jesus, who had a high reputation among moderate and pious Jews in Jerusalem. Two procurators followed, Albinus (62–4) and Gessius Florus (64–6), who scarcely pretended to govern and plundered both communities and individuals, becoming accomplices of the already existing bandits and *sicarii*. During the chaos of the time of Florus some moderate Jews sought the intervention of C. Cestius Gallus, the governor of Syria. He sent a tribune Neapolitanus; he and Agrippa did their best to prevent the open rebellion now fast becoming inevitable.

VII. *The First Jewish Revolt (*AD *66–74)*

It seems appropriate that the revolt when it came should begin from the Temple; Eleazar, son of the high priest and himself captain of the Temple guard, persuaded the priests to accept no offering or gift from aliens. Josephus says this made war inevitable 'for they abolished the sacrifice of Caesar on behalf of them' (i.e. the Romans). The meaning, if the text is correct, seems to be that there was a sacrifice on behalf of Caesar usually offered and thought to be on behalf of all Romans, and now deliberately discontinued. However, this was the formal side of activity already much in evidence, for the city was in open revolt against Florus and at the same time as the Temple act of defiance some Zealots surprised the Roman garrison in Masada, killed them, and put in a force of their own.

Jerusalem was to be the victim both of foreign oppression and of one of the worst examples of internecine strife. The series of events which ensued was of such appalling cruelty between different parties of Jews that it is hard to believe they were conscious, as they must have been, of the enemy at the gates. The hardest choice, as so often, was to support the moderates, who now made an effort of unity and tried to stop the revolt, on the grounds that it would make bad worse, not for any love of Roman rule. Events were too much for them. A former high priest named Ananias (48–55 or perhaps 59) lost his house, and Agrippa and Berenice their palaces. In the meantime Menahem, son of Judas the famous rebel of AD 6, went to Masada and returned with a considerable supply of arms which had been Herod's. He had at first great success; with his followers he managed to turn out the Romans who had taken refuge in the upper palace, butchering those who did not run fast enough to the towers of Hippicus, Phasael and Mariamme. Ananias was found in hiding and murdered along with his brother. Then Menahem himself was opposed by other forces under Eleazar and was killed. One of his followers, another Eleazar, escaped and became the leader at Masada.

Ill-starred and self-destructive as the rebellion was, it appeared at first to be part of a general uprising of Jews in different places where they had settled and lived in uneasy rivalry with the non-Jewish population. In some cities, such as Caesarea, it was the gentile population who began the fighting. There the Jewish population was massacred. Cities which saw similar events included Scythopolis and other Decapolis cities, Ascalon, Ptolemais, and Alexandria in Egypt. Cestius, the Roman legate of Syria, seems to have been slow to act; at first he may have been held up by the necessity to restore order in Galilee. When he moved on to Jerusalem he suffered a defeat, seemed to be reversing it, and then unexpectedly withdrew. It was naturally a signal for pursuit by Jewish forces, which they continued as far as Antipatris. The Twelfth Legion, concerned in this rout, was now in disgrace and not used for some time.

Moderates now began to melt away, either ceasing to be moderate or escaping from the city if they could. An attempt was made by the remaining defenders to organize the campaign not only in the city but also in the rest of the country, including Galilee where the historian Josephus was in charge. Neither the course of events nor the conflicting motives of Josephus and his assistant John of Gischala can be entirely understood. Both seem to have been convinced that the eventual victory of the Romans was inevitable, and to have striven to outwit one another in trickery with scant concern for the populations whom they were supposed to defend. Both had dissidents to deal with. In Gischala John had to rebuild the city after it had been destroyed by extremists, and Josephus actually looted Tiberias and Sepphoris after quelling opponents in them. But when threatened with removal from command Josephus asserted his position as general and prepared to defend the town of Jotapata, which became an important centre of resistance.

Nero had received the news of Judaea while in Achaea, and appointed Vespasian, a general of experience and distinction (much of it won in Claudius' invasion of Britain) to replace the failed Cestius, who died at about this time (67) perhaps by suicide. Vespasian collected a large force which included a legion brought from Egypt by his son Titus to add to the two already with him, and auxiliary troops from Judaea, Commagene, Emesa and Arabia. Sepphoris went over to Vespasian immediately and people in the countryside took refuge in Tiberias and Jotapata. Other towns remained in the hands of the rebels, namely Tarichaeae, Gischala and Gamala in Gaulanitis, as well as the vantage point of Mount Tabor.

After a terrible siege, which Josephus describes in full, Jotapata fell. The end was marked by the death of many by a suicide pact which included Josephus, but he dodged death by a trick and then surrendered to the Romans. As a prisoner he rather successfully donned the mantle of a prophet, foretelling for Vespasian the destiny of emperor. After enquiry into Josephus' reputation as a seer, Vespasian was inclined to think there might be truth in his prisoner's claim to special powers, and this cautious entertainment of possibility became high hope and finally conviction as, first, events revealed the opportunity to contend for the throne, and then the prophecy was quite fulfilled. Josephus' own fortunes increased by stages which corresponded, and he was treated with special courtesy from the first. Later he was to live in Rome under the patronage of Vespasian and Titus.

Titus proved efficient in the task set him by his father, and Tiberias and Tarichaeae fell into his hands without trouble. Gischala also fell to him after John had secretly escaped. In the meantime Vespasian took Gamala, though only after heavy losses, and Mount Tabor.

In the next year, 68, Vespasian had little difficulty in reducing Peraea and the countryside of Judaea in a wide-ranging campaign which included apparently the destruction of the Qumran settlement and its inhabitants. During this campaign the people in Jerusalem were quarrelling about the leadership and policies for defence. Among those who had taken refuge there and thus swelled the population to unmanageable numbers was John of Gischala, who aspired to the leadership, and believed or pretended to believe that Jerusalem was destined never to fall. Many of the moderates lost their lives at the hands of his supporters who gave to the cause that maniacal devotion typical of fanatics which manifests itself in fury against the non-fanatics who in action would have been their best helpers. The Zealot party had taken over and accentuated the divisions which were a pledge of the city's destruction. It was at this time, according to Eusebius, that the small Christian community escaped to Pella in Peraea.

Something of a pause followed, while Vespasian busied himself with preparation at Caesarea for attacking Jerusalem. Here he received news of the death of Nero, and suspended operations to see what would now happen on the wider stage of the Roman Empire. Titus set out for Rome to take loyal greetings to Galba when the latter's accession was known, but heard at Corinth of his murder and so returned to Caesarea. Again therefore Vespasian waited, but then further activity in Judaea compelled him to act. The new force was that of Simon bar Giora, a lawless bandit of towering personality who ravaged the countryside and reduced the people to fearful submission. Vespasian had perforce to take the field against him, and the year 69 saw the resumption of Roman military activity in the country, leaving only Herodium, Masada, Machaerus and Jerusalem in the hands of the Jews. Simon was not caught, and managed to get himself invited into Jerusalem by those who were made desperate by the tyranny of John. The result was not to rid themselves of one tyrant but to saddle themselves with two. Vespasian's renewed campaign was just ended when the news of Vitellius' accession arrived. Then the legions, foreshadowing much history to come, took a decisive step. Beginning with those in Egypt, then Palestine and Syria, they proclaimed Vespasian emperor. He sent Mucianus to Rome with an army from Antioch, and himself left for Alexandria.

There he heard of the success of his cause and the murder of Vitellius at the end of 69, but stayed on until the summer of 70 (pp. 64–7).

Titus was therefore entrusted with the siege of Jerusalem, within which the internecine strife had reached almost incredible dimensions of lunacy. A third party was added to those already in rivalry, under Eleazar, and so bitter was the mutual hostility that a precious store of grain was set on fire to prevent its use by fellow-citizens of other factions. The siege, described by Josephus, lasted five hideous months, during which all the usual horrors of such events took place. They were occasionally offset by acts of fierce bravery, while the afflictions of the people led them to greater obstinacy and to refuse ever more boldly any suggestions of surrender. The city fell bit by bit, the last days increasing the hatred and bitterness on both sides, until the final fall in September 70. Of the survivors many were put to death, others enslaved (some of the strongest being reserved for gladiatorial shows) or sent to the mines. John of Gischala was spared only to spend the rest of his life in prison. Simon bar Giora was reserved as a victim for the triumph of Titus in Rome. The triumph was anticipated by Titus' progress through a number of cities in the east before returning home, where festivals were held at which Jewish prisoners figured in the barbaric shows which so often adorned the might of Rome.

After the war, governors of senatorial rank were allotted to Judaea. They were no longer subordinate to the legate of Syria, but themselves commanded the legion which garrisoned the country. Even after the fall of Jerusalem and its Temple the fortresses of Herodium, Machaerus and Masada remained to be reduced. Lucilius Bassus, governor of Judaea, succeeded with the first two, and then died; he was replaced by Flavius Silva whose name is associated with the destruction of Masada and its siege, as grim in its way as that of Jerusalem. The defendants were Zealots, with a small admixture of refugees from Qumran; many amongst both groups no doubt believed to be imminent that last stand which their shared eschatological beliefs led them to expect, but their main driving force was desperation, as the oration of their leader Eleazar showed near the end of their resistance. The eight camps built by Silva and the ramp on the west side which rendered the approach of an attacking force less difficult may all still be seen. Again, the refusal to surrender and the discovery on the final morning, when the Roman forces broke in, of the death by suicide pact of 960 persons (all the inhabitants except two women and five children) impressed the conquerors with the fear and hatred which they inspired. The date has long been taken to be 73 but newly discovered inscriptions which date the beginning of Silva's governorship to 73 suggest that it must have been in 74 that this last fortress fell.

VIII. *Judaea* AD 70–135

The destruction of the Temple marked with terrible certainty the end of an epoch for the Jewish people in their long and disaster-filled history. A passage in the Mishnah (Soṭ. 9:12) says gloomily among other things that 'When the Temple was destroyed ... faithful men came to an end' and since then 'there has been no day without its curse'. The desert in time and place is matched even in historical sources, for there is no continuous history of the area after 70, and we gather facts from casual references in classical and church historians writing on other subjects, a few inscriptions, coins and rabbinical literature, which is written from its own unique point of view and pays little attention to the order in which events happened.

After exacting the cruel and ruthless punishments which followed the defeat of Judaea, the Romans did their best to rebuild life among those who remained in the ruined province. Even the procurators appear to have been of a quite different stamp from those who misruled in the years which led to the destruction. Vespasian founded military colonies at Emmaus outside Jerusalem (probably though not certainly the Emmaus of Luke 24:13) and Flavia Neapolis (the modern Nablus) near the ancient Shechem. Other cities followed at rather later dates. Of already existing cities Jamnia must rank as historically the most important at this time, for it had been captured by Vespasian early in his campaigns and from 67 had been used as a refuge for Jews who remained loyal to the Romans during all the succeeding hostilities. The establishment there with his approval of an academy of rabbinic learning thus becomes intelligible as part of a policy for the rehabilitation under Roman rule of a Judaism separate from the Temple, which had been the centre of the revolt. Whatever the amount of truth in the legends associated with this establishment, R. Johanan ben Zakkai obtained permission for such an academy and settled in Jamnia as its leader even before the fall of Jerusalem. His teaching included a touch of genius in his profound acceptance of the end of the Temple and his skilful transference of its sacral character and authority to the assembly which formed the academy.

The sanhedrin was suspended as definitely as sacrificial worship. There are a number of references in both Jewish and Christian literature which suggest that sacrificial worship may have been restored, but all may best be explained as describing what is correct according to the Torah rather than what was actually happening. In fact, Johanan taught and legislated in such a fashion as to make the way of life enjoined at Jamnia a supersession of the practices centred upon the Temple. He therefore tacitly took over the leadership, since his rabbinic school was the natural successor to that which had flourished in Jerusalem and whose last president was Simeon son of Gamaliel, who seems not to have survived the destruction in AD 70. The academy appears to have been constituted of seventy elders as a deliberate copy of the old sanhedrin.

Lack of references to any high priest after 70, together with the apparent and natural cessation of the system of worship belonging to the Temple, lead to the conclusion that the high-priesthood came to an end. Josephus reviews its history in *Ant.* xx.10.1–5 (224–51) and seems to imply clearly enough that it is a thing of the past without specifically stating the fact, which may well have been obvious to him and to his contemporaries. Ironically, this was not true of the Temple tax, which Vespasian exacted as the price of being regarded as a Jew with licence to practise Judaism, of being an adherent of a *religio licita* (allowed religion). He used it avowedly as a tax for the benefit of the temple of Jupiter Capitolinus in Rome, whereas the site of the Jerusalem Temple remained for the time being in ruins.

It was consistent with the policy of the Flavian emperors, which thus allowed a scholarly and domestic Judaism to flourish, to suspect and to discourage any tendency towards messianism, which for them must have been synonymous with military aspirations to victory and freedom. In this connexion it is interesting to read in Eusebius (*Eccl. Hist.* 3.12 and 3.19–20) of two events which may or may not be connected. Hegesippus is quoted as the authority for both. The first is said to be under Vespasian and immediately after the capture of the city, when a search was made for any of the family of David in case there were anyone of 'the royal tribe'. This led to a persecution of the Jews. The story sounds as if it happened more probably under Titus, when there was a population of Gentiles of some kind, who could persecute their Jewish neighbours. The second was the order by Domitian to execute all of David's line, which caused an accusation by some 'heretics' against the grandsons of Jude the brother of Jesus. These were brought before Domitian and had no difficulty in convincing him that they were working men with no political ambitions, and that in their belief Christ's kingdom was to come at the end of the world; accordingly they were dismissed from his presence. It is hard to credit the historicity of this story since Domitian is not described either by Suetonius or Tacitus as ever being in the east, and no explanation is given of the men being available for questioning by him. It is easy to imagine Vespasian acting in the manner of the incident, but his time is perhaps early for a meeting with Jude's grandsons. If then the incident is historical, it too may belong to Titus' story.

Judaea and the Unrest of 115–17. There is no real evidence for a rising of Jews in Judaea itself at this time of widespread revolt in the Diaspora, though the statement of the *Historia Augusta* that at Hadrian's accession Libya and Palestine were in a rebellious frame of mind is credible enough. It is doubtful if the Jews in Judaea were in any position to express their discontent in action. Lusius Quietus was made legate of Judaea as a reward for his success in Mesopotamia, and it is probably wrong to alter the sense of this to mean that he was appointed to put down a rebellion, for which the other evidence is confused and slight.

The Second Revolt (132–5). Josephus' account in the *War* ends with the disturbances in Cyrene in the early seventies, immediately after the First Revolt. For the period of the Second Revolt we have only references in Dio and in Eusebius, and one sentence in the *Hist. Aug.* Jewish literature tells the story only of the end of the revolt at Bethar, but in recent times papyri from the wadis bordering the Dead Sea, especially Wadi Murabbaʿat and Nahal Hever, have thrown some light on the conditions of the rebels and the extent of their domination under the leadership of Bar Kokhba. On monuments Hadrian is often celebrated and his achievements extolled; he is there the restorer *par excellence*, and both buildings and games are recorded as instituted by him. Aelia

Capitolina (Jerusalem) was part of this widespread programme, which included in Palestine a Hadrianeum in Caesarea and in Tiberias, and Sepphoris was renamed Diocaesarea. In the capital, building began in 130 while Hadrian was in Syria (129–30). If the original plans had included some restoration of the Temple as a Jewish place of worship, hopes were dashed when during Hadrian's absence in Egypt (autumn 130) the plans were seen to replace the Temple with a typical Roman complex of forum and pagan temple. Whether there had ever been any promise to rebuild the Jewish Temple is very doubtful, and belongs· perhaps to Jewish legendary tradition rather than history. Dio says that the emperor's plans for Aelia Capitolina were the cause of the revolt, but the *Hist. Aug.* says it was a prohibition of circumcision. Certainly such a prohibition had angered the Jews, but it had not been aimed only at them.

Revolt broke out in 131–2, and met with some success, as its duration implies. Jerusalem may well have been occupied by the rebels, as implied by Appian's clear reference to its 'destruction' three times, by Ptolemy I, Vespasian, 'and again in my time by Hadrian', that is on the conclusion of the revolt. This is supported by coins, some of which may indeed imply only aspiration to 'the freedom of Jerusalem', but some seem to have been minted in the city itself. The Bar Kokhba documents show that there was a strong and centralized military government with the leader in genuinely supreme control and districts administered by leaders who were both civil and military. The existence of instructions in connexion with feasts among purely military matters seems to imply both confidence and the religious character of the rising which we have learnt to regard in connexion with Jewish nationalism. It was a religious war supported by a famous rabbi, Akiba (p. 194), who at the end of the war in 135 died a cruel and true martyr's death at the hands of the Romans. Akiba even seemed to see Bar Kokhba as a messianic deliverer. The name means 'Son of a Star', based on Num. 24:17ff. His enemies have called him Bar Koziba, 'Son of a Lie'. From the newly found documents we now know his true name and title to be Simeon bar Kosiba, Nasi' (leader) of Israel. He seems to have demanded acknowledgement of his own messiahship, to judge by the context in which Eusebius quotes Justin's statement (*Apol.* 1.31.6) that Bar Kokhba persecuted Christians who refused to deny Jesus as Christ.

The religious character of the revolt is reflected in the appearance on some coins of the name of Eleazar as priest. That he is not called high priest is no doubt due to the fact that only the sanhedrin could according to the Torah constitute a high priest, and we have seen that the sanhedrin disappeared along with the Temple.

Probably the rebels held at least for one or more short periods the whole of Judaea, including strongholds, except Herodium and apparently Masada. The Romans found it necessary to bring troops from many places in the Empire, and the most important commander sent to assist the legate Tineius Rufus was Sextus Julius Severus from Britain. Perhaps Severus' first success was the capture of Jerusalem in the third year of the revolt, when the patriotic mint appears to have closed. The war was of guerilla type and pitched battles were avoided by both sides, but in 135 the territory held by the rebels was reduced to the mountain area of Judaea. The discovery of possessions in inaccessible caves in the Dead Sea area bears out Dio's description of the rebels at the end as being refugees rather than fighters. The final phase was the siege and capture of Bethar seven miles south-west of Jerusalem, but we do not know more than that it was the last stronghold left in the hands of the rebels. Bar Kokhba was killed and the same kind of miseries were endured by the vanquished as in the case of Jerusalem in 70.

Jewish tradition speaks of the 'ploughing up' of Jerusalem and the Temple. Perhaps the same ritual ploughing and sowing with salt as took place in Carthage in 146 BC was administered here, but it may be rather that the ploughing was the marking of the *pomerium* or boundary of the new city from the religious point of view. Such *circumductio* (driving round) is witnessed by coins celebrating a refounding of the city Aelia. From it Jews were excluded except to make a ritual wailing on the ninth of the month Ab, a date which marks a number of disasters in Jewish history, including the fall of Jerusalem and of Bethar. This exclusion applied equally to Jewish Christians, and the church in Judaea now became more gentile in character, especially in leadership (Eusebius *Eccl. Hist.* 4.5). Temples of Jupiter and Hadrian were built on the site of the Temple, and new buildings included a circus, baths, amphitheatre and theatre. Jerusalem became a colony and its territory was formed of three toparchies, the Oreine (the area of the actual city and its immediate environs), Gophna and Herodium. (Luke mentions the Oreine in this sense in his gospel, 1:39, 65, where NEB translates 'uplands of Judah'.)

The province became Syria–Palaestina. There was clearly a thorough attempt to exterminate the god of the Jews, which extended even to measures against the Samaritans, the most obvious being the building of a temple of Jupiter on Mount Gerizim. It is small wonder that Jewish tradition is bitter against Hadrian, for such measures were naturally accompanied by much persecution, of which the death of Akiba is an example.

IX. *Judaea in the Antonine Period* (AD 138–92)

Antoninus Pius (138–61) relaxed the ban on circumcision for Jews. Some continuous discontent on this matter may be the historical ground for the unsupported mention in *Hist. Aug.* of Jews among others who rebelled and were quelled by this emperor. The removal of the ban may have been enough to remove the discontent; but circumcision was still forbidden for non-Jews, which was a measure against proselytizing, forbidden explicitly under Septimius Severus.

The Jewish people had suffered a chain of disasters to their nation during the first two centuries AD until within a few years of Antoninus' reign, through death, deportation, sale of prisoners into slavery, poverty and deprivation of land. Consequent emigration tipped the balance of population even in Judaea itself in favour of Gentiles, and Galilee, once 'Galilee of the Gentiles', became the only area with an overwhelmingly Jewish majority, and so became the stronghold of Judaism. The rabbinic school removed from Jamnia to Galilee after a conference in Usha. Academies were established in Sepphoris and Tiberias. The sanhedrin was set up at Usha, then moved to Beth She'arim, afterwards to Sepphoris and then to Tiberias. Presidency of the sanhedrin had lapsed after the death of Gamaliel II in about AD 110; now his son Simeon III was appointed, and the *nasi'* thus filled the gap left by the disappearance of the high priest. Simeon's successor was R. Judah I who energetically restored religious observances, including the calendar and correct procedure. *Apostoli* or emissaries ensured contact with the Diaspora, and the joint observance of the calendar. Jews everywhere in the Empire continued to pay a tax 'for being a Jew', now politely called the *aurum coronarium*, originally the name for a 'golden crown' offered to Roman generals on victory, which through various stages in which it became an exaction had sunk to being a form of common or irregular taxation on a community. The *nasi'* (sometimes called the Patriarch) was accorded real respect by the Romans, and the community, organized as a religious rather than a political entity, gradually recovered, though emigration was common either to other provinces or to Parthian territory. When the tide of prosperity turned, Diaspora Jews began to enter Palestine from Babylonia, Asia Minor and Alexandria, settling in Sepphoris, Tiberias and especially Joppa. Aelia Capitolina remained officially out of bounds, and the land was heavily garrisoned, so that it became like the Danube provinces a strain on the resources of the Empire. In 175 Avidius Cassius, legate of Syria, rose against M. Aurelius (161–80) and was supported in his bid for the throne by the eastern provinces. Cassius was murdered before battle was joined, but the emperor, who had been busy with the Danube frontier, hurried in alarm to the east and toured through Syria and Egypt, to return to Rome for a triumph technically deserved only for the settlement on the Danube, which however was abandoned by his son Commodus whom he had left in charge.

X. *Judaea in the Severan Period (*AD *193–235)*

From the late second century there was evidently much building of synagogues; some were rebuilt, especially in Galilee, where there was now the highest concentration of the Jewish population. The architectural style is uniform throughout the area. It is not very Jewish, but generally conforms to the lines of Syrian architecture, datable to the Severan period or sometimes later.

The richness of sarcophagi in Beth She'arim also shows that Judaism flourished in this period. R. Judah I moved there with the sanhedrin (p. 194) and the catacombs became his family's burial-place; as a result burial there became the fashion for some time to come. In this period there seems to have been a *de facto* relaxation of the ban on Jewish entrance into Aelia, and some Jews even lived there, but the ban on proselytism imposed by Septimius Severus remained firm.

From about 230 onwards the troubled changes on the eastern frontier, where the new Persian dynasty had overthrown Parthian supremacy, affected all populations. (For its effect upon Jewish life in the frontier town of Dura-Europos see p. 30.) Provision of the *annona* (supplies to the army exacted from local populations – see p. 53) became an even greater burden than usual; and we find that R. Judah I and Gamaliel III relaxed the laws governing sabbatical years for the land.

EGYPT

Outline of History 304 BC to AD 284

After the death of Alexander the Great one of his generals named Ptolemy secured for himself the satrapy of Egypt. In 306 BC Antigonus of Macedonia took the title of king, and his rivals followed suit. They included Seleucus of Syria (p. 12) and Ptolemy I (Soter, 304–283), who was content with his fertile land and did not threaten the ambitions of the other Diadochi. Antigonus was a Macedonian soldier and a man of some culture, author of an account now lost of Alexander's campaigns, used by Arrian and thus to some extent preserved at second-hand. He founded only one city, Ptolemais on the west bank of the Nile in Upper Egypt, settling his Greek mercenaries among the Egyptian population in already existing towns or on the land near them. The conditions in Egypt, including a neglected and therefore inefficient irrigation system, demanded Greek technical ability and energy. So did land reclamation schemes, more advanced agriculture, and reform of the old bureaucratic system by which Egypt was administered. Moreover the Ptolemies regarded their territory as part of the world of the Mediterranean, and as the source of their wealth, largely in the form of corn, and did not aspire to absorb Egyptian culture, still less to become Egyptians.

The Egyptians had welcomed Alexander as a deliverer from the Persian Empire, but had in reality exchanged one overlord for another. Although some high-born and better educated Egyptians occupied a number of important offices in the administration, the people of the land as a whole felt themselves to be of inferior status, an impression strengthened by economic inequality. They were artisans and tenants of land regarded as owned by the king, or if holders of allotments bestowing an almost private ownership, they received less extensive holdings than Greeks. There was therefore a considerable amount of hostility, but only expressing itself spasmodically in anything like active rebellion. For their part, the Ptolemies, while willingly adapting the autocratic government of ancient Egypt into a hellenistic mould, did not wish the Egyptians to feel inferior, but rather to join the new civilization offered them, as all enlightened persons in their estimation surely must. In one sphere there was improvement on the past; the old rivalry between the Pharaoh and the priests of the temples disappeared in a new policy which confirmed the priests in their privileges and maintained the fabric of the temples. Thus it was true that an Egyptian might flourish if he were willing to accept the superiority of hellenistic culture. Manetho, an Egyptian priest, compiled under the first two Ptolemies (about 290 to 250 BC) a history of Egypt from ancient records, probably rather like the court annals of other near eastern countries such as are mentioned in the Old Testament (1 Kings 14:19 and elsewhere; 1 Chron. 27:24; Esther 2:23; 6:1). He dedicated his work to Ptolemy II. It was used much by ancient historians but has disappeared apart from fragments.

If Egyptians only rarely rose to high rank in the administration, in the remoter countryside the division between them and the Greeks was less marked; intermarriage was common and local gods were accepted. Ptolemy I indeed fostered and may have introduced worship of a special god, Sarapis, who seems to have combined the attributes of a number of Greek gods, including Zeus and Aesculapius, with the Egyptian Osiris and Apis the bull-god. A magnificent temple was erected for him in Alexandria. If the intention was to offer a focus for joint Hellenic–Egyptian feelings and aspirations, the cult was not very successful, for after a time little enthusiasm was shown by Egyptians outside Alexandria. It succeeded however in presenting to the world outside Egypt a god with the glamour of that country in a guise acceptable to hellenistic civilization, and his worship spread through all the Mediterranean lands, and even reached Britain. It was one of the pagan cults still rivalling Christianity in the fourth century.

The famous city Alexandria was founded by Alexander himself on the site of a small fishing village called Rhacotis. The city occupied a strip of ground between the sea and Lake Mareotis. Out in the sea the island Pharos supported a lighthouse, and was reached by a mole seven furlongs in length on either side of which lay a harbour. There was another harbour at the mouth of the Nile, that is on the north side of Lake Mareotis and south of the city. Alexandria was a Greek city and its population was at first mainly Greek, organized like a Greek city-state, although its original constitution for government is not known. There was a large number of Egyptians, and one of the five 'quarters' into which the city was divided, and part of another, were occupied by Jews, who were to be found in other parts also and played an active part in the history of the city.

Alexander had entered the temple of Ammon in the oasis of Siwah in the western desert and had there been greeted by the priest as son of the god. It is probable that the incident introduced or fostered in Alexander's mind the idea of his own divinity, and he expressed a desire to be buried in the oasis. Ptolemy shrewdly brought his body to Egypt, and buried it not in the oasis but in Memphis; his son transferred it to a tomb in Alexandria. This *sema* (the word is Greek for 'tomb') was a famous building in the city which boasted also the famous Sarapeum, a gymnasium, stadium, hippodrome, theatre and royal palace. We do not know when the city became the capital, taking over the honour from the ancient Memphis, but the change seems inevitable. Close to the palace were the Museum and Library, both centres of learning with which are associated famous names of antiquity, such as Aristarchus who proposed many centuries before Copernicus the heliocentric universe and the rotation of the earth on its axis, Euclid, and many other scholars, including famous fathers of the Church. Ptolemy III ordered all travellers who disembarked at Alexandria to deposit any books in their possession for copying. The traveller received the copy and the Library retained the original; this was true even of some state copies of classical tragedies from Athens whose loan was obtained by paying large sums as pledges and forfeiting them while keeping the originals.

After the death of Ptolemy I in 283 BC there were three main rivals, Antigonus of Macedonia, Antiochus I of Syria, and Ptolemy II (Philadelphus, 283–246). It was Ptolemy II who, abandoning the peaceful policy of his father, began a long struggle against both Macedonia and Syria. At first unsuccessful, he changed his fortune by marrying his full sister Arsinoe. This action was strange since it would be regarded by all except the Egyptians as scandalous and unnatural. Arsinoe was as remarkable a woman as her situation. To marry her Ptolemy had to dismiss his wife, who was also called Arsinoe and was the daughter of Lysimachus, another of Alexander's generals and ruler of Thrace. His sister whom he now married, Arsinoe II, was the widow of Lysimachus and of Ptolemy Keraunos (Ptolemy I's son by his wife Eurydice). She was one of the remarkable women of antiquity, evidently possessing a personality more than a match for any opposition which might arise through her scandalous position. Her conduct of the war – the First Syrian War, 276–272 – which Ptolemy had seemed to be losing, ended by the acquisition of Phoenicia and the coast of Asia Minor. She received unique honours from many cities and is often mentioned alongside Ptolemy as the ruling king; she is sometimes even thought of as a goddess. The period of her successes was the golden age of Ptolemaic Egypt but she died before realizing her ambition to set Ptolemaeus, her son by Lysimachus, on the Macedonian throne. Her death was indeed the end of effective opposition to Antigonus of Macedonia. After it Ptolemy encouraged a disastrous alliance of Greek cities to resist Antigonus which ended in a triumph for the latter. In the years 259–255, he and Antiochus II attacked Ptolemy who however resisted successfully but died in 246. His son Ptolemy III had even better success after Antigonus' death. In 246 he was able to march through Syria and Cilicia with little opposition and to extend his empire as far as Thrace, but after a defeat at sea he ceased his expansionist activity.

The first three Ptolemies had been active and able, Ptolemy I being probably the wisest in that he adopted a non-threatening attitude towards other countries. Under Ptolemy IV (221–205) there came a decline, although he had in Sosibius an able if unscrupulous minister who energetically prepared for and then won a victory at Raphia in 217 over Antiochus III. The times were unpropitious, for Rome was already on the scene, having made a treaty with Ptolemy II in 273, at first confining her activity to using Egypt as a counterweight to the Seleucid power and not threatening her independence. Raphia had an unexpected result: restoration of Egyptian confidence led to nationalist unrest which was hard to check, so that the accession of a boy king, Ptolemy V (205–181), gave an opportunity to Philip V of Macedon and Antiochus III to rob Egypt of all her possessions. Most important for our purposes was the battle of Panion (p. 13) which did more than reverse the victory of Raphia and lost Syria–Palestine for all time from Egyptian control. Antiochus IV contemplated a conquest of the entire country of Egypt but was rudely warned off by the Roman representative. Nevertheless even after this Rome left Egypt officially independent.

Ptolemy V reigned until 181 when he died of poison. He had mastered the native unrest which he inherited but evidently not secured the throne, which now became ever weaker. He left three young children, a daughter Cleopatra, and two sons, the elder of whom succeeded though still only a boy and reigned 181–145, in due course marrying his sister. He is known as Ptolemy VI Philometor. During the time when Antiochus IV was beginning the campaign in Egypt which was to be so decidedly cut short (169–168) the Alexandrians made the younger son king. He is usually known as Ptolemy VII Euergetes II, but sometimes as Ptolemy VIII (to acknowledge the claim of Ptolemy Neos, son of Ptolemy VI, who reigned briefly in 145 and is sometimes called Ptolemy VII). Ptolemy VII (to give him the usual number) was acknowledged by Ptolemy VI Philometor, so there were two kings in Egypt at this time. In 163 the Alexandrians drove out Philometor, and later under Roman arbitration a sharing took place, according to which the latter ruled Egypt and Cyprus, while Euergetes (Ptolemy VII) ruled Cyrene and Libya. Philometor intrigued with Alexander Balas and Demetrius II (p. 14) and attempted to gain control of Syria but died of wounds in 145, thus leaving Euergetes king of the whole of the Egyptian possessions. On Philometor's death Euergetes married the widow Cleopatra II who was his own sister, and subsequently married also Philometor's daughter Cleopatra III. Whether these personal matters were the cause or not, a civil war broke out between Euergetes and Cleopatra II which was so protracted as to cause the breakdown of proper administration in the whole country. When he was able to deal with this situation Euergetes published and enforced a number of decrees which tell us less about the system than about the more honest ways in which he demanded that it should be applied. Although these measures had some effect, a more radical change was needed, and Euergetes was not popular. His character and intentions are something of an enigma; he extended the privileges and powers of the priests and was favourable to Egyptians. He was hated by Greeks for this, because he damaged the Museum in Alexandria, and because he let his troops loose on a hostile mob in Alexandria during the civil war. He perhaps envisaged a Graeco-Egyptian state in which Greeks and Egyptians would be true partners, but he failed largely because he did not tackle the necessary economic reforms of a system which bore hard on the native Egyptians.

Internecine strife continued under Euergetes' successors. The inhabitants of the Thebaid were at times virtually a separate state; this southern district was centred upon Thebes, once the ancient capital of all Egypt. It stretched from Hermopolis in the north to Elephantine in the south. In 85 Thebes was destroyed and reduced to a number of ruined villages. The successors of Euergetes included none of any note for a generation or two. Euergetes' illegitimate son Ptolemy Apion was given Cyrene to govern, and in 96 he bequeathed it to Rome. Of Euergetes' sons by Cleopatra III the elder was Ptolemy IX Soter II (b. 141; d. 81). (Again the numbering is not unanimous; that followed is from *The Oxford Classical Dictionary*.) He shared the rule with his brother Ptolemy X Alexander I (b. *c.* 140; d. 88), whose son Ptolemy XI Alexander II (b. *c.* 100; d. 80) was made by Sulla joint ruler with his step-mother Cleopatra Berenice whom he murdered. He was afterwards himself killed by the Alexandrians. Ptolemy IX (who was nicknamed Lathyrus) had an illegitimate son Ptolemy XII Neos Dionysos (called 'Auletes' – 'the flautist') who succeeded to the kingship in 80 and was friendly towards Rome. The Alexandrians expelled him in 58, but he was restored by Gabinius in 55. This Ptolemy was the father of Cleopatra VII, born about 69 BC and destined to become the most famous of all her line.

Cleopatra became joint ruler with Ptolemy XIII in 51. In 49 they were supporting Pompey with supplies but in 48 he was murdered by Ptolemy's ministers, who expelled Cleopatra from the throne. Ptolemy opposed Caesar but was defeated and ended his life by drowning in the Nile. This was in 47 when Caesar restored Cleopatra and gave her Ptolemy XIV, another brother, as joint ruler and husband. He left three legions for their defence and departed for Rome. Subsequently Cleopatra bore a son which she claimed was Caesar's, and next year she visited Rome with her son and her husband, but on Caesar's assassination in 44 returned to Alexandria. Her husband then died by poison, it is thought at her instigation. In 41 Mark Antony came to Alexandria and Cleopatra began her famous association with him. She bore him twins, a son and daughter, and in 37 joined him at Antioch where they formed an alliance with comprehensive plans for the future. In 36 she bore him another son.

Caesar had restored Cyprus to Egypt in 48 and Antony now added further territories including Cyrenaica. Cleopatra supplied his army, making up for the great losses he had incurred in Parthia (p. 17). Their vision of empire, an eastern-based alternative to Rome, was proclaimed from Alexandria in 34 in what were called 'the Donations'. The lands which Alexander the

Great had ruled were theoretically distributed, those east of the Euphrates to one child, those west to another, with the daughter as 'Queen of Cyrenaica'; Antony and Cleopatra themselves were the overlords of the entire empire. The idea, ornamented with symbols and religious notions, was welcomed by many in the east, but was never realized. In 32 Rome declared war on Cleopatra (not mentioning Antony and thus avoiding the taint of civil war) and in 31 the battle of Actium brought an end to their ambitions, and to their lives. Cleopatra took her own life in 30 and her eldest son Caesarion, claimed to be Caesar's son and called in the Donations 'King of kings', was executed by Octavian later in the same year.

The unique character of Egypt among all the nations was reflected in its ill-defined status in the Roman Empire when Augustus, as he says in his *Res Gestae*, 'added Egypt to the dominions of the Roman people'. It may be loosely called a province, noting that it was administered as if part of the personal estate of the emperor, producing corn and money for the Roman state. It was naturally fertile and rich and could become a stronghold for a usurper; Augustus therefore shrewdly entrusted it to a prefect who was an *eques*, since a senator might more easily become a rival. The prefect however, as viceroy in a country accustomed to autocratic rule, had very extensive powers, being commander-in-chief, civil head, chief financial officer and supreme dispenser of justice. Revolts in the Thebaid against the Roman taxgatherers at the beginning of the Roman rule were soon crushed, and a strong government brought its rewards. Piracy in the Mediterranean was abolished; an increase in trade resulted, and was enhanced by a growth of trade with India and the east, due to the discovery about this time of the monsoon, whose changing winds facilitated sailing from the south-west and later returning from the northeast. Irrigation canals were repaired and deepened, so that the rise in the Nile on which Egypt had always depended for its prosperity was guaranteed to be sufficient even in a relatively poor year. Much of the bureaucratic system used under the Ptolemies remained, and the hellenistic rather than the Egyptian population enjoyed favour.

Roman administration was always harsh, but it was often in the long run beneficial, especially to provincials willing to adapt and indeed to bow to it. Egypt to an extent conformed to this pattern, but there was an important difference which operated in her case. Much more than with other provinces, her produce was absorbed in excessive measure by Rome so that Egyptians felt an extra bitterness when faced with the burden of taxation. This often included being forced to undertake the collection of local taxes, which might well mean paying the bulk oneself. Along with this burden stood that of the liturgies. This term, *liturgy*, far from its modern meaning, was used in the ancient Greek city-states in its literal meaning of 'work performance', the work in question being public work such as the provision of a warship or its equipment, or of a chorus in a drama festival. Especially at first, liturgies were undertaken voluntarily by wealthy aristocrats, but by degrees easily imagined became a burden which the state demanded from those whom the people thought wealthy enough to undertake them. In Egypt the term was used, more comprehensively, of the burden of being a village elder, then of higher financial officer, and finally that of being a district tax-collector. The extreme result of the compulsion system was for some individuals to withdraw – to 'go underground' or disappear from official sight. Tiberius Alexander, nephew of Philo, procurator of Judaea 46–8 (p. 113) and prefect of Egypt 66–70, seems to have corrected some obvious abuses such as compulsion to undertake tax farming, informing and imposition of new and illegal taxes, but a reformation both of the system and of those who administered it was as improbable as it was necessary.

The picture should not be painted too black. The dry climate of Egypt and its dry sand have preserved innumerable fragments of literature and letters. Many fragments have been found at Oxyrhyncus which was the capital of a nome (district) and not a Greek settlement. This witnesses to the wide influence of Greek culture and to interest in its classical literature. Such flourishing of culture is not likely to have been accompanied by extreme poverty, and the quality of municipal buildings supports the inference that not only in Alexandria but also elsewhere in Egypt there was a lively cultural life in the Ptolemaic period, and this included the athletic elements typical of Greek education.

Becoming part of the Roman Empire did not at first make a great difference to the character of life and its amenities in Egypt. Augustus divided the land into three: the Thebaid, Middle Egypt and the Delta. Special privileges were enjoyed by citizens of the capitals of these districts, Thebes, Arsinoe and Alexandria, and these were the most hellenized parts of the population. In these cities various magistracies were introduced, and while at first they bore individual responsibility they came to form corporations which afforded the nuclei for the local senates established by the emperor Septimius Severus (193–211). A census was held every fourteen years, and some land could be privately owned, which meant that there might be people rich enough to pay taxes.

By degrees the one-sided nature of the Roman administration had its effect. Taxes became too heavy and the disappearance of taxpayers became acute. The phenomenon of withdrawal from sight was called *anachoresis*, which was to be used extensively later on to designate those who escaped military service thereby, and which also became a technical term for religiously motivated retirement from normal life, giving us the word 'anchorite'. Viewed from the official standpoint it posed an acute problem; suitable candidates for magistracies became hard to find. When therefore Septimius Severus established senates in 202, he created a further problem rather than solved that of local government. Membership involved financial reponsibility which was ultimately personal, and escape was hard, since to decline the honour cost a sum equivalent to two-thirds of one's property. In Egypt the disadvantages of Caracalla's measure in 212 bestowing Roman citizenship on all inhabitants of the Empire outweighed the advantages to a much greater degree than elsewhere in the Empire. In this situation ingenious and unscrupulous men contrived to make themselves wealthy by managing the taxes in ways unexamined by the governors, and a division between rich and poor became acute. The reforms of Diocletian in 284 simplified the tax system but the tendency towards a sort of feudal system continued into the Byzantine period.

Jews in Egypt

According to the Bible the stories of the patriarchs and Moses relate the earliest contacts of the Israelites with Egypt; the traditions of the Exodus indeed form the basis of much of Israel's faith and liturgy. In the period of the monarchy, from Solomon onwards, many contacts with Egypt can be traced more precisely.

At the time of the Exile some Israelites fled to Egypt (Jer. 41:16–44:30); after the Persian conquest of Babylon and Persia's annexation of Egypt in 525, more Jews settled there, probably including some from Babylon and Mesopotamia. Firm evidence of actual

Jewish settlement is afforded by the Aramaic papyri, legal, epistolary and religious, dating between 495 and about 87BC and found at Elephantine, an island in the Nile opposite Assuan (ancient Syene) (*Making*, pp. 38–40). Its beginnings may date from a nucleus earlier than the Exile, perhaps the Jewish mercenary force employed by Psammetichus II (594–589). The fact that these documents come to an end at 400 BC may suggest that the community was destroyed; there is clear evidence of Egyptian hostility to it.

In the Ptolemaic period Egypt, of all countries of the Diaspora, was the most fully populated by Jews, the inevitable result of the constant changes of fortune in the frequent wars between the Seleucids of Syria and the Ptolemies of Egypt. Some Jewish immigrants were prisoners of war, the others no doubt including some who found that they had supported the wrong side in political or military warfare. Alexandria with its trading facilities was a natural attraction to immigrants at all times. From the reign of Ptolemy I Jews were among them, attracted by opportunities for work. An example of the constant movement between Egypt and Palestine was the flight to Egypt of the deposed high priest Onias III (murdered 171 BC, p. 87; or of his son Onias IV – Josephus is authority for both – about 167 BC). There the latter rebuilt and adapted a ruined temple granted him by Ptolemy VI Philometor at a site called Leontopolis in the south of the Delta. The associated settlement became a military colony, guarding the road from Memphis to the frontier at Pelusium. Its inhabitants were typical of many Jews, who were often used as police and mercenaries by the Ptolemies. The activity of such Jews, supporting causes (such as that of Cleopatra III in 108–107) against rivals backed by the Greeks of Alexandria, sharpened racial feeling both in Alexandria and in other parts of Egypt. It was no doubt largely in the hope of support against the Greeks that Egyptian Jews helped the Roman invaders in 55 and 48 (p. 96).

Inter-racial ill-feeling did not lead to actual hostilities under the Ptolemies, who protected their Jewish subjects. Evidence of such activity occurs only in the Roman period. The seeds of violence were sown effectively from 55 onwards, when the Egyptian Jews, at the instigation of Antipater, father of Herod the Great, gave support to the Roman army, and expressions of open hostility began with the Roman annexation in 30 BC. From AD 30 matters between Greeks and Jews became increasingly serious, especially after Agrippa I's visit to Alexandria in 38. Under the Ptolemies anti-Jewish feeling was expressed in local quarrels and in literature. An example of the latter was Manetho, a Greek-speaking Egyptian. The hostility to Jews shown in his history became common in writers from his time onwards, and gave a strong motivation to Josephus, whose care to refute anti-Jewish slanders and wilful misunderstanding appears on nearly every page of his works, not only in the *Against Apion* which is devoted to the cause. Actual violence, with attacks on Jewish people and their property, began in the early Roman period in Alexandria where it exemplified the very common situation in so many hellenistic cities of mixed population throughout the Middle East.

Jews and Greeks in Alexandria. The situation and its terrible outcome in Alexandria deserve special mention, partly because of the importance of Alexandria and its history, and partly because of their frequent repercussions in later history. It is important to remember that Alexandria was a Greek city proud of its ancestry and its character. In it Jews had rights of residence, which was not confined to the two districts called Jewish, just as the residents of these were not exclusively Jewish. The Jewish rights were those of members of a *politeuma*, which they constituted as a corporate body; it was an officially recognized corporation of aliens enjoying the right of residence in a foreign city. Within it the ethnic unit conducted its own affairs and administered its own religious and social laws among its own people. In Alexandria, as sometimes elsewhere, the *politeuma* was presided over by an ethnarch, assisted by a council of elders, which in Alexandria numbered seventy-one. An individual Jew's right to protection therefore rested on membership of a *politeuma* with its right of residence. It did not bestow citizenship of the city (although this has often been argued), but some Jewish individuals did hold Greek citizenship and held office in the municipality. Such was Philo's brother Alexander in the thirties AD, who was alabarch or customs officer.

Greeks in Alexandria do not appear to have been anti-Jewish from the first, but they resented Roman favouritism and perhaps the help which Jews had given to the original Roman encroachment on Egypt. They resented also the insinuation into the ephebate, the organization of Greeks for education and athletics, of those Jews who joined it in order to escape the *laographia*, the census for capitation tax from which Greek citizens were exempt. Such Jews must have been well hellenized, since while they did not wish to abandon their faith they were willing to adapt their religion far enough to allow them to take part in the social and religious observances and gymnastic exercises involved. Non-Jews would view this ability to make the best of both worlds with some jealousy, so that the growth of Egyptian nationalism, in which some Greeks were involved, was both anti-Roman and anti-Jewish.

In AD 38 A. Avillius Flaccus, the prefect appointed in 32 by Tiberius, fearing deposition and perhaps execution by Caius, accepted the proffered help of the Greek community at the price of the 'surrender' of the Jews. It is doubtful what he would have done, but in August 38 Agrippa I arrived in Alexandria and the Jews begged him to intercede with his friend the emperor. He did no more apparently than make some sort of parade through the streets and disappear when the Greeks staged a mocking counter-demonstration which Flaccus tolerated in the belief that Agrippa's parade had been a provocation to his authority. The situation then went from bad to worse; Flaccus was persuaded to proclaim that Jews were aliens and foreigners in Alexandria, thus destroying the basis of their *politeuma*. The pogrom which followed was nasty, brutish and long, including robbery, torture, humiliation and brutal executions. During the peace of exhaustion in the following autumn soldiers arrived from Rome to arrest Flaccus. The Jews gradually recovered under the new prefect C. Vitrasius Pollio, but their rights were not explicitly re-established until Claudius' accession in 41. The only authority for the detailed events is Philo in his *Against Flaccus* and *Legatio ad Caium* (p. 140). Philo was the leader of the Jewish delegation to Rome which followed the unrest, probably in the winter 39–40. It was while they and the rival Greek delegation were waiting for a full hearing that news came of Caius' outrageous proposal to paganize the Temple at Jerusalem (p. 112). Caius' death was the solution to that problem, but the Jews of Alexandria had to wait for Claudius, who on his accession made a sensible pronouncement enjoining on all the duty to respect the rights of the Jewish race, and the Jews to respect those of others, a clear warning against reprisals. The same declaration of principle was sent also to other cities in the Empire. Nevertheless in Alexandria it appears that Jewish vengeance was feared, and indeed threatened. In reply to a Greek delegation in 41 Claudius sent a *Letter to Alexandria* published there by the prefect L. Aemilius Rectus. The emperor was again impartial and diplomatic in urging live-and-let-live conduct, but referred to the Jews as living 'in a city not their own' and threatened action against any disobedience from them for 'making a general nuisance of themselves throughout the empire'.

Throughout the disturbances the leaders of the Greek nationalists were Lampo and Isidorus, each in his time a gymnasiarch. They were misguided enough to attempt to impeach Agrippa (probably Agrippa I in 41 but possibly Agrippa II in 53). By an unknown turn of events their efforts led to a trial of themselves and ended in their execution. Some details, largely incredible, are related in the *Acta Isidori*, part of a very fragmentary series of documents called *The Acts of the Alexandrine Martyrs*, which make heroes of a number of Greek nationalists on trial before Roman emperors.

Racial rivalry, expressing itself from time to time in open hostility, with glorification of its 'martyrs' by each side, now became endemic not only in Egypt but elsewhere in the Empire, where indeed it had already shown itself; it now became sharper, more violent, and more openly anti-Jewish. Claudius' warnings fell on deaf ears. It was natural that Jews in Egypt should wish to exact vengeance, and when Trajan was absent in Mesopotamia in AD 115 they rebelled. Our sources, Eusebius (AD *c.* 260–340), Dio (*fl.* AD 200), Orosius (*fl.* AD 415), and archaeological evidence including papyri, fail to supply us with an adequate account of the immediate causes. The nature of *The Acts of the Alexandrine Martyrs*, making heroes of one's own side, and the incredible conversations purporting to have taken place between accused and emperor–judge, prepare the reader for disappointment when examining for instance an ancient papyrus such as P. Ox. 1242, which gives an account of delegations of Greeks and Jews at Rome whose details are obviously fictional though revealing the different nationalistic attitudes. It is safe however to say that the 'rebellion' was at first against Greeks rather than against the Roman authority, which was involved rather as the force attempting to keep the peace.

The Jews in Egypt suffered a complete military defeat in 119, but some evidence suggests that the Jewish *politeuma* survived.

Nevertheless, after Hadrian's settlement we have no evidence for the following century about the Jewish community in Alexandria.

Philo of Alexandria (c. 15 BC to c. AD 45)

Philo was a member of a distinguished family in Alexandria and took part in its political life, being in fact the leader of the delegation to the emperor Caius in Rome, defending the rights of Jews in Alexandria. In the larger part of his works he combined philosophy with biblical interpretation, and both his thought and method in these spheres are of the first importance. In addition his exegesis of the books of Moses involved him in a version of biblical history at least as far as the death of Moses.

Philo wrote other treatises invaluable for our understanding of the history and thought of the period. His *De vita contemplativa* describes the beliefs and life of the sect called the Therapeutae, and sheds light on the ascetic life and theology of Jews of his time, including the Qumran community (p. 172). Important for history is what Eusebius describes as a five-volume work, whose general theme was the eventual triumph of righteousness over wickedness. If there were indeed five volumes, only two, both written after the death of Caius, survive. One is *Against Flaccus*; it describes the persecution of the Jews in Alexandria in AD 38 and the final deposition of the governor Avillius Flaccus by Caius himself. The other is the *Legatio ad Caium* (*Embassy to Caius*) which describes the joy felt at the accession of Caius, and pleads for the rights of Jews following the subsequent change in his mentality and life, with its fearful consequences for them. Philo describes his meeting with the emperor and the events in Alexandria which led to the embassy, and gives a striking (and probably factual) account of Caius' attempts to set up his statue in the Temple in Jerusalem (p. 112).

CYRENE

'The districts of Libya around Cyrene' (Acts 2:10), or Cyrenaica, form a country of fertile territory separated from other civilized parts of Africa by tracts of desert, and therefore forming its most natural links across the sea with Crete and Greece. Cyrene was a Greek city founded in the seventh century BC, which developed well enough to found other cities in the region. This formed the Pentapolis ('Five Towns') of Greek cities: Berenice, Teuchira (Arsinoe), Apollonia and Ptolemais with Cyrene itself. Part of the Persian Empire after Cambyses' conquest in 525 BC, Cyrenaica was independent from about 475. It submitted to Alexander and after his death was governed by a liberal constitution, whose officials acknowledged the king of Egypt as overlord. This lasted until the Roman senate gave it in 163 as a separate entity to Euergetes II, brother of Ptolemy VI, on whose accession to the throne in 145 BC it was joined to Egypt.

Jews in Cyrene

Cyrenaica was one of the territories where the Jewish population was greatly enlarged by the policy of Ptolemy I and his use of Jews as trustworthy settlers and mercenaries. He sent Jewish colonists thither, especially to the city of Cyrene itself, and immigration continued while Ptolemaic rule lasted. There was unrest in 87–86 BC, early in the period of direct Roman rule which began in 96. Later, a successful appeal for freedom from molestation and for the right to send the Temple tax to Jerusalem produced relative peace after some other trouble, but we hear again of disturbance in about AD 72, caused by refugee nationalists from Judaea. The result is unknown and the next landmark is the revolt of 115. The immediate causes are obscure, but it is probable that dissatisfaction with Vespasian's Jewish tax and hostility between Jew and Greek were permanent undercurrents of life here as elsewhere in the Diaspora, and it is possible that there was an opportunist connexion of timing with the revolt in Mesopotamia. In Cyrenaica the rising took on the colour of a religious–nationalistic rebellion against Rome, and wanton destruction and atrocities were many and immense. The archaeological evidence reveals great damage to temples in the city of Cyrene.

It is possible that there was a messianic rising in Cyrene which spread eastwards into the Delta. Further examination of the archaeological evidence may make this clearer. The revolt was put down only after persistent and bitter warfare by Q. Marcius Turbo, sent to the task specially by Trajan and later entrusted with the same authority by Hadrian. The result of the campaign was the death of many thousands of Jews, in battle or by execution.

There is archaeological evidence for thorough restoration and rebuilding in Cyrenaica under Trajan and especially under Hadrian, the latter arranging for repopulation and the founding of at least one new city, Hadrianopolis. Historically the region then lapses into obscurity.

5. The Jewish Diaspora and Roman Empire in Later Centuries

We have seen that in the period of about 100 BC to AD 100 there were Jewish populations in cities of many parts of the Roman Empire. They were often in a state of unrest or open conflict with inhabitants of other races, or with Rome, or with both. No doubt many such conflicts have gone unrecorded, and uncertainty attends any enquiry into the relations between Jews and the Roman administration in the second and following centuries of our era.

There seems to have been a general movement towards revolt by Jews in the Empire in the time of Trajan and Hadrian, but the sources are so thin that it is impossible to give an accurate or full account of it. It seems that there was a fierce revolt in Cyprus, but how it was ended is not known, though a decree was made which forbade any Jew for the future ever to set foot on the island. Dio implies that this ban was in force a century later (early third century) and it is not known to what extent it was ignored, or if it was repealed, and if so at what date.

In Mesopotamia the Jews revolted in the rear of Trajan's advance into Parthian territory, but it is far from clear whether they were joining in a general rebellion or initiating their own. Lusius Quietus is reported to have obeyed Trajan's order to sweep Jews out of the province so well that he was made legate of Palestine as a reward (*c.* 117). It is certain, however, that when Hadrian renounced claims to Parthian territory, Jews were able to return and to reorganize themselves again under Parthian rule.

The exodus of Jews into other lands after the sufferings of 70 and 135 had the permanent effect of increasing the Jewish population in the many countries where they went. By enactments of Severus and Caracalla (especially of the latter in 212 – p. 70) people of Jewish religion could (i.e. must) serve on local councils and hold magistracies, but were liable only for those duties which did not conflict with their religion. It is probable therefore that *politeumata* membership had become unnecessary, and if lists of members still existed they were absorbed into the larger lists of all citizens.

Part II

6. The Synagogue

In the Diaspora exiled Jews, loyal to the one-sanctuary law (Deut. 12:2ff), still looked to Jerusalem as their cultic centre and appear only in Egypt to have provided any substitute for the Temple. Even there the two exceptions are susceptible of explanation. The temple at Elephantine, of which the fifth century papyri tell us, was more than an exception in being syncretistic (*Making*, p. 38), while that constructed at Leontopolis by Onias III or IV in 167 BC (p. 136) may be regarded as due in the main to the personal demand of an exile who thought of himself as the true high priest of Israel.

Even in Palestine the Temple could not meet the needs of those who lived at a distance from the capital and, when the need to know and obey the Torah was impressed upon them, the system of sacrifices was hardly adequate. It is therefore possible that the need for local meeting-places became acute after the Restoration, but also possible that it had been felt in the homeland before the Exile. Certainly after the destruction of the Temple in 587, both there and in the Diaspora there was a need for places of assembly where children and the unlearned could be taught and the experts could debate and consult. Another and perhaps earlier need was for a place which could be used for prayer. This may have been a root of the synagogue's growth, for 1 Chron. 24:4ff divides the priests who were to officiate at the Temple into twenty-four courses, and the Mishnah (Ta'an. 4:2) explains that for every course there was a *ma'amad* consisting of priests, levites and lay-men. When it was a course's turn to officiate the priests and levites went up to Jerusalem, and the laymen assembled in their own towns to read the Torah. Ta'an. 4:3 goes on to relate this reading to times of prayer, which correspond to times of sacrifice at the Temple. In the Diaspora private prayer was apparently made at similar fixed times and in fixed places. Dan. 6:10–13 reflects the custom of Babylonian Jews in the second century BC, and Josephus in *Ant.* IV.8.13 (212) inserts an instruction to pray twice daily into an extended homily by Moses drawn largely from Deuteronomy (cp. 1 Kings 8:27ff). It was perhaps a very early habit to add readings from the Torah to private prayer; this would foreshadow the office of the *ma'amad* and lead to such an assembly as is described in Neh. 8:1–18, which suggests an early stage of synagogue worship. The procedure on this occasion is conducted by returned exiles, and it may be that the synagogue developed earlier in the Diaspora; but it seems natural that the destruction of the Temple would create the need for meeting-places for prayer and reading in the homeland also.

EVIDENCE OF VOCABULARY

The words used in connexion with the synagogue and its worship are significant. The Greek word *sunagoge*, often used in the LXX (Septuagint, p. 153) in its natural meaning of 'assembly' or 'gathering' in a quite general way, is not used there of a religious meeting-place, and there is no passage where any other word can be said to foreshadow the concept. (The AV rendering 'synagogues' in Ps. 74:8 is anachronistic and not justifiable for either Hebrew or Greek; a better translation is 'meeting-places'.) It is perhaps significant that in the Diaspora the Greek *proseuche* (lit. 'prayer') is the earliest word used for a synagogue building. The later universal term almost always means the assembly which used it. In time, from roughly the second century AD, *sunagoge* replaces *proseuche* for the actual building.

In the homeland the sequence of word-usage was different. A prophet of the exilic period or perhaps later could look forward to a restored Temple as a 'house of prayer for all nations' (Isa. 56:7; cp. 60:7 LXX and 1 Macc. 7:37), perhaps thus unconsciously making Babylonian Jews think of the Temple as a meeting-place rather than as the divinely ordered centre of the cult. The Temple as a place of prayer is certainly the most important theme of the Deuteronomic chapter 1 Kings 8. When the Temple had been so designated, it may have seemed disrespectful as well as confusing to use the same word for a local meeting-place, so that in Palestine after the Restoration the term *sunagoge* was more widely used, and prevailed as late as early Christian times (though *proseuche* is found in the New Testament in this sense, Acts 16:13).

146

ARCHAEOLOGICAL EVIDENCE

The survival of Judaism in Babylonia would be hard to explain without the existence of some institution comparable to the synagogue known from later evidence, but no firm evidence for the existence of buildings is available till much later.

The earliest inscriptions denoting buildings as synagogues (using the term *proseuche*) appear in Egypt, beginning in the third century BC, mentioning Ptolemy III Euergetes (246–221 BC). Similar archaeological evidence witnesses to the continuity of synagogue building in Egypt into late Roman times.

There is indeed abundant evidence from inscriptions for the existence of synagogues from every quarter of the Diaspora, though none early enough to illustrate the origins of the synagogue in Babylonia. Among the earliest is an inscription from the island of Delos, about 100 BC. In Rome the evidence bears out the increase in Jewish population from Pompey's prisoners of war in 63 BC as mentioned by Philo. In various parts of Asia the remains of buildings with inscriptions suggesting synagogues are found from the time of Julius Caesar onwards. Sardis is particularly rich in them. In the Bosporus evidence stretches from the first century AD to Diocletian. It is possible that excavation will eventually yield evidence of synagogues from periods much earlier than that of the original synagogue at Dura-Europos (probably first century AD, see p. 30).

Josephus mentions synagogues in Syria–Palestine only at Antioch, Dora, Caesarea and Tiberias, so that the New Testament is the earliest witness to the widespread existence of synagogues in Palestine, especially in Galilee. This may be due to the setting of the gospel stories, and we should not necessarily conclude that they were more plentiful there than in the south. It has been suggested that they became necessary in Galilee after its conquest by Aristobulus I (104–103 BC). The many remains, some substantial, which are visible today, especially in Galilee, are the result of much later history. In the third to seventh centuries AD Galilee became the centre of Judaism, resulting from the flight of dispossessed and insecure Jews from their native Judaea after the failure of the Second Revolt (p. 125).

Some synagogues early enough to be known to Philo and Josephus were sufficiently imposing to be famous as buildings, but this was exceptional, since most were strictly functional and their use was such that no rivalry with the sacredness of the Temple arose in the minds of those who used them. Of these greater synagogues the main synagogue in Alexandria, as known to Philo and the Tosephta (p. 197), must be mentioned. These literary references indicate that it was a magnificent building, like the sixth-century Church of the Nativity at Bethlehem a five-aisle basilica with two double rows of columns, but it was used not only for religious purposes but also as a general meeting-place for Jews where administration and business could be conducted. The old synagogue in Antioch may seem an exception to the rule that synagogues in the ancient world were not sacral buildings. In *War* VII.3.3 (43–5) Josephus records the gift to this synagogue by Antiochus Epiphanes' successors of the bronze offerings looted by him from the Temple at Jerusalem, and further gifts of ornaments by later kings. In this connexion Josephus calls the building 'the temple' (*to hieron*), but the Greek word means 'the sacred place' and could presumably be used in a general way which the context explains. The more elaborate synagogues built after the destruction of the Temple acquired only gradually a sacral character, with the 'ark' or cupboard housing the Law Scrolls being assimilated mentally to the ark of the covenant. This was a natural development, but the Essenes, according to Philo and the Damascus Rule (CD 11:22), saw their synagogue as in conscious opposition to the Temple. This was perhaps not because a synagogue was intrinsically sacred, but because for them the Temple had become defiled.

7. Law, Prophets and Writings

The Pentateuch consists of Genesis, Exodus, Leviticus, Numbers and Deuteronomy. Their composite nature is here taken for granted, and no explanation is attempted of the processes by which these books were given their present form. It suffices to remark that the whole Pentateuch was formed largely by replacement of older bodies of law by new ones, but this replacement took place in practice and not in the actual literature, which was enlarged to incorporate new collections with the old rather than to discard the old. The Laws of Deuteronomy (D) may most readily be seen as offering an extension of earlier material such as is found in the so-called 'Book of the Covenant' in Exod. 20–3. An alternative or replacement for the D material is in some respects offered by the 'Priestly Code' (P) which is to be found in parts of Exodus, Leviticus and Numbers, and incorporates an independent collection usually termed 'The Holiness Code', Lev. 17–26. Only minor additions and alterations followed, and the text norm was fixed by 350–300 BC. This is evidenced by its recognition by the Chronicler and by the Samaritan version (for the latter does not deviate substantially from the Masoretic version, and the Samaritans separated from the Judaeans *c.* 300), and by the similar parallel between the Masoretic text and the Septuagint (p. 153).

These comprise Joshua, Judges, the books of Samuel, the books of Kings (each of these two latter items counting as one book), Isaiah, Jeremiah, Ezekiel, the Twelve Prophets (counting as one book though including Hosea, Joel, Amos, Obadiah, Jonah, Micah, Nahum, Habakkuk, Zephaniah, Haggai, Zechariah and Malachi). The historical books which open this list were thus allotted to the Prophets. We have already seen that the tradition thought of as the Oral Law was regarded as handed on after Moses by Joshua, the

Elders and the Prophets. It is but an extension of this idea which makes them tradents (handers-on) of events, i.e. God's dealings with the nation, and so into what we should call historians. Ben Sira (whom we can date to about 180 BC for his original composition in Hebrew) implies by his treatment of scripture that there was in his time agreement about which books in this 'Prophets' category, like those of the Pentateuch, 'defiled the hands'; that is, they were sacred and demanded a washing-off of their dangerous holiness. Put technically, the canon (list of sacred scriptures) was closed about 200 BC. This is confirmed by Daniel (written about 164) being still in the third part of the canon and not yet promoted to the Prophets, in which section of the Hebrew canon it was for a short time included, though in the Septuagint (see p. 153) both Daniel and Lamentations are among the Prophets.

WRITINGS

Ben Sira's grandson translated his grandfather's book into Greek in Egypt in 132 BC. In a preface from his own pen he refers to the Law, the Prophets and 'other traditional books' or, in another sentence, to 'the rest of the books' as an already existing category to which his grandfather aspired to add. These books were: the Psalms; Proverbs; Job; the five 'Megilloth' or 'scrolls', i.e. Song of Songs, Ruth, Lamentations, Ecclesiastes, Esther; then Daniel; Ezra; Nehemiah; and Chronicles. The Megilloth illustrate this category usefully in one respect: they are readings for major festivals (or a fast in the case of Lamentations) and so won their place in the canon *de facto* – they were used for a sacred purpose on a sacred occasion. The Song of Songs celebrates the Exodus, Ruth celebrates Weeks (and the giving of the Law), Lamentations celebrates the ninth of Ab (date of the destruction of the Temple), Ecclesiastes celebrates Tabernacles and Esther celebrates Purim. From Josephus *Against Apion* 1.8 (38–42) and from 2 Esdras 14:19–48 we see that the list is fixed (though not the order in the collection) by AD 100. Luke 24:44 refers to the tripartite division of scripture, the third being called the Psalms, the first book in the collection, much as collections of short stories are today often published under the title of the first in the collection.

Ezra–Nehemiah, Song of Songs, Ecclesiastes and Esther all fail to be mentioned in the New Testament. This may well be fortuitous, but accords with the fact that the Song of Songs, Ecclesiastes and

Esther at this time were, like Proverbs – and in some quarters at some periods, Ezekiel – still controversial in relation to the canon.

The manuscripts of the Septuagint do not directly reflect the tripartite division of the Hebrew canon, but divide into narrative, poetical and prophetic books. Of the Writings of the Hebrew canon, Ruth, Chronicles and Ezra–Nehemiah (2 Esdras) are in the narrative, while Ecclesiastes and Song of Songs are in the poetic section. Daniel and Lamentations are among the Prophets. Davidic and Solomonic authorship claims are probably responsible for the group after the histories being the poetic books of Psalms, Proverbs, Ecclesiastes and Song of Songs, to which Job is added. Then follow the Prophets, the Twelve leading and followed by Isaiah, Jeremiah now succeeded by Lamentations, Ezekiel and Daniel. Samuel, Kings, Chronicles and Ezra–Nehemiah are all divided into two books.

TEXT TRANSMISSION

In the first century AD, and almost certainly earlier, three forms of the Hebrew text of the sacred books were distinguishable, although not all the manuscripts (such as those of Qumran) fit into one of them. They may be characterized thus:

1 A preliminary stage of the later standard – Masoretic – text (see below)
2 A precursor of the Hebrew original of the Septuagint
3 An early stage of what became the Samaritan text

Masora means transmission, with the underlying suggestion of responsible and careful transmission, as when Akiba speaks of the *masora* being a 'fence for the Torah' (Ab. 3:14). The Masoretic text is that preserved with great care and detailed study of words, letters and syllables by the Jewish scholars of AD 500–1000 who were called Masoretes. They were the spiritual descendants of men such as Akiba, whose care for the text is evidenced as early as the Mishnah (Ab. 3:14; Pes. 9:2; Soṭ. 5:5). The desire, which Akiba fostered, to fix a standard text, is an aspect of the desire to fix a canon, the work of the Council at Jamnia *c*. AD 100.

TRADITIONAL JEWISH UNDERSTANDING OF THE CANON

To comprehend how the sacred and allied literature of the Jewish tradition has come down to us in the existing order and arrangement, it is necessary to know not only the facts outlined above but also the traditional Jewish beliefs about the canon, since these are by no means defunct and have strongly influenced the world of scholarship and left permanent marks upon knowledge and understanding of the writings themselves.

Josephus (*Against Apion* 1.8 (38–42)) argues that there were twenty-two canonical books; five were written by Moses and cover as well as the Law the tradition from the creation of mankind to the death of Moses. The period from his death to the time of Artaxerxes I (465–424) is covered by thirteen books written by the prophets after Moses. These are Joshua, Judges with Ruth, Samuel, Kings, Isaiah, Jeremiah with Lamentations, Ezekiel, the Twelve (as one book), Job, Daniel, Esther, Ezra–Nehemiah, Chronicles (thus Job is among the historical books, and the order may have as a rule placed Chron.–Ezra–Neh. after Kings; Dan. sometimes before and sometimes after Ezek.; the Twelve perhaps before Isaiah). The remaining four make a sort of David–Solomon canon: Psalms, Proverbs, Song of Songs, Ecclesiastes. Josephus adds that 'from Artaxerxes to our own time everything has been written down' – but not given the same credence, as there was 'no longer a reliable succession of prophets'. According to this view of the canon, writings known to exist but later than the fifth century BC are outside it.

This tradition appears in a variant form in the Babylonian Baraita to the Baba Batra 14b–15a (for Baraita see p. 197), according to which authorship is allotted as follows: Moses was the author of the Pentateuch and Job; Joshua of Joshua and Deut. 34:5–12; Samuel of Samuel, Judges and Ruth; David of the Psalms; Jeremiah of Jeremiah, Kings and Lamentations; Hezekiah and his associates of Isaiah, Proverbs, Song of Songs and Ecclesiastes; the Men of the Great Synagogue of Ezekiel, the Twelve, Daniel and Esther; Ezra of Ezra–Nehemiah and the genealogies in Chronicles. 2 Esdras 14:19–48 makes Ezra responsible for the recreation of the canon after the destruction of the Temple and the Exile. The number of the books there is twenty-four, Ruth and Lamentations being given separate status. This tradition has been handed on into modern times in a slightly new form, with the three divisions reimposed.

8. Greek Versions, Apocrypha and Pseudepigrapha

'Septuagint' is from the Latin for 'seventy'. It is not certain how it came to be attached to the Greek version of the Hebrew scriptures. In the Letter of Aristeas, which contains some historical among many legendary elements, the task of translation was entrusted to seventy-two, six from each tribe. If this was the original traditional number, it may have changed to seventy by association with the elders who accompanied Moses on Mount Sinai (Exod. 24:1, 9) and with the number of the sanhedrin (Sanh. 1:6). Luke 10:1, 17 with their variant readings illustrate the tradition of the delegates to the seventy other nations (Gentiles) wavering between seventy and seventy-two. The Letter of Aristeas is the main early document which asserts an origin for the LXX (to use its constant symbol), and the main points in its story may be summed up thus:

An official translation, of Alexandrian origin, was initiated by Jewish authority, and the Pentateuch (with which the Letter is concerned) was the first part of the Jewish scriptures to be translated. The event is associated with Ptolemy II Philadelphus (283–246 BC) and this is a fair indication of the date, even when the legendary character of the king's involvement is accepted. The translation was made, not for the edification of Gentiles, but for Jews to use in their synagogues in worship and instruction. The translation would show that this was in the mind of the scholars concerned and so take on something of the character of a Targum. It seems very probable that it was made by Jews in Alexandria, and not for them by a learned team from Jerusalem as the Letter narrates. Nevertheless, it may be accepted that relations between the Jews in Jerusalem and those in Alexandria were good.

It has been claimed that the Alexandrian LXX was an official translation provided to standardize the text, in view of the existence of a number of other translations (of some if not all the books) which were current in the Diaspora. The evidence does not admit of any comprehensive theory of this kind, since the early Greek manuscripts old enough to represent these 'other translations' are very fragmentary. The most significant fact about the LXX, once it was established, was its eager adoption by Christians, who were able to use to their own advantage nuances of translation and variant readings, of which the most famous is that which made Isa. 7:14 prophesy the birth of the Messiah from a virgin. Such interpretations were made in good faith, and the Hebrew scriptures in their Greek form were inherited by the Christian church as their own, since they believed themselves to be the true Israel. It was in reaction to the LXX therefore that alternative translations were made by scholars in the tradition of Jamnia. Though many may have worked at this task, we know certainly of only three, and there remain only traces of their productions. These are Aquila, Theodotion and Symmachus. (For the first two see pp. 193 and 191.) For a long time Aquila's translation was known only in incidental citations, but a hoard of ancient manuscripts from the lumber room of a building, formerly a synagogue, in Cairo has yielded palimpsests with fragments of Aquila's translation of Kings and the Psalms. (Such a room, attached to a synagogue and used to house documents too sacred to destroy but too worn to use any more in worship, was called a *genizah*; those just mentioned are published as documents from the Cairo Geniza.) It is also thought by some that Ecclesiastes and Song of Songs in the LXX are in the Aquila style and that these translations are in fact his.

Theodotion had been dated to the first century AD, but it has recently been claimed that the influence of his translation can be perceived in the New Testament. His translation of Daniel obtained particular regard in the early Church. This with other evidence suggests that he was earlier than Aquila and a pioneer of the literal school of translators, or that there was such a translator, name unknown but tentatively called Ur-Theodotion (*Ur-* is the German for 'original'), who makes a fourth to precede the trio Aquila, Theodotion and Symmachus.

Symmachus is placed by Epiphanius in the time of Severus (AD 193–211) and said to be a Samaritan who became a proselyte, while Eusebius calls him an Ebionite and author of some memoirs opposed to the gospel of Matthew which, with other 'interpretations' by him, came through one Juliana into the hands of Origen (*c.* 185–255). He does not receive any identification with any rabbinic translator. All three translators were preserved by Origen in his Hexapla. This was an arrangement in six columns of as many different versions of the Old Testament. The first column showed the Hebrew version in Hebrew letters, the second the same transliterated into Greek letters; the third was devoted to Aquila, the fourth Symmachus, the fifth the Septuagint (in a text regarded as authoritative for many years), the sixth Theodotion. Unfortunately the Hexapla survives only in fragments and quotations, but these have enabled some of the characteristics of the different columns to be known.

The Septuagint is important also because it has preserved a number of books rejected from the Hebrew canon, and preserved only in Greek and by the Christian church. This brings us to the Apocrypha.

A *genizah* was used for storing or hiding away. Some writings were also called *genuzim* ('hidden') for other reasons than hidden because worn out. For example, they might be thought to contain dangerous material, perhaps abstruse and easily misunderstood by the unlearned, or apparently contradicting the Law. They might be read by scholars but should be kept from the uninstructed. The Greek equivalent term for such writings was *apocrypha* ('hidden'). The scholarly attitude to them was not necessarily hostile; they might, like Daniel, be deliberately addressed only to the initiated (see Dan. 12:8f, and cp. 11:33; 12:3 for the 'wise', i.e. instructed; and 2 Esdras 14:46f). The term could therefore be applied to material in the Hebrew canon and was not always derogatory; its Hebrew equivalent was not used as a division in the Hebrew canon, which consisted as we have seen of the Law, the Prophets, and the Writings. Rejected books were not *genuzim* or apocryphal but *ḥiṣonim* ('outside').

Where Greek and Latin were current the term apocrypha underwent important changes in meaning. It might refer to books with messages for the initiated (such as Revelation in the New Testament) but was used also in an unfavourable sense, meaning books excluded from the canon, and then extended to spurious or heretical books. Jerome (*c.* AD 342–420) uses it for uncanonical books, naming Wisdom, Ecclesiasticus, Judith, Tobit, the Shepherd of Hermas, and 1 and 2 Maccabees.

The term Apocrypha, following a development of Jerome's usage, is now the title of a collection of documents, some separate books, some additions to books whose main text is in the Hebrew canon. From the point of view of the latter, they are all officially 'outside' books. They have been preserved in the manuscripts of the LXX, which contain the books of the Hebrew canon and vary as to other books outside that canon. A list of those printed in standard editions is given below.

N.B. Only very brief notes as to character and content will be given for books of the Apocrypha and the New Testament. For fuller information see the appropriate volumes of the Cambridge Bible Commentary series.

The Septuagint Apocrypha, or Books not in the Hebrew Canon Preserved in Manuscripts of the Septuagint

Esdras A (First Book of Esdras in English Apocrypha). An alternative recension of part of the story in Chron.–Ez.–Neh. (2 Chron. 35, 36; Ezra 1–10; Neh. 7:73b – 8:13), including a passage without parallel in the Hebrew, 3:1 – 5:6.

Esdras B. LXX version of Ez.–Neh. Not in English Bible.

Tobit. A folk-tale with religious teaching whose scene is laid in Mesopotamia and Media, written probably in Judaea between 250 and 200 BC.

Judith. Religious novelette about a Jewish resistance heroine who kills an Assyrian general, written probably in the first century BC, or perhaps in the second.

Additions to Esther. Six passages not in the Hebrew version of the canonical book, inserted into the LXX text soon after the latter's compilation in the middle of the third century BC.

Wisdom of Solomon. A commendation of Judaism in the hellenistic world of Alexandria, probably written there mid-second to early first century BC.

Ecclesiasticus or the Wisdom of Jesus Son of Sirach. Miscellaneous 'wisdom' and advice and condensed Jewish history. Hebrew original written *c.* 180 BC by Jesus Ben Sira. LXX version made by his grandson in Egypt *c.* 132 BC.

Baruch. A penitential psalm, a hymn of praise, and a song of encouragement, claiming to be written by Jeremiah's secretary Baruch in Babylon *c.* 583 BC, but probably completed after AD 70.

Letter of Jeremiah. Early recognized as pseudepigraphic, based on Jer. 29:1–23. Original written in Hebrew between 300 and 100 BC.

Additions to Daniel:

> *Prayer of Azariah* probably from the first century BC, interpolated after Dan. 3:23 in some Greek versions.
> *Song of Three Children* (the Benedicite). Inserted about the same time as the Prayer of Azariah, after it, but originally independent.
> *Susanna.* Folk-tale about innocence and detection at least as early as the second century BC, interpolated to enhance Daniel's reputation.
> *Daniel, Bel, and the Snake.* Tales originally of the early second century retold in favour of Daniel and Judaism.

Prayer of Manasseh. Inspired by 2 Chron. 33:11–13, of Jewish origin, but first appears in the Christian Didascalia of the second or third century AD.

1 Maccabees. Original dated between 100 and 70 BC. History of *c.* 176–135 BC, narrating heroic Maccabaean resistance to Seleucid rule.

2 Maccabees. Dated *c.* 100 BC, commends Hannukah and Nicanor's Day by telling story of Maccabaean resistance from 187 to 161 BC.

The above form the list of those books usually regarded as the true Apocrypha, but there are others which occur in some LXX manuscripts, and are generally relegated to the list of Pseudepigrapha. These are: 3 Maccabees, 4 Maccabees, Psalms of Solomon, Odes and Psalm 151.

Vulgate Apocrypha

The canon of the Latin Bible, formed by Jerome and called the Vulgate, included in its Apocrypha the following: Tobit, Judith, Additions to Esther, Wisdom of Solomon, Ecclesiasticus, Baruch, Letter of Jeremiah, Additions to Daniel, 1 Maccabees, 2 Maccabees.

It omits 3 and 4 Maccabees and Psalm 151 and does not officially include 1 and 2 Esdras or the Prayer of Manasseh but places these as an appendix after the New Testament.

English Bible Apocrypha

This list follows the Vulgate but restores 1 Esdras (the LXX Esdras A) to the main list, followed by 2 Esdras, which is the 4 Ezra of scholars and not in the LXX list. It includes also the Prayer of Manasseh in the main list. Of the books of the English Bible Apocrypha there therefore remains for brief comment:

2 Esdras (4 Ezra). Extant fully only in Latin. Chapters 1 and 2 are a Jewish Christian tract, 3–14 the Ezra Apocalypse, and 15–16 a Christian appendix.

PSEUDEPIGRAPHA

The term is used rather arbitrarily. If used strictly, it would denote 'writings falsely entitled', which is its literal translation. Since in the ancient world a title almost always included the author's name, the term Pseudepigrapha has been used to embrace writings falsely attributed to an author. In this strict sense it could be logically applied to some books in the Old Testament and Apocrypha, but it is not normally so used. Its use has been traditionally extended to cover writings connected with biblical books, personalities or themes, which failed to be included in any canon, even among the Apocrypha. Many of these books are associated, quite unhistorically, with famous names.

Greek- and Latin-speaking churches preserved some apocryphal books in those languages; so did oriental churches speaking other languages, e.g. Syriac, Coptic, Armenian, Ethiopic and Slavonic, usually in only one of these languages.

The Main Pseudepigrapha

This list includes:

1   Pseudepigrapha which occur in LXX manuscripts; they include therefore those accepted as part of the LXX Apocrypha in the revised edition of the LXX of Swete (1914) and the edition by Rahlfs (1935), but excluded by the Vulgate and the English Bible (3 and 4 Maccabees, Psalms of Solomon, Odes, Psalm 151);

2   Those printed by Kautzsch in his two volumes of 1900. Kautzsch's list is followed, with the addition of 2 Enoch, by Eissfeldt–Ackroyd (*The Old Testament*, 1965). This addition is made also by R. H. Charles in Volume II (Pseudepigrapha) of his two-volume *Apocrypha and Pseudepigrapha*, which he edited in 1913. We accept also Charles' addition of Ahikar. From Charles' list we omit Aboth as being part of rabbinic literature (p. 184) and Fragments of a Zadokite Work, which is now known to belong to Qumran, consistently with his assessment of it long before the discoveries there.

Letter of Aristeas (printed by Swete in an appendix to his edition of the LXX). The main story is of a journey of Aristeas and Andreas, officers of Ptolemy II (283–246 BC), to Jerusalem to fetch the Pentateuch and men able to translate it, so that it could be included in the royal Library at Alexandria. The Letter may be divided into: 1–12, dedication of the book to Philocrates and Demetrius' proposal of the translation enterprise to the king; 13–28, emancipation of Jewish captives; 29–50, Ptolemy's letter to the high priest Eleazar and the reply with names of translators; 51–82, description of the royal gifts to Eleazar; 83–120, description of Jerusalem; 120–7, Eleazar's farewell to the translators; 128–71, Eleazar's defence of the Jewish Law; 172–86, reception of the translators at Alexandria; 187–300, banquet at Alexandria; 301–22, translation and reception of Pentateuch. The story is a fabrication and cannot have been written before the end of the second century BC. The existence of a Greek Pentateuch is evident from 57–8, where specifications are given for the Bread of the Presence table donated by the king (Exod. 25:23–30). An account of a release of some Jewish prisoners (13–28) and the penultimate scene of table-talk at Ptolemy's banquet (187–300) are insertions into the original story.

Jerusalem is idealized (83–106), and throughout the story the author's intention to exalt Judaism is obvious; so also is his main object, to insist on the reliability of the Greek version of the Pentateuch current in his time and originating in Alexandria. In the table-talk scene (187–300) the superiority of Jewish wisdom, identified with the Torah, is repeatedly demonstrated.

Jubilees. Extant in full only in Ethiopic. The original, probably Hebrew, dates from the second century BC; fragments in Hebrew have been found among the scrolls from Qumran, with whose ideas Jubilees has much in common. Recognizable as a rewritten Genesis, it is presented as a revelation to Moses by the Angel of the Presence on the occasion of Moses' reception of the Law on Mount Sinai. It embraces all Genesis and part of Exodus, showing awareness of certain difficulties and smoothing some away, but emphasizing the validity of the Law. It introduces some interesting beliefs of the later period, such as the creation of angels among the creative acts on the first day; the history of the world arranged in a series of jubilees (49 years) or jubilees of jubilees; an apparently solar calendar of 364 days in the year, regarding the moon as misleading; and the attribution of the corruption of creation to the progeny of fallen angels and human mothers.

Martyrdom of Isaiah (and Ascension of Isaiah). The Ascension of Isaiah is almost universally accepted as composite and containing the Martyrdom of Isaiah (1:1–3:12; 5:1–14), the so-called Testament of Hezekiah (3:13–4:22) and the Vision of Isaiah (6:1–11:4). Only the Martyrdom is of Jewish origin, existing in fragments and only in Greek, Ethiopic and Latin, originally probably from the second century BC. The author of A Letter to Hebrews may have known it (Heb. 11:37), but perhaps derives his knowledge from the Lives of the Prophets. The story has affinities with traditions about Isaiah in the Talmud. It begins with a scene in which King Hezekiah gives orders to his son Manasseh in the presence of Isaiah, who prophesies his own death at the hands of Manasseh. After Hezekiah's death Manasseh leads Israel into apostasy and Isaiah retires into the wilderness. A false prophet Belkira moves Manasseh to seize him, and on doing so the king is prompted by Beliar to saw Isaiah into two with a wooden saw, the prophet continuing to speak until the end.

The Testament of Hezekiah is an allegorical history of the early Church in the form of a vision of Isaiah which provokes the anger and opposition of Beliar. The Vision of Isaiah is an account of Isaiah's rapt ascent through the heavens, in which he receives glory and joins in praise to the Father, Christ and the Holy Spirit, and has a vision of the descent to earth and ascent again to heaven of Jesus. Both these are of obvious Christian origin and only the Martyrdom may be regarded as having affinities with Jewish canonical and apocryphal writings. A complete recension of all eleven chapters of the Ascension has survived only in Ethiopic, but fragments of Greek and Latin versions are also known, as well as a separate Latin and a Slavonic version of chapters 6–11 (the Vision of Isaiah).

Psalms of Solomon. Included by Swete and Rahlfs in their editions of the LXX, thus by implication for them part of the Apocrypha. The Psalms are listed as a book in the catalogue at the beginning of the fifth century Codex Alexandrinus (A) after the books of the Old and New Testaments. PssSol is a collection of eighteen psalms dated to the middle of the first century BC, 2:30–5 apparently referring to the death of Pompey in Egypt (48 BC). It is generally agreed that they were originally written in Hebrew; they are extant now in Greek and Syriac. They emphasize Israel's covenant with God, the coming destruction of sinners, and the resurrection to eternal life of God-fearers. The 'Messiah of the Lord', active but not necessarily militant, is expected according to 17:23–51.

Odes (of Solomon). Of the forty-two OdesSol, five are extant in Coptic, one in Greek, and 40 in Syriac, which is probably the original language of them all. There is general agreement in dating them to AD 70–125. They show affinities with Qumran, Johannine literature and Ignatius of Antioch, and may be described as Jewish–Christian psalms on Christian themes, especially those connected with baptism.

3 Maccabees. A legendary account of an unsuccessful attempt on the part of the Egyptian king Ptolemy IV (221–205) to annihilate the Jews in Egypt, and of his divinely effected change of heart. Nothing to do with the Maccabees, but part of the literature of defence against hatred of the Jews in the early centuries of our period. It is widely agreed probably to have come from Alexandria, written in Greek in the first century BC or AD.

4 Maccabees. Most critics agree in dating the original Greek writing to AD 40–118, perhaps inspired by Jewish martyr deaths in the time of Caligula. It forms a diatribe, i.e. an ethical treatise or lecture, often denunciatory and repeating its main lesson, in the form of a speech. This example reiterates that reason can triumph over the passions, by recalling the martyrdoms of Eleazar, his seven sons and their mother as narrated briefly in 2 Macc. 7:1–42. The full story in 4 Macc. 5:1 – 17:6 crowns the philosophical introduction in 4 Macc. 1:13 – 3:18. Reflection on the value of these martyrdoms closes the book, which represents a remarkable use of Jewish traditions forcibly to argue a Greek, indeed Stoic, doctrine.

Odes (or Canticles). A collection of songs and prayers, other than the Psalms, which occur in the Bible and are used in the Church's liturgy. The collection differs in various manuscripts of the LXX. (Not to be confused with the *Odes of Solomon*.)

Sibylline Oracles. Sibylla was originally the name of a legendary prophetess in ancient Greek tradition, and became a generic term for a number of such women, some historical, many of whose utterances were preserved at their native places. In quite early times 'prophecies' were attributed to a supposed original sibyl in classical verse, both Greek and Latin; these were in reality 'prophecies after the event', elements in a kind of history writing which lent authority to the warnings which it uttered in apocalyptic fashion. The genre was taken over by Jewish authors, both in its own apocalyptic literature and in imitation of Greek collections of sibylline oracles. A daughter-in-law of Noah was cast in the role of sibyl (SibOr 3:823–7). Christians took over the genre from Jews and have been uncritical in embracing some sibylline oracles from Latin sources. In about the sixth century AD Jewish and Christian oracles were collected together; from the collection of fifteen books twelve survive, 1–8 and 11–14. Books 6–8 and 13 are Christian; 3, 4 and 5 are mostly Jewish. Book 3 contains elements from Roman and Egyptian history from the time of Ptolemy VII (170–164 and 145–116 BC) and from 43 and 30 BC; Book 4 reflects historical events of AD 68–79 with no indication of place of origin; Book 5 is concerned with Jerusalem soon after the destruction of AD 70, and also with Hadrian and the three emperors after him (i.e. AD 117–180) and seems to have been composed in Egypt.

1 Enoch (Ethiopic Enoch). Fully extant only in Ethiopic. According to views now widely held it falls into five sections: 1–36, Enoch's journeys into the underworld; 37–71, Similitudes or Parables; 72–82, Astronomical Treatise; 83–90, Visions of the Future; 91–105, Admonitions; 106–7, an appendix from the lost Book of Noah, known also from Jub 10:13; 21:10, to which also Charles ascribes 1 Enoch 6–11; 54:7 – 55:2; 60; 65:1 – 69:25. Apart from the Parables, 37–71, the material dates from the first half of the second century BC, some perhaps from the third century, and fragments in Hebrew and Aramaic have been found at Qumran. The Parables have been suspected to be later and their apparent absence from Qumran has encouraged speculation about the date of this section, even as late as AD 270. In this section occur the Son of Man sayings which, if sufficiently early, may be held to throw light on the meaning of the phrase in the gospels. Enoch's journeys owe something to the Greek underworld speculation and stories, like the eleventh book of Homer's *Odyssey*, associated with the Nekuia, or ceremony of calling up and questioning the dead. The astronomical treatise enjoins the solar calendar probably used at Qumran.

The mysterious nature of Enoch (Gen. 5:24; Ecclus. 44:16; 49:14) occasioned a cycle of literature about him, 2 Enoch being another example. 1 Enoch is referred to in the New Testament in 1 Peter 3:19; 2 Peter 2:4, 9f; Jude 6, 14f.

2 Enoch (Slavonic Enoch). Extant in Slavonic manuscripts from a probably Greek original of a date some time before the destruction of the Temple in AD 70; usually thought to have been written in Egypt. It exists in two recensions, one shorter and apparently incomplete. Enoch is taken up into heaven and has revealed to him secrets of the creation and order of the universe, with some religious and ethical instructions for Israel.

Assumption of Moses. The title is misleading and has been dropped by scholars in favour of the Testament of Moses. Moses on the approach of death delivers instructions to Joshua and prophesies the future, reviewing history until the time of Antiochus Epiphanes and the martyrdoms of Eleazar and his seven sons (2 and 4 Maccabees), who are his heroes rather than the Maccabees whom he does not mention. Joshua expresses sorrow and is being consoled by Moses when the text breaks off. As far as this point it is clearly a Testament of Moses. Parallels between the New Testament Jude (16, 19) and this extant Testament have given support to the testimony of some church fathers that Jude 9 refers to a passage in the following lost Assumption. If the text of TMos was leading to such a passage, the two books were being read consecutively, or more probably as one composite work. This would explain the title Assumption given to a book whose extant portion contains only the Testament of Moses. The existing form of it survives in a difficult Latin manuscript with the AsMos known only from a few quotations in Greek. TMos seems to have been written between AD 7 and 30, and its point of view, supported by some parallels with the Qumran literature, suggests Essene origin.

4 Ezra (Ezra Apocalypse). 2 Esdras of the Apocrypha (see CBC volume) divides naturally into three works obviously originally separate: chapters 1–2 (Christian), 3–14 (a Jewish apocalypse) and 15–16 (Christian). 4 Ezra is the usual label given to chapters 3–14, the Jewish Apocalypse, which is treated by itself as a Pseudepigraphon. It is written as though thirty years after the destruction of the Temple in 587 BC, but clearly with that of AD 70 in mind, in the form of revelations to Ezra by the angel Uriel. Internal references suggest, if not exactly thirty years afterwards, yet about AD 100. Acute and searching questions are raised about the eternal destruction of so many of God's people and the unfulfilled wait for restoration; hope is placed in a Messiah of supernatural origin, and in the meantime Ezra, warned of his own coming translation to heaven, restores the sacred books (p. 152) before this translation takes place and ends the story. Originally in Hebrew or Aramaic, the book is preserved in Latin, Syriac, Ethiopic, Arabic, Armenian, Sahidic and Georgian translations.

2 Baruch (Syriac Apocalypse of Baruch). Part of the Baruch cycle of which 1 Baruch is the book in the Apocrypha. 2Bar begins with a prophecy to Baruch, Jeremiah's secretary, of the coming destruction of Jerusalem. After the departure of Jeremiah to Babylon, Baruch remains among the ruins of the city and receives revelations of the coming age which will solve the problem of injustice in this world, but according to a determined order, the events of which will include the coming of the Messiah and the rebuilding of Zion, its further destruction and final restoration for ever. Further visions provide details in symbolic forms. Before the coming of the Messiah Baruch must instruct the people, and the book concludes with his exhortation and a letter of a similar kind to the exiles. The book faces the same problems as 4 Ezra but with less profundity, and may be partly dependent on it. It appears to have been written between AD 100 and 130, probably originally in Hebrew or Aramaic; it survives in a few Greek fragments, but entire in Syriac.

3 Baruch (Greek Apocalypse of Baruch). Extant in only two Greek manuscripts and two Slavonic versions. Of Jewish origin, incorporating some Greek ideas, worked over by a Christian, the book begins with Baruch's complaint to God at the fate of Jerusalem. He is promised a revelation of divine secrets, but when given, these do not refer to Jerusalem. Baruch is led on a journey revealing the structure of the universe, described in a poetic manner. It shows knowledge of 2Bar, so dates after AD 130.

4 Baruch or *Paralipomena of Jeremiah.* Paralipomena means 'things omitted', i.e. by previous narrators. Probably originally a Jewish story which has been worked over by a Jewish Christian, the original belongs to the first half of the second century AD. It is preserved in Greek, Ethiopic, Armenian and Slavonic and there is also a Rumanian translation. Jeremiah and Baruch lament over the fate of the Temple and the holy vessels are buried (cp. 2 Macc. 2:1–8); the Chaldaeans take Jerusalem and the people go into exile in Babylon. Abimelech sleeps for sixty-six years and awakes to a vision. Baruch receives an angelic answer to prayer and writes a letter to Jeremiah which is carried by an eagle and read by Jeremiah to the people. Jeremiah sends a reply by the eagle. The people return to Jerusalem and half of them are rejected. Jeremiah prays and finally is martyred. The story is related to other works in the Jeremiah cycle and perhaps to 4 Ezra.

Testaments of the Twelve Patriarchs. Each of the twelve sons of Jacob delivers an exhortation to his own sons about the conduct of their lives after his death. In form reminiscent of the Blessing of Jacob in Gen. 49 (cp. that of Moses in Deut. 33), these testaments are in content rather different, taking as text a famous (or infamous) action of the patriarch in question, but adding much haggadic material, and some which seems not to be based on

Genesis at all but to represent later Jewish traditions. Important doctrinal passages include the importance of the high-priesthood and the priesthood (Levi) and of the Davidic monarchy (Judah), high ethical teaching, the Two Ways, and the two inclinations in man. Some elements have led to theories of Christian authorship, whether of the whole or of elaborations from a Jewish core consisting of the Testaments of Naphtali and Levi, or of interpolations into a Jewish work already complete. Some theory falling within the last category is favoured by many scholars, who differ widely as to details.

The debate about the extent of Christian redaction or interpolation continues. The problems are inseparable from those of the manuscript tradition. There are apparently eleven Greek manuscripts (excluding those of extracts and fragments) and Armenian and Slavonic versions, of which the former, represented by some fifty manuscripts, is the most important. The T12P were originally written in Greek; they do not in themselves provide evidence for any Semitic original or originals, while the relation of recently discovered fragments to the T12P as we know them is hard to determine. The only Hebrew fragment is one claimed to be of TNaph, found at Qumran Cave 4. Aramaic fragments of a text about Levi have been found in the Cairo Geniza and in Qumran Caves 1 and 4, but they are not necessarily part of a Testament and their relation to TLevi is uncertain. Finally, there is an allusion in the Damascus Covenant (CD 6:10) to a writing of 'Levi, son of Jacob', so far unidentified.

Life of Adam and Eve (and Apocalypse of Moses). This is the oldest example of the literature inspired by consideration of the post-Fall lives of Adam and Eve; most of the later of these writings are Christian, but this early example probably had a Jewish origin and a text in Hebrew not now extant. Two recensions exist, the first in a Latin version of a Greek exemplar, the second a Greek version misnamed the Apocalypse of Moses. The two are parallel but occasionally one or the other alone supplies an incident. It is generally thought that the original dates from 20 BC to AD 70, since Herod's Temple is apparently presupposed.

Ahiqar. Since the folk-tale of Ahiqar is found in an Aramaic papyrus from Elephantine, it dates from before the period under examination to at least as early as the fifth century BC, but it is included because of its probable influence on some literature of these four centuries, e.g. Tobit 1:21f and 2 Peter 2:22. Acts 1:18 also reflects the manner of death of Ahiqar's ungrateful nephew. Further, there are parallels with sayings of Jesus, whether due to Christian interpolation or not. Ahiqar is the very wise and rich vizier of Sennacherib king of Assyria who, lacking a son, adopts his nephew Nadin who returns evil for good by lying and betraying Ahiqar. On his way to execution Ahiqar is saved by the executioner whose own life he had earlier saved. Restored to office Ahiqar executes vengeance on Nadin. The story contains narrative and much teaching including parables, and is known in Syriac, Arabic and Armenian as well as in the Aramaic which may be the original version.

Psalm 151. The Qumran Psalms Scroll (11QPs^a) includes in addition to forty-one canonical psalms four not normally included among the 'Psalms of David' (see p. 157). Some of these were already known in ancient translations and one, Ps. 151, appears in some LXX manuscripts. It was excluded from the Vulgate canon but was known in Latin and Syriac versions. The Hebrew version from Qumran is two poems, designated as 151A and 151B, and this apparent revelation of the original form would make the Greek version seem to have been a short amalgamation of the two. Sanders, editor of the 11QPs^a scroll, describes 151A as 'a poetic midrash on 1 Sam. 16:1–13'. David tells the story in the first person, including in 151B, which is very fragmentary, his encounter with Goliath from 1 Sam. 17:41ff. The LXX version may reflect this in the title of the psalm, which says it was written 'outside the number' specially for David when he fought Goliath, although the brief text does not mention that event.

This concludes the list of those Pseudepigrapha which have traditionally been published and studied in accounts of the religious literature of the period, but a large number of others are known and probably many are as yet unidentified in unstudied ancient manuscripts.

The order in the above list and in that which follows implies nothing with regard to importance or extent of influence on other literature. Although a limited number of Pseudepigrapha have in the past attracted the attention of scholars, and these have been listed above as the Main Pseudepigrapha, there is a strong tendency today to study the whole field anew without prejudice as to which writings have been most influential in the development of ideas and beliefs. This leaves editors free to list and arrange this various and wide-ranging literature by more objective standards. Thus the contemporary collection of *Jüdische Schriften aüs hellenistisch-römischer Zeit* (begun in 1973) distinguishes five sections: Historical and Legendary Narratives; Teaching in Narrative Form; Teaching in Didactic Form; Poetical Writings; Apocalypses. The collection being published by Doubleday uses another arrangement: Apocalyptic and related works; Testaments (often with apocalyptic sections); Expansions of material from the Old Testament and other legends; Wisdom and philosophical literature; Prayers; Psalms and Odes; Supplement. Again, different editors may assign any particular work to different categories. It remains to give here a short list of some which certainly have significance for study of the thought of the period.

Other Pseudepigrapha

A considerable literature has grown up round some famous names and some less famous from the Old Testament. Such are Abraham, Adam, Asenath, Baruch, Daniel, David, Eldad, Elijah, Enoch, Eve, Ezekiel, Ezra, Hezekiah, Isaac, Isaiah, Jacob, Jeremiah, Job, Jonadab, Joseph, Manasses, Modad, Moses, Noah, Rechab, Shadrach, Shem, Solomon and Zephaniah. But some are of slight importance, very often because surviving in residual form and perhaps incorporated in other writings.

The material is often referred to as haggadic midrash, that is, material in the form of a story expressing some teaching and filling out the original canonical story which it takes as its point of departure. The Qumran Genesis Apocryphon is a clear example, but is not technically pseudepigraphic since it does not borrow a name as authority.

Apocalypse of Abraham. Extant only in old Slavonic manuscripts but originally in a Semitic language. Written about AD 80–100, a haggadic midrash on Gen. 15:9–17, it has a Christian interpolation.

Testament of Abraham. 'Testaments' – deathbed speeches as in T12P, usually of prophecy - are often occasions for apocalyptic prophecy, but the apocalyptic (i.e. revelation) may contain cosmic and ethical matters also. This Testament is an account of the last days of Abraham to whom Michael the archangel and Death appear, in which Abraham is granted visions of judgement and finally, after refusing to die, is taken by Death and receives great honour at his burial. The story is told with much power and depth of feeling. Generally regarded as a Jewish composition of the first century AD, it reads at times like parts of the New Testament (especially apocalyptic and parabolic passages). Extant in several languages, it has been edited chiefly in two Greek recensions.

Apocalypse of Adam. Extant in Coptic, being one of the Nag Hammadi codices (p. 204), but currently regarded as originally one of the non-Christian writings of the first or second century AD.

Jannes and Jambres. Extant only in fragments in Greek and Latin, but from an original apparently of the first century AD at latest, since it is referred to by 2 Tim. 3:8. The two names are those given to the Egyptian opponents of Moses in the Jerusalem Targum on Exod. 1:15; 7:11; Num. 22:22. They are mentioned also in CD 5:17–19. We know of the existence of the apocryphal writing through the Elder Pliny, Apuleius and Origen. 'An apocryphal book which is called the Penitence of Jannes and Mambres' (a form of the second name met also elsewhere) is expressly rejected by the Decretum Gelasianum, a list of canonical and non-canonical books of the sixth century AD.

Testament of Job. A virtual retelling of the story of Job, the date being disputed, whether the first century BC or AD. The main version is in Greek but the original may have been Hebrew or Aramaic.

Joseph and Asenath. Preserved in several languages, the main textual tradition being Greek, it had an origin in Greek and a date in the first century AD according to the usual opinion. One of a number of apocryphal legends about Joseph now mostly lost, it is haggadic midrash on Gen. 41:45 and has a strong romantic and religious appeal. Asenath, at first repelled by the idea of marrying a Hebrew but strongly attracted to Joseph on meeting him, is refused by him as being an idolater. On breaking her idols and repenting she is told by an angel that she has been given to Joseph in marriage. She undergoes elaborate purifications and wedding ceremonies. Subsequently Asenath bears Manasses and Ephraim (cp. Gen. 41:50–2) and the couple visit Jacob. Pharaoh's son, desiring Asenath, plots Joseph's death, but fails and is himself killed.

Liber Antiquitatum Biblicarum (or Pseudo-Philo). The only important recension is in Latin based on a lost Greek version which may itself have been a translation from Hebrew or Aramaic. This version of Jewish history from Genesis to 2 Samuel (as far as the death of Saul inclusive) contains elements of early haggadic exegesis, and itself dates from at least as early as the first century AD; as such it is a valuable document for study of the development of this form of literature, which includes 1 and 2 Chronicles and the *Antiquities* of Josephus.

Pseudo-Phocylides. Verses extant in Greek and wrongly attributed to Phocylides, a poet of Miletus in the sixth century BC who wrote verse in a gnomic manner. It seems to be an example of Jewish missionary writing of the first century AD but may be early Christian. Influenced by Exodus, Deuteronomy and by 4 Maccabees and Jewish Wisdom literature, it contains a number of moral exhortations of a lofty character.

Lives of the Prophets. Preserved in various versions, the most important being Syriac, Armenian and Greek, this material was probably originally written in Hebrew; it was composed from various traditions, some oral, in the first century AD or earlier.

Treatise of Shem. Known in only one manuscript, Syriac of the fifteenth century AD. An astrological and calendrical treatise, it may be from Egypt in the Roman period, or possibly of much later origin.

Apocalypse of Zosimus. A composite work extant in various ancient languages whose Christian core may belong to the first century AD, and even owe its own Jewish core to the earlier half of that century. Zosimus is distinct from the Roman bishop, the Greek historian, and Zosimus of Panapolis, all of the same name.

9. The Qumran Writings

The Qumran literature consists of a number of manuscripts of books of biblical and para-biblical literature, some of which were already known and some hitherto unknown. Many of the manuscripts are very fragmentary; they are written for the most part in Hebrew, but there are some in Aramaic and a few small fragments in Greek (see list p. 183). They were found in caves at a desolate spot on the north-west shore of the Dead Sea known as Qumran, close to the ruins of a set of buildings. It is impossible to understand the Qumran literature except against the background of the appropriate period in the history of Israel. After the scrolls were first discovered this was difficult to determine, until de Vaux and Harding undertook a thorough archaeological investigation of the ruins in 1952–6, and at the neighbouring Ain Feshka in 1958. These investigations made clear that the period in question was the end of the Hasmonaean and the beginning of the Roman period (roughly 160 BC to AD 68).

De Vaux has given a lucid account of his findings in his Schweich Lectures for 1959, published in French in 1961; they were 'reissued with revisions in an English translation in 1973', the revisions leaving the main findings unaltered. They have well stood the test of examination by scholars, and the vast majority accept de Vaux's conclusions as correct and build upon them, a process to be followed here.

The following is a summary of the history of the site at Qumran stated in archaeological terms by de Vaux.

(i)	Israelite Remains:	
	Iron Age II	End of monarchy and downfall of Judah
(ii)	Period 1a	Small beginnings of occupation by covenanters, difficult to date. End determined by beginning of Period 1b
(iii)	Period 1b	Certainly includes reign of Alexander Jannaeus 103–76 BC, and may be as early as John Hyrcanus, 135–104. Period therefore begins probably c. 135; it ends 31 BC (earthquake and fire)

(Period of abandonment until about 1 BC or AD 1)

(iv)	Period II	Reoccupation about AD I and destruction AD 68
(v)	Period III	Roman military post occupies the ruins AD 68–73
(vi)	The Second Revolt	End of Period III when groups of insurgents were hunted down as at Muraba'at in 135

This leaves the date of the beginning of occupation by the covenanters as known only approximately, but the 'small beginnings' may have been as early as 150 BC; the effective end of the life of the community on this site was AD 68. Before summarizing the history as far as evidence allows, it is necessary to say something about the religious element in the situation. I Macc. 2:42 (see note in CBC *1 and 2 Maccabees*, p. 40) introduces fairly early into the story of Judas' patriotic struggle the people called Hasidaeans, which corresponds to the Hebrew *ḥasidim*. Their chief virtue was to show *ḥesed* (faithful or loyal love, such as is shown by those who adhere to a covenant) to the Law. This defined their position; it was to obey the Law as absolutely as possible when others were adopting hellenstic lives and practices. As the term is generally used they did not share the belief of those who afterwards came to be called Zealots, namely that their duty was to resist by arms the claims to authority of a foreign ruler, but they believed strongly that they should obey only God as ruler, and the legitimate earthly authority which had the divine sanction. They objected strongly therefore to high priests who were not true Aaronites and therefore not descended from Zadok (who had been given an Aaronite ancestry in the traditional genealogy, I Chron. 6:1–15) and who according to the Law had no right to be chosen for the high office; to be *high* priest it was not enough to be a Levite. The Hasmonaeans were Levite but not Aaronite. Thus according to I Macc. 7:12–16 the *ḥasidim* were willing to make peace with Demetrius I when an Aaronite high priest was presented to them. There can be little doubt that the *ḥasidim* were the spiritual ancestors of the Essenes as these are known from the writings of Philo and Josephus.

Philo (*c.* 15 BC to AD *c.* 45) in his *Quod omnis probus liber sit* (12–13) says of the Essenes that they live in villages and not in towns, pursue agriculture, possess very few goods, and carry on no warlike crafts or commercial activities. They do not keep slaves and they abhor slavery. They are interested in theology, not in philosophy or science. They follow their ancestral customs and receive instruction on them, especially on the seventh day. On this, the sabbath, they go to their synagogues and listen to the reading of the scriptures with an interpretation, in which they use allegory. They exhibit a variety of virtues which are summed up by love of God, love of virtue, and love of man; they avoid oaths, and show great friendship for one another. They have everything in common; each opens his house to the others; they have common meals; and share the produce of their toil alike. They care for their sick, and the younger members show great reverence to all the aged members. No ruler of Palestine, however cruel, was ever able to bring a charge against the Essenes.

Josephus gives a long account in *War* II.8.2ff (119–66), which is summarized in the following, based on G. A. Williamson's translation in the Penguin Classics:

Scorning wedlock, they choose other people's children while still pliable and teachable. They do not wish to do away with marriage which is necessary to continue the race, but they are afraid of the promiscuity of women and convinced that none of the sex remains faithful to one man. Novices admitted to the sect must surrender their property to the order, so that among them neither poverty nor excessive wealth is seen, but each man's possessions are pooled so that there is one property for them as though they were all brothers. They possess no one city but have large colonies everywhere. When they travel they carry no baggage, but only weapons to keep off bandits.

On their worship and daily routine Josephus says:

Before the sun rises they do not utter a word on secular affairs, but offer to (God) some traditional prayers as if beseeching him to appear. After this their supervisors send every man to the craft he understands best, and they work assiduously to an hour before noon, when they again meet in one place and donning linen loincloths wash all over with cold water. Thus purified they assemble in a building of their own which no one outside their community is allowed to enter ... they go into the refectory as if it was a holy temple and sit down in silence.

The meal which follows is preceded and ended by grace said by a priest. They return to work until the evening when they take supper in the same way. Shouting and disorder are never heard among them, each giving way to the other in conversation. Rules for entering are strict. There is probation for a year, during which the novice keeps the same rule as the members. If he has been satisfactory during the year 'he is associated more closely with the rule and permitted to share the purer waters of sanctification, though not yet admitted to the communal life'. The further period of testing now follows, and Josephus says it is another two years. When they are over, if the novice has stood the test, 'before touching the communal food' (i.e. entering on full membership) he swears solemn oaths 'to revere God and to deal justly with men'. Within the latter principle is included obedience to rulers, since all power is conferred by God. Men convicted of major offences are expelled, and Josephus concludes by saying that this often means death, since the expelled man is prevented by his oaths from eating outsiders' food, and he avers that charity has often compelled the members to readmit an offender who was at his last gasp.

Their observance of the sabbath is strict, and their laws of ceremonial cleanness are obeyed with meticulous care. It is these rather than hygiene in the modern sense which govern their sanitation rules, which curiously enjoin the individual use of a trenching-tool (it is among the few simple objects with which a novice is issued). This implies the absence of a common latrine, and thereby perhaps a relatively small community, though they would probably have in any case regarded a latrine as bringing defilement on the camp. The Essenes were divided into four grades and 'uncleanness' resulted from contact with one of a lower grade. To this strict Jewish principle the Essenes, according to Josephus, added a hellenistic belief of considerable importance, that 'bodies are corruptible and the material composing them impermanent, whereas souls remain immortal for ever'. This very un-Jewish belief was already present in the Judaism of the Wisdom of Solomon, but is unexpected in such a strictly orthodox brotherhood. Perhaps the explanation for Josephus' claim that it was part of Essene teaching lies in his intended audience; for he compares it to that of the Greeks quite expressly, saying that the Essenes too looked for a pleasant home after death for the righteous, situated beyond the Ocean, while the wicked are to be confined to a stormy abyss with unceasing punishments.

Equally important for understanding the character of the Essenes is their claim to foretell the future through a prolonged training in scripture, various purifications, and the utterances of the prophets. Josephus says 'rarely if ever' do they prove wrong. He closes this account with a short statement about 'another order of Essenes' who include marriage in their way of life, strictly regulating its conduct for their members on the basis that it is not for pleasure but for the production of children.

Pliny the Elder adds an interesting piece of evidence in view of the site which he seems to allot to the Essenes as a whole. He wrote in his *Natural History* a sort of gazetteer of the places which he visited; he was in Judaea about AD 75, and perished in the eruption of Vesuvius in 79. When describing the Dead Sea region he writes:

On the west side the Essenes avoid the baneful shoreline. They are a race by themselves ... they have no women, they abjure sexual love, they have no money, and they live among palm-trees. Still their membership is steadily recruited from the large number of people who resort to their mode of existence because they are wearied of life's struggle with the waves of adversity. In this way the race has lasted ... for thousands of ages, though no one is born in it; so fruitful for them is the dissatisfaction with life which others feel. Below them lay the town of En-gedi, once second only to Jerusalem in fertility and palm-groves, now simply a second sepulchre. Then comes the rock-fort of Masada, which is not far from the Dead Sea. (*Nat. Hist.* v.17.4 (Loeb edn v.15.73).)

Pliny evidently thought this was the only place where Essenes lived, and knew nothing of an order which tolerated marriage, to which the people of Qumran seem to have belonged. But his indication of the site is of the utmost importance, hardly weakened by the fact that it is likely that he was only told about it; for he writes as though they were still there, even though conscious of the terrible destruction wrought by the war of 66–70.

The next step is to see if any features in Qumran writings tally with the information in Philo, Josephus and Pliny. The main scrolls which we should use for this purpose are the Damascus Rule, the Commentary on Habakkuk and the Commentary on Nahum.

Historical information in the usual sense of straightforward narrative is almost non-existent in the extant Qumran documents, being confined to the short opening passage of the Damascus Rule. Even this is hardly historical writing as we understand it!

Hear now ... and consider the works of God; for he has a dispute with all flesh and will condemn all those who despise him. For when they were unfaithful and forsook him, he hid his face from Israel and his

Sanctuary and delivered them up to the sword. But remembering the Covenant of the forefathers, he left a remnant to Israel and did not deliver it up to be destroyed. And in the age of wrath, three hundred and ninety years after he had given them into the hand of king Nebuchadnezzar (Nebuchadrezzar) of Babylon, he visited them, and caused a root of planting to spring from Israel and Aaron to inherit his Land and to prosper on the good things of his earth. And they perceived their iniquity and recognized that they were guilty men, yet for twenty years they were like blind men groping for the way. And God observed their deeds, that they sought him with a whole heart, and he raised for them a Teacher of Righteousness to guide them in the way of his heart. (CD 1:1–7, Vermes' transl.)

The passage goes on to speak of the 'Scoffer' and 'those who sought smooth things'. This illustrates well the difficulties faced by modern interpreters when they see their material apparently promising identification with already known facts or persons but then lapsing into the use of hints and nicknames.

The 390 years is taken from Ezek. 4:5 (390 days; NEB follows LXX and has 190). Jewish chronology of the period cannot be correlated with that of modern scholars, but the date suggested by 390 years from the Exile, *c.* 197 BC, points sufficiently closely to some time in the second century BC, which seems on historical and archaeological grounds to be the nearest we can discover for the beginnings of the *hasidim*. It coincides with the supersession of Egyptian overlordship by the Seleucids in Syria, and may be taken as consistent with a period when hellenization received a new impetus and provoked their pious reaction. According to the Damascus Rule another twenty years were needed before the appearance of the Teacher of Righteousness who is often mentioned in the literature as the leader of the community *par excellence*. The Damascus Rule is so called because of its reference to the New Covenant made 'in the land of Damascus'. There is much debate as to whether this is a true geographical or a metaphorical term; in either case it refers to a step taken away from the headquarters of the main population of Judaea, whether outside the borders of the country or not. If it may be taken as referring to a desert place, it may denote Qumran; certainly the Rule of Qumran is evidence for a going into the desert, in obedience to Isa. 40:3, of a number of dedicated people, to rebuild Israel.

The general situation is then intelligible enough. There was a vigorous reaction to foreign domination and to hellenization; some rebelled with arms, others trusted in their observance of the Law to ensure divine intervention at God's own time. These last would include many who did not withdraw from public affairs, meeting the times with adjustment and compromise. Their more intransigent fellow-countrymen might well call them 'seekers after smooth things', and they would inevitably show gradations of loyalty and disloyalty to the Law. Others who were obedient to the Law would be those already described (p. 172), both the men willing to fight for freedom in both national and religious fields, and those who would not at any rate use force as their usual weapon and whose faith was placed in their extreme obedience to the Law. Among these were various types of Essenes, and among them it is natural to place the men of Qumran.

THE WICKED PRIEST AND THE TEACHER OF RIGHTEOUSNESS

Is it possible to go further along the path of historical identification, in spite of the inexact, allegorical and allusive nature of the references in the documents? There is one direct identification in the surviving documents: it occurs in the Commentary on Nahum where 'Demetrius the king of Greece' is claimed to be the *pesher* (the divinely ordained secret meaning) of a Nahum prophecy. The statement and the following passage are recognizable as referring to the events in 88 BC when Demetrius III tried to overthrow Alexander Jannaeus, who is 'the furious young lion who executes revenge on those who seek smooth things and hangs men alive, a thing never done formerly in Israel'. It looks therefore as if sometimes 'those who seek smooth things' are in the eyes of the writer the Pharisees; but we must remember that neither the term, nor the body of people which it represents, was so well-defined as it is for us. It is also legitimate to remark that, on the occasion of the atrocity committed by Alexander, the phrase could be used as a description only by those who were implacably opposed to them, and who ignored the manner of their deaths and dangerous activity which had led to it. Indeed it is probable that the phrase arose out of disagreement in interpretation of the Law, rather than out of actual situations in political life. The author of the Commentary on Habakkuk explains many passages in the first two chapters of the Old Testament book of Habakkuk by saying that they refer to one whom he calls without explanation the Wicked Priest. Alexander Jannaeus was officially high priest and acted with great cruelty and disregard for the sacredness of this office, and we have seen that in the Commentary on Nahum he is described as 'the furious young lion'. It is therefore tempting to identify him with the Wicked Priest, and this is done by some scholars, who thus date the events concerned with the Wicked Priest to the reign of Alexander, 103–76 BC.

There is however a difficulty in the identification; the Wicked Priest is characterized largely by his opposition to the Teacher of Righteousness, with whom therefore he was contemporary, so that the chronology must suit both. Can we then date the Teacher of Righteousness? The passage already quoted from the Damascus Rule suggests the time round about 170 BC, but this is certainly not exact. There is archaeological evidence of an expansion and flourishing of the community in Period 1b, which may be due to the influence of the Teacher of Righteousness. This would mean that the Teacher began his decisive activity about 150 BC, and the events which concern him and the Wicked Priest would belong to roughly the same period, half a century earlier than the reign of Alexander Jannaeus.

If the Wicked Priest was active as a persecutor from about 150 onwards, can we find a high priest of this period who deserves such a title? Many of the facts about him are provided by the Commentary on Habakkuk; taking these into account, we have to look for someone who was high priest between 200 and 90 BC, accepted as the highest political representative of Israel in his time, but regarded as so unworthy as to be an illegitimate holder of his office. It is stated of him that he died outside Jewish territory, and by a violent death. But it was not during his term of office that the Temple treasure was plundered, for the Commentary places this event among the days of the 'last priests of Jerusalem'. The list of high priests is given on p. 227, and the dates within which we have to search extend from Joshua (Jason), 175, to John Hyrcanus (d. 104). The only one who fits all the data given is Jonathan (152–142). According to this theory the Teacher comes into the list just where we have the gap of the so-called Intersacerdotium. This is the seven-year period during which Josephus says the city was without a high priest after the death of Alcimus (*Ant.* xx.10.3 (237)). These are the years 159–152. Many have expressed doubt as to the possibility of Josephus being right about Jerusalem having no high priest for this time. Alexander Balas won over Jonathan by giving him the high-priesthood (1 Macc. 10:18–20), and this means that the existing high priest was expelled, not that the post was vacant. The name of the deposed high priest remains unknown; according to this interpretation of the data from the scrolls and from the few historical references, he was the famous Teacher of Righteousness who adopted the Qumran community and gave so decided an impulse to its development. We may compare his position as a deposed high priest with that of the earlier Onias III (d. 171, p. 87), or of his son Onias IV and his establishment of a temple at Leontopolis *c.* 160 BC (p. 136). But for the Teacher of Righteousness the Temple was to be the community, and he joined it as a leader on being deposed in 152 BC. Jonathan, the usurper in 152, is the Wicked Priest.

There can be no certainty about the right interpretation of the evidence. To sum up briefly, we have to attempt to relate the scrolls references to known history largely through the Wicked Priest and the Teacher of Righteousness, neither of whom is explicitly identified by name in the scrolls. If we make the Wicked Priest our starting-point, the current view is that he was probably either Jonathan, Simon or John Hyrcanus (the 'Maccabaean' theory), though some think he was Alexander Jannaeus. If we make the Teacher of Righteousness our starting-point, we find that characters in history with whom we might identify him are not recorded in any known literature as having carried out the work with which he is so warmly credited in the Qumran scrolls. It is therefore hazardous to seek to advance beyond the identification of the Teacher with the unnamed high priest of the Intersacerdotium. This identification is after all with an unknown person. Some have tried to take further steps; they see in a number of rather obscure references the reflection of the history of an original community of 'pious ones', and especially of that of a split of this community into two distinct communities, that of Qumran and that of the movement which we call the Pharisees.

This is too speculative, but some individual identifications are virtually certain, whether we try to weave them into a historical pattern or not. We have seen that Demetrius III Eucaerus (95–88) is mentioned without disguise, and the Lion of Wrath (or Furious Young Lion) is safely identified with Alexander Jannaeus. The *kittim* are always enemies, almost always foreign and usually

Roman. 'Seekers after smooth things' are perhaps not the exact equivalent of Pharisees, but the strict Essenes, including those at Qumran, may have included them among those too weak in loyalty to the Law, and regarded them as typical of such renegades.

THE MAIN QUMRAN DOCUMENTS

These are arranged here according to character and content; in each case the conventional abbreviation indicates first the number of the cave at Qumran in which the document was found. 'Q' is for Qumran (so that, e.g., 1Q means 'from Qumran Cave 1') and is followed by a letter or syllable whose significance is given on its first occurrence, unless already obvious.

Texts of the Hebrew Bible

Every book of the Hebrew Bible is represented among the finds, except Esther. Many occur only in fragments, but many in a number of fragments some of which are extremely small.

Those which are specially important are listed below.

The Isaiah Scrolls. The larger was at first known as *The St Mark's Isaiah Manuscript* (now 1QIsa^a) which is of the entire book although it lacks a few words at the foot of some columns. The other was called *The Hebrew University Manuscript* (1QIsa^b) and is of various passages beginning with Isa. 7:22–8:1 and ending with 66:1–24. The earlier part of the book is represented by fragments which with the more continuous latter part are regarded as one manuscript.

Bible Commentaries. Qumran has provided examples of a kind of writing not known before. These are commentaries which cite short passages consecutively from a book of the Prophets or Psalms and place after each section of text a commentary which begins: 'Its *pesher* is ...'. *Pesher* is 'meaning' or 'interpretation', with the nuance of true or real interpretation. The *pesher* thus offered links the passage receiving comment with some milestone or crisis in the history of the sect, and disregards the original meaning entirely. Such commentary or *pesharim* scrolls consist mostly of small fragments, but the Habakkuk Commentary from

Cave 1 is almost intact and contains the text of Hab. 1–2 (there is nothing to suggest that Hab. 3 was ever included), alternating with commentary. In 1QpHab, 'p' stands for *pesher*.

Other surviving texts of this character include some substantial fragments, viz. 4QpIsa^a, 4QpIsa^c, 4QpNah, 4QpPs^a (this last being some verses with *pesher* of Ps. 37).

Apocryphal or Para-Biblical Texts (in Hebrew unless otherwise stated)

The Rule of Qumran 1QS ('S' is for *serek*, 'order') or *Manual of Discipline*. Finds in Caves 4 and 5 show that at least thirteen other manuscripts existed at Qumran. It was certainly a foundation document, containing doctrine, rules and liturgy for admission and for life as a member, and religious and liturgical instruction. The MS has two appendices: The Rule of the Congregation (1QSa) which prescribes procedure for the reconstituted Israel at the end of the age, and Collection of Blessings (1QSb).

The Damascus Covenant or *Damascus Rule* (CD). Known fully only from the Cairo Geniza rather than from Qumran, where fragments of it have been found in Caves 4, 5 and 6, and where it undoubtedly belongs. It has much the same character as the Rule but opens with a cryptic historical passage (pp. 175 f.).

The Genesis Apocryphon 1QapGen. In a poor state of preservation and lacking both beginning and ending, only columns II, and XIX–XXII are so far published. In Aramaic, these retell and add to the story of Noah the vinedresser (rather than the Ark captain) and of Abraham as far as the divine promise in Gen. 15:4. It opens with a story whose remnants suggest that it is about the character of Noah at his birth, and is like 1 Enoch 106:1–2, itself thought to come from the now lost Book of Noah. The scroll is here very fragmentary, but the teller of the story is clearly Lamech, whose name was attached to the whole scroll at first by a number of scholars. Short haggadic insertions occur in the story of Abraham, e.g. his route when obeying the injunction to 'walk through the land' in Gen. 13:17. There is also an uninhibited description of the beauty of Sarah.

The War Scroll or *The Scroll of the War of the Sons of Light with the Sons of Darkness* 1QM ('M' is for *milḥamah*, 'war'). A probably composite document comprising distinct sets of documents with instructions about the conduct of the last and decisive war on earth. Some are military and some liturgical, and the final war is given almost the character of a ceremony, appropriate to the cosmic dimension which it is given as the final battle between good and evil and the final triumph of good.

The Thanksgiving Psalms (Hodayoth) 1QH ('H' is for *hodayoth*, 'thanksgivings'). A collection of religious songs reminiscent of the biblical psalms, showing deep religious and poetic feeling towards God and towards the community. Apparently written by a leader of the community, some or all perhaps by the Teacher of Righteousness himself, the collection contains some searching autobiographical passages.

Texts of Apocrypha or Pseudepigrapha Already Known

Fragments of 1 Enoch, Jubilees, Noah; and in Aramaic of Levi (possibly the Testament – see p. 166; for the Book of Noah, see under 1 Enoch, p. 163).

Some fragments from Caves 1, 4 and 6 of the Book of Giants, preserved with fragments from 1 Enoch 6–36 (1, 4 or 6QEnGiants), a book destined to have a great influence on Mani and Manichaeism in the late fourth century.

Further New Material

The very numerous fragments, not all yet reliably interpreted, show an originally extremely full and widespread library, the greater part of which has perished. Many fragments represent other copies or recensions of the Rule, the Damascus Rule, the Genesis Apocryphon, the War Scroll, the Thanksgiving Psalms, and much material unknown hitherto, in the form of liturgy, blessings, prophecies, calendrical instructions, etc.

Other material new to scholarship was yielded by Cave 11 from 1956 onwards. The Psalms Scroll (11QPs^a) has already been mentioned. Besides some of the canonical psalms and some already known apocryphal psalms (p. 167), it contained compositions now called a Plea for Deliverance, an Apostrophe to Zion, a Hymn to the Creator, and a piece of prose about David's Compositions.

Also from Cave 11 are a fragment of a treatise on Melchizedek

(11QMelch) which has been claimed to be important for the understanding of the New Testament Letter to Hebrews, and the Aramaic Targum of Job (11QtgJob). Most extensive is the Temple Scroll (11QTemple). Making full use of the Pentateuch, the author puts together the laws and regulations for the construction and administration of the Temple, the status and duties of the king, feasts with their sacrifices, and laws of purity. More than half is devoted to the Temple, describing an ideal building, differing in some respects from any actual model.

The Copper Scroll (3QTreasure). A roll of copper sheet – the copper now completely oxidized – originally formed from three strips making one long strip, on which has been inscribed a list of about sixty treasures (gold, silver and perfumes) hidden in carefully described places, valuable less for any possible discovery of treasure than for ancient topography. Dated between AD 70 and 132 by Milik who believes the list to be a fantasy.

Finally, mention should be made of phylacteries found in several caves. These are remarkable as including the only specimens from antiquity which have survived in their original leather holders, with the threads used for closing and donning them. They are also striking in that they often contain texts additional to the standard texts used in phylacteries.

Greek Manuscripts

In the Nahal Hever cave in the Dead Sea area were found extensive fragments of the Minor Prophets in Greek. In Qumran a few fragments in Greek were found; they are listed as follows:

4QLXXLev[a]	Fragments of Lev. 26:2–16
4QLXXLev[b]	Fragments of Lev. 2–5
4QLXXNum	Fragments of Num. 3:40–2; 4:6–9, 11–12

10. Early Rabbinic Judaism

Josephus presents the Pharisees as a school of thought among the Jews; this rendered them intelligible to his hellenistic readers at the cost of some distortion. But it is hard to know 'how to describe them, for their activities before AD 70, as met in the pages of Josephus, suggest a party in the political sense, though distinguished by their religious enthusiasm. Yet apparently in the gospels and in much of the Mishnah they are a quietist sect, in whom it is difficult to imagine anything like political activity. Nevertheless many Pharisees clearly played as active a part in politics as the subject position of Judaea allowed. The Mishnah is a law-book with no occasion to report such activity, but some rabbis who appear in its pages are known from Talmud and midrash to have been involved in politics through their profound religious convictions. Such were Akiba (p. 194), Meir and Simeon b. Yochai (c. 140–65). It must also be acknowledged that desire to defend Jesus as the founder of Christianity against ill-informed Roman prejudice has strongly influenced the attitude of the gospels. They appear to be occupied only with religious matters, but cannot altogether conceal strong political undercurrents in such passages as that concerning the tribute money (Mark 12:13–17, etc.) and the accounts of the arrest and execution of Jesus.

Josephus makes it clear that the Pharisees were very influential with the majority of the people, who admired their strict loyalty to the Law, while the Sadducees were followed by the rich. The earliest story about them in Josephus occurs in *Ant.* XIII.10.5 (288–92): when some Pharisees were present at a feast at the table of John Hyrcanus (135–104 BC), one of them, by name Eleazar, rebuked John for taking the high-priesthood, on the ground that his mother had been a captive at the time of Antiochus Epiphanes (so that he was not of pure descent). Josephus goes on to say that the story was false, that it enraged John, and aroused the anger of the other Pharisees, adding unexpectedly that John was one of their disciples. The story is surely based on hostility to John Hyrcanus and is retold in bQid. 66a, where the king is Alexander Jannaeus (103-76); but this is well accounted for by the later custom to call all kings of the period Jannaeus and enemies of the Pharisees, a natural result of Jannaeus' actions towards them. (See p. 92.)

In *War* I.5.2 (110–12) the Pharisees are a body of people 'with the reputation of excelling the rest of their nation in the observances of religion and as exact exponents of the laws'. Salome Alexandra (76–67) listened to them and they took advantage of her favour to become the real administrators of the state: 'she ruled the rest, the Pharisees ruled her'. They therefore put to death a man who had advised the king to crucify eight hundred victims, and 'proceeded to kill whomsoever they would'. The picture is quite different when Josephus is writing about the Pharisees' religious beliefs. His fullest statement is in *Ant.* XVIII.1.3 (12–15): They simplify their living, making no concessions to luxury. They follow the guidance of that which their doctrine has selected and transmitted as good, attaching chief importance to the observance of those commandments which it has seen fit to dictate to them. They show respect and deference to their elders … Though they consider that everything is brought about by fate, still they do not deprive the human will of the pursuit of what is in man's power, since it was God's good pleasure that there should be a fusion and that the will of man with his virtue and vice should be admitted to the council-chamber of fate. They believe that souls have the power to survive death and that there are rewards and punishments under the earth for those who have led lives of virtue or vice; eternal imprisonment is the lot of evil souls, while the good souls receive an easy passage to a new life. Because of their views the Pharisees are influential among the townsfolk and all the prayers and sacred rites of divine worship are performed according to their exposition.

In *Ant.* XIII.10.6 (297–8), after the account of the Pharisees under Salome Alexandra, another passage mentions as important 'certain legal practices which the Pharisees have handed on to the people by succession from their forefathers, which were not written in the laws of Moses'. These 'regulations' are in Hebrew terms the *halakoth* or laws derived from the Mosaic Law. Considered as a collection they form the Oral Law, which demands some explanation.

THE ORAL LAW

At the Restoration, traditions of belief and practice were reintroduced; laws and customs of the land were taught to returned exiles, and the latter taught theirs to the people of the land. (The books of Ezra and Nehemiah give the impression that the returned exiles did all the teaching.) Versions of history, the story of God's dealings with the nation through the patriarchs, Moses and later leaders, began to be edited and combined, and above all both the ancient and more recent recensions of the Torah, as believed to have been given to Moses, were amalgamated and consolidated. In addition there were a number of traditions created by the answers of priests and scholars of the Law to questions concerning the right application and interpretation of the Mosaic Law. This diffuse and miscellaneous tradition was preserved alongside the Mosaic Law; how it was preserved is debated, but the Academy set up by Johanan b. Zakkai in Jamnia seems to have set great store by the belief that it was preserved exclusively orally. It was – and is – known as the Oral Law. Every 'school' or 'sect' within Judaism treasured its own part or version of this mass of tradition. In the gospels Jesus is represented as criticizing the traditions of the Pharisees as the 'traditions and teachings of man', i.e. without Mosaic, and therefore without divine, authority (cp. Mark 7:8f).

The gospels suggest that the concerns of the Pharisees were ritual purity, agricultural taboos, sabbath and festival observance and the like. These are certainly subjects met in the Mishnah, but it is concerned also (as in the Order of Nezikin) with social justice, business ethics, administration of public affairs, and the rights and duties of government. Laws of charity as well as agricultural taboos are enjoined in the Order of Zeraʿim, whose opening tractate Berakot deals not only with liturgical matters but also with spiritual questions touching the relation of man and God. The passage in Matt. 23:1–36, much of whose material is peculiar to that gospel, would seem to reflect a later stage in the history of the Church and in any case the reproach that the scholars and Pharisees 'have overlooked the weightier demands of the Law, justice, mercy and good faith' cannot be true of all Pharisees contemporary with Jesus, even in the eyes of the evangelists. See for example Mark 12:28–34 and the instructive difference in the later versions of Luke 10:25–8 and Matt. 22:34–40, both of which impute to the scribe a hostility absent from Mark. Without entering further into this complicated subject, we may say that it is probable that the criticisms voiced by the historical Jesus were not addressed to Pharisaism as a whole but to some of the Pharisees who opposed him. Not all held belief in an imminent Messiah, but they were united on many subjects, not all of which are mentioned in the gospels. Much in Josephus' account contrasts with both gospel and mishnaic evidence, such as their alleged belief in fate. Their high influence in public affairs was more limited by the occupying power than Josephus sometimes implies, though he was well aware of these limitations.

Such an account of the matter assumes acceptance in general of some critical view of how writings of very different origins and dates received their present form. Traditional Jewish belief is very different: the Torah given to Moses on Mount Sinai was twofold, the Written and the Oral, and God taught both to Moses. In the Mishnah and Talmud (p. 195) 'the Law' usually means the Oral Law, of divine origin like the Written Law and derived from it. But the 'traditional' belief that all the Oral Law was given to Moses was not held by scholarly rabbis, who of course knew the post-Mosaic origin of Purim and Hanukkah, as of even later rulings and practices which the Mishnah attributes to various decision-makers.

THE CHAIN OF TRADITION

'Tradition' means 'handing on' or 'what has been handed on'. The Law has been the subject of handing on or tradition; and there is a tradition about this tradition, set down at the beginning of the Mishnah tractate Abot ('Fathers', sometimes called Pirqe Abot, or 'Sayings of the Fathers'). This passage says of the Oral Law, 'Moses received the Law from Sinai and committed it to Joshua, and Joshua to the Elders, and the Elders to the Prophets; and the Prophets committed it to the men of the Great Synagogue' (Ab. 1:1). These last were the Elders thought of as having accompanied Ezra on the return from Exile.

This is a condensed and formalized view of history; it makes us cautious in our attitude to its continuation (Ab. 1:2–18) which gives the names of the human links in the subsequent handing on of the Oral Law. The links are joined by saying in each case that the last named received (it) from the previous named or 'from them' (for the list ends with a series of pairs). Each individual is credited with a saying specially his. This tradition can therefore be summarized in a list of names, with comments giving the very little known of each one:

Simeon the Just	Either Simeon I, high priest *c.* 280 BC under Ptolemy II Philadelphus (*Ant.* XII.2.5 (43)), or Simeon II *c.* 200 BC (Ecclus. 50)
Antigonus of Soko	(elsewhere only in Abot deRabbi Nathan)

The pairs follow:

Jose b. Joezer	*c.* 160 BC
Jose b. Johanan	(never mentioned apart from his partner)
Joshua b. Perahyah	
Nittai the Arbelite	*c.* 120 BC
Judah b. Tabbai	
Simeon b. Shetah	*c.* 80 BC, successful leader of Pharisees in reigns of Alexander Jannaeus and Salome Alexandra
Shemaiah	probably the Samaias who intervened against Herod
Abtalion	*c.* 47 BC according to *Ant. xiv*.9.4 (172–6). These two are almost always cited together. Josephus links Samaias with Sameas of *Ant. xv*.1.1 (1–4) who is there associated with Pollion, and some identify the latter with Abtalion; but Josephus is probably mistaken
Hillel	
Shammai	both *c.* 30 BC to AD 10
Rabban Gamaliel	*c.* 30–40
Simeon b. Gamaliel	d. AD 70

The list is part of the heritage of the Pharisees from the years before the disasters of AD 70 and 135. It is as remarkable for its gaps as for its contents, and covers the years from *c.* 160 to 40 BC with the six names of the first three pairs. Very little is said about Hillel and Shammai who are frequently cited in the Mishnah; Johanan and his disciples are omitted altogether. The last four names, i.e. the last two pairs, are regarded in the tradition as in each case the president and vice-president (who bore the title of 'Father of the Court') of the sanhedrin, as is clearly stated in Mishnah Ḥag. 2:2. The presidency continued in fact from Hillel through his descendants until AD 415, with the interludes of Johanan in Jamnia and of the temporary deposition of Gamaliel II. We can therefore continue the list of presidents begun by the opening of Abot (noting shifts of place, first from Jerusalem to Jamnia), beginning again with Shammai and Hillel, and including Johanan.

Jerusalem	*Jamnia*
Shammai	
Hillel *c.* 30 BC to AD 10	
Gamaliel I (grandson, possibly son of Hillel) *fl.* AD 30–40	
Simeon d. 70	
*Johanan (assisted Simeon) *c.* 50–70	*Johanan 70–80
	Gamaliel II (deposed for a time in favour of Eleazar)
	Simeon III (moved from Jamnia to Usha)

In Beth She'arim, then Sepphoris, Rabbi Judah ha-Nasi, 135–219, chief compiler of the Mishnah.

This brings us to the end of our period. Judah's son, Gamaliel III, was president of the Academy; a fellow-student and subsequent pupil, Abba Areka, almost always known as Rab (180–247), moved from Sepphoris to Sura on the Euphrates, where he founded an academy.

This amended list is historically more reliable than those which continue after Hillel in Abot; the latter show grave aberrations in chronological order. It should be noted also that the names at all periods are more safely understood as those of *de facto* acknowledged leaders rather than as of official presidents and vice-presidents.

The title 'rabbi', not found in the Old Testament, means literally 'My Great One' and was used to address a teacher. At first informal, after the fall of Jerusalem it was given to all qualified scholars, in Babylonia taking the form of 'rab'.

EARLY RABBIS

In the Mishnah, opinions from the old Pharisaic traditions ('the sages') are often quoted as being from the schools of Shammai or of Hillel, and both are often quoted on a particular point in order to show their differences. (See Argyle on Matt. 5:32 in CBC

Matthew, p. 51.) Both schools were represented by scholars in the early Jamnia period (from AD 70); it is therefore strange that we can discover very few details about the actual lives of these two masters, Shammai and Hillel, both of whom lived in the period *c.* 30 BC to AD 10.

Shammai and his School. Material in the Mishnah concerning Shammai himself (as distinct from his school) is very sparse, but many passages about his school imply that the school of Hillel had to make headway very gradually against that of Shammai, and we may fairly conclude that Shammai was earlier widely accepted as authoritative. In a number of debates Hillelites yielded repeatedly to the Shammaiites ('Ed. 1:12–14). None of the few mentions of Shammai as a person enables us to link him with history, although he is sometimes identified with the Samaias of *Ant.* XIV or XV or both (see list p. 188), an identification by no means universally accepted. Shammai's reputation in the Mishnah, intensified in the Talmud, is for strictness in application of the Law and severity in manner. We have no means of knowing whether this reputation was deserved or simply reflects the comparative severity in most instances of the school of Shammai when set alongside Hillelite decisions.

Hillel. Hillel is not mentioned either in the New Testament or by Josephus. From rabbinic sources we know that he (or his immediate ancestors) came from Babylonia. This would be in accordance with Herod's policy of settlements in the north (p. 26). Hillel may therefore have been from Bathyra, but we have no direct evidence of this. From the Herodian period to his death in about AD 10 Hillel gradually won a dominant position as an halakhic (legal) interpreter. We have to guess how this happened; he showed lack of militancy during the times in which the Pharisees changed under the pressure of circumstances from an active sect and party into a quietist group. Perhaps these conditions enabled him to emerge as the ideal leader, once the opportunity for a quiet life became not only possible but the only possibility. He prepared for this emergence by a long, skilful and diligent study of the Law, both Mosaic and traditional or 'Oral'. It is virtually certain that many of the decisions which are attributed to him are those of the Hillelites at Jamnia, and that his name is attached to many from Jamnia onwards by disciples in his tradition.

Johanan b. Zakkai. We have seen (p. 120) how Johanan moved from Jerusalem to Jamnia in AD 70 and established the Academy there, apparently with the approval of Vespasian. Tradition tells of his early discipleship of Hillel when the latter was an old man and of a not very successful time in Galilee. In Jamnia he presided over the heroic and successful task of transforming a Judaism centred on the cult in Jerusalem into a Judaism centred on the community (the new 'temple') represented by the Academy with its court. Johanan showed both skill and determination in directing decisions after debate upon differing traditional interpretations of Jewish law, i.e. different 'traditions of the fathers' within Pharisaism. At first the Shammaiites prevailed, but by degrees the Hillelites became the accepted authorities, reflecting Johanan's adherence to that tradition, and either reflecting or creating the tradition of his having been a disciple of Hillel.

Jonathan b. Uzziel. Another disciple of Hillel, of interest in literary history because he has been identified with Theodotion (Greek form of the name Jonathan) who translated the Old Testament into Greek. The identification is by no means universally accepted, and requires a relatively new theory that the original Theodotion belongs to the early first century AD rather than the second (p. 154).

Among contributors from their own knowledge to the Mishnah may be mentioned:

Hanina (or *Hananiah*). Prefect of the Priests towards the end of the Second Temple, i.e. deputy high priest. His special saying in Ab. 3:2 may well be historically significant: 'Pray for the peace of the ruling power, since but for fear of it men would have swallowed up each other alive.' The cessation of sacrifice on behalf of Rome accelerated the outbreak of war in AD 66. Hanina is able to give descriptions of parts of the Temple as well as of customs.

Eliezer b. Jacob. His uncle had served as a Levite in the Temple; he contributes some interesting details of architecture which smack of personal reminiscence, as does also his recollection, concerning Levite duty in the Temple: 'They once found my mother's brother asleep and burnt his raiment.'

The Five Disciples of Johanan b. Zakkai. These five, active at
Jamnia, came with Johanan from Jerusalem. They were Joshua b.
Hananiah, Eliezer b. Hyrcanus (these two were the most famous),
Jose the priest, Eleazar b. Arak and Simeon b. Nathanael.

Joshua maintained a reputation for humility and gentleness. His
goodness was almost proverbial. He apparently lived part at least
of his life in Peki'in in Galilee, and he is said to have had conversations with the emperor Hadrian. His gentle nature may have
helped keep the peace between him and the overbearing Gamaliel.
He often debated with Eliezer, perhaps the most famous of Johanan's
disciples, and was in contact with Gamaliel. No such contact is
reported of Eliezer himself, who appears to have been excommunicated by Gamaliel. Eliezer was stubborn where Joshua was
flexible; he was renowned for his retentive memory, his master
Johanan likening him to a cistern coated with lime which does not
lose a single drop of water. With his knowledge went an unwil-
lingness to change or modify. He lived in Lydda. It is related that
when he found himself before a gentile court he attributed this
misfortune to the sin of having admired a legal decision which a
Jewish Christian had told him had come from Jesus. Such an
attitude, combining hostility with occasional unwilling admiration, is typical of the half-hidden references to Jesus which appear
sparsely in the Talmud. Both Joshua and Eliezer conversed with
their younger contemporary Akiba (see below).

Gamaliel II (c. 90–110). Son of Simeon and grandson of Gamaliel
I, he succeeded Johanan as president of the Academy, thus restor-
ing the family succession from Hillel. The later tradition that he
excommunicated Eliezer, already mentioned, would account for
the apparent lack of contact with the latter, but a sufficient
explanation lies in his autocratic behaviour, which caused him to
be temporarily replaced at the instance of the seventy Elders of the
Academy by Eleazar b. Azariah, but penitence secured his return to
office. Eleazar was then his deputy, 'Father of the Court', and both
are said to have travelled with Joshua and the young Akiba by ship
to Rome. Reporting of this event is very characteristic of rabbinic
writing; 'Er. 4:1-2; M.Š. 5:9; Šab. 16:8 all refer to it, giving the
opinions of each on legal religious points which their journey
raised at various stages, but never telling us the reason for their
journey, perhaps as a delegation to obtain some dispensation for
Jewish religious practice from the emperor Trajan.

Aquila (*c.* 117–38). According to Epiphanius (*c.* 315–403) a Gentile from Sinope in Pontus and therefore a proselyte. His translation of the Old Testament into Greek was intended to meet the Jewish need for help against Christian appropriation of the Septuagint. Nowadays he is often identified with Onqelos, the translator of the prophetic literature into Aramaic. His Greek translation was pedantically literal, under the influence of Akiba and his extreme reverence for the divine text.

Ishmael b. Elisha. Ishmael (d. 135) was probably of priestly descent and his father may have officiated as high priest in the troubled times at the end of the Second Temple. As a boy he was released from Roman captivity by Joshua b. Hananiah, Johanan's disciple. Sometimes at Jamnia, he lived mostly in Kephar Aziz on the Edomite border with ancient Judah. The facts about him illustrate the process of imposing a relatively ordered written form upon the complex interrelation and miscellaneous mass of traditions of different rabbinic schools. That is the process, which occupied several generations, of reducing the Oral tradition to a written form acceptable to the majority and which produced the Mishnah that we know. Ishmael was concerned to show the link between traditional laws (*halakoth*) and scripture. He discharged this task from a relatively commonsense point of view, and Thirteen Rules for such interpretation (*middoth* or 'measures') are associated with him. They are an extension of the seven *middoth* traditionally attributed to Hillel. Ishmael claimed, against more fanciful ways of treating scripture, that 'the Torah speaks the language of men'.

His exegesis is often quoted in the Mekilta, a *midrash* (roughly equivalent to 'commentary') which presents with comments the legal material of Exodus (Exod. 12:1 – 23:19; 31:12–17; 35:1–3). The Mekilta is often called the Mekilta ('rule' or 'measure') of R. Ishmael. Much of the Sifre (lit. 'books', meaning midrashic presentation of the original books) on Numbers and Deuteronomy also derives from him or his school. The most famous pupils of this school were R. Josiah and R. Jonathan, and the absence of their names from the Mishnah illustrates its descent through R. Meir from R. Akiba, a rival school to that of Ishmael. He appears to have been more of the age of Tarphon and Akiba than of older contemporaries such as Eleazar b. Azariah and his benefactor Joshua. According to tradition Ishmael was one of the many rabbinic martyrs of the war of 132–5.

Akiba. After Hillel, Akiba (d. 135) was perhaps the most famous of all rabbis of the generations before the Mishnah of R. Judah (i.e. of the years before *c.* AD 200). He appears to have lived in Lydda and at Bene Barak, and to have visited Jamnia. His reputation is that of a gentle zealot. He combined religious devotion with patriotism, but was born to contemplation, scholarship and heroic suffering rather than to heroic political activity. His patriotism led him to accept Bar Kokhba as the Messiah, and he was and is criticized for naïveté on that account. Perhaps it was rather a measure of both his own submissiveness to authority·and of the extent to which Bar Kokhba for a considerable time succeeded in establishing his authority. Akiba was martyred by a most cruel death in 135.

His devotion to the details of the text, not only the principles, of the Mosaic Law was extreme; for him not a single word of the sacred text was superfluous, and this led to fanciful uses of it and to his fostering an absurdly literal translation into Greek. Aquila's translation was carried out under his influence. Akiba gave great impetus to collection and assessment of the halakhic tractates and the eventual Mishnah bears the stamp at many places of his extreme reverence for, and sometimes extreme interpretations of, the Hebrew scriptures.

Meir (*fl.* 140–65). A man of peace and holiness who was occupied largely with the formation of a written version of the traditions, in other words with a Mishnah. He was a pupil at first of Ishmael, then of Akiba on whose recension he based his own, which was in its turn to be used by Judah. Meir married Beruriah, whose good character won her fame in Jewish tradition. She was the daughter of Hananiah b. Teradion, a martyr of 135. Her gentle exposition of Ps. 104:35, that it forecast the abolition of wickedness rather than the wicked, once moderated his wrath and incidentally showed her skill in pointing Hebrew words. The story of her breaking the news to her husband of the death of their two sons reveals spiritual understanding of the Law as well as great tenderness, and is unsurpassed for its brief beauty.

Judah ha-Nasi (135–219). (*Nasi³* means 'chief' or 'president'; in connexion with Judah often translated 'prince'.) Said to have been born on the day of Akiba's death in 135, Judah lived in Usha where he was taught by Judah b. El'ai. His studies included Greek which he liked. He had other teachers, including his father Simeon, son of Gamaliel II, and after his death he moved to Beth She'arim, which by its association with so famous a man became afterwards a fashionable place of burial for pious Jews. Finally he moved to Sepphoris. He was a man of great influence through the holiness of his life as well as the possession of a most able mind. His fame rests primarily on the definitive recension of the Mishnah which he created, although it has undergone much editing since it left his hands.

GENERATIONS OF RABBIS

The exact dates of individual rabbis are seldom known, and they are divided generally into three periods: before AD 10, i.e. from about 200 BC to AD 10, pre-Tannaim; AD 10 to 220, Tannaim; after 220, Amoraim, of which there are both Palestinian and Babylonian. Both Tanna and Amora mean 'teacher' (more literally 'reciter' or 'repeater').

Our period embraces the pre-Tannaitic (*c.* 200 BC to AD 10) and the Tannaitic (AD 10–220) generations. Of the latter there are six, denoted thus:

T1	(AD 10–80)	T4	(AD 140–65)
T2	(AD 80–120)	T5	(AD 165–200)
T3	(AD 120–40)	T6	(AD 200–20)

The Amoraim added to the Mishnah further teaching and traditions, called the *gemara* ('completion'). The whole makes up the Talmud ('learning' or 'study', i.e. of the Law).

This work of forming the Talmud proceeded in both Palestine (chiefly at Caesarea, Sepphoris, Tiberias and Usha) and Babylonia (chiefly at Nehardea, Sura and Pumbeditha). Frequent movement of scholars between the two countries meant mutual influence, but there grew up a Palestinian Talmud and a Babylonian Talmud. The Palestinian Talmud is often cited as the Talmud Yerushalmi (i.e. of Jerusalem). In references the letters M, b, y, or t preceding the name of the tractate indicate that the reference is from the Mishnah (M), the Babylonian Talmud (b), the Palestinian (or Jerusalem) Talmud (y, short for Yerushalmi), or the Tosephta (t). Bar. indicates a Baraita (see below).

TARGUM, MIDRASH, HALAKAH, HAGGADAH, MISHNAH,
BARAITA, TOSEPHTA

A *targum* usually means a translation into Aramaic, but with the
implication of interpretation. A targum has been defined as 'a
translation of the Hebrew Bible into the Aramaic language for
liturgical use in the synagogue'. When translations of the Hebrew
Bible into Greek are referred to as 'targums', the implication is
that they contain a strong element of interpretation, which sometimes involves change and addition.

Aramaic targums were originally not a substitute for the
Hebrew text, but a portion of them would be read after a portion
of text. Efforts to standardize the texts of targums made in the
second and third centuries drew on previous material, and
whether any of the early miscellaneous material can be recovered
from known texts is an all-important question for scholarship.

The main targums on the Pentateuch include some whose
origin may well lie within the dates of our period. One is Neofiti I,
recently discovered and thought by some to be a recension of a
pre-Christian targum, but by others to be not earlier than the
third century. The fragmentary targum is preserved in five different manuscripts. The Cairo Geniza fragments have not yet been
grouped satisfactorily. The Targum of Onqelos is a fairly literal
translation and so might be by Aquila (p. 193). It is usually
regarded as of Babylonian origin, but may be Palestinian. The
Pseudo-Jonathan Targum is awkwardly named: it was originally
called Targum Jerushalmi, being Palestinian, and 'Targum J' was
misinterpreted as 'Targum of Jonathan'. 'Pseudo-' has now been
added to acknowledge the error.

Written targums exist for all biblical books except those
already with substantial portions in Aramaic (Ezra, Nehemiah,
Daniel). The dates of their origin vary greatly. A targum of Job
has long been known from rabbinic writings to have existed in
the first century. One has also been found among the Qumran
documents.

Midrash is a word occurring in the Bible only in 2 Chron. 13:22
and 24:27, where it seems to indicate some kind of addition to the
official Annals of the Kings. These additions may have been
explanatory, for midrash later became the term for explanatory
commentary or exegesis. Midrash material varies in length from
very short to very long. When applied to legal matters it

conveyed *halakah*, lit. 'way', and thus regulation or law; but midrash is often in the form of story (and therefore may sometimes not immediately appear to be midrash but seem to be continuation of the text). It can be parable, proverb, anecdote, illustrative example, or indeed anything not classifiable as halakah. It then conveys its meaning by *haggadah*, i.e. 'telling' or story, and haggadah is the term used to cover this very wide range of material.

The Oral Law thus consisted of halakah and haggadah; it was largely handed on by oral repetition, and a teacher was a 'repeater', a Tanna (p. 195).

Mishnah means 'what is repeated', hence Oral Law or Teaching. The term has several applications but is used primarily as the title of the collection of Oral Law and derived teachings made by Judah ha-Nasi. The material which he excluded but which some rabbis thought valuable was termed *baraita* (external); some collections were made of such material which was often of the sort to serve as explanation, illustration or interpretation of material merely recorded in the Mishnah.

A collection of this kind is the *tosephta* ('Addition' or 'Supplement'). In the opinion of some it is an alternative Mishnah, similarly divided as it is into Orders and Tractates, and not a mere supplement, its original relation to R. Judah's Mishnah being complicated and obscure. It seems to have been in the main edited by R. Hiyya, a friend of R. Judah, who came from Babylonia to live in Tiberias at an advanced age and was active in the mid-second century. Like his friend and master R. Judah, he was a teacher of Rab (Abba Areka, 180–247), his nephew, the influential founder of the academy at Sura on the Euphrates.

11. Christian Writings

The Letters of Paul. The career of Paul as a Christian missionary began about AD 35, and he wrote a number of Letters to the early churches at times which are impossible to determine exactly. They are the earliest documents of the Christian Church. The following approximate dates would command considerable assent:

49	1 and 2 Thessalonians
54–8	(from Ephesus) 1 Corinthians, Galatians, 2 Corinthians, Colossians, Philemon
58 or 59	(from Corinth) Romans
61-4	(in Rome) Philippians

At least one of his letters to the Corinthians is lost, and the extant Corinthian correspondence may be the amalgamation of three, four or more originals. Col. 4:16 refers to a non-extant Letter to the Laodiceans (which has however sometimes been identified with Ephesians or even Philemon). Ephesians and the Pastorals are now widely regarded as post-Pauline on grounds of theology and vocabulary.

The Rest of the New Testament. The date of Mark, the earliest gospel, is disputed. A probable date is just before or just after AD 70, followed by Luke and Matthew 85-95, and John and the rest of the Johannine literature *c.* 100.

69(?)	Hebrews
85-95	Acts, Revelation, Ephesians, the Pastoral Letters (1 and 2 Timothy, Titus), James
c. 112	1 Peter
c. 115	Jude, 2 Peter

NEW TESTAMENT APOCRYPHA

We have seen that manuscripts of the LXX sometimes contained non-canonical ('outside') books, some of which are now accepted as a collection of Apocrypha, the list of them differing a little according to time and place. In a roughly parallel way the Codex Sinaiticus, the only uncial manuscript which contains the whole of the Greek New Testament, contains also two apocryphal books, the Letter of Barnabas and the Shepherd of Hermas. Moreover, canonical lists of various dates, some of the early second century, show that: (1) in the first centuries there were at least some differences in the canon in different localities; (2) a number of 'apocryphal' books (i.e. books not finally included in the canon of AD 367 recorded by Athanasius) were often read and venerated in the early centuries AD. The following list is of the most important:

Letter of Barnabas. Included by the Codex Sinaiticus but mentioned by Clement of Alexandria (*c.* 150–215) as 'disputed'. Certainly not written by the Barnabas of Acts 4:36 etc., since the events of AD 70 are treated as past. It is in the main a homily arguing that the Jews failed to understand their own Law and its significance, obeying it literally and missing its foreshadowing of the new covenant in Christ. The last chapters are a short treatise on the Two Ways (see Didache below).

Shepherd of Hermas. The other apocryphal writing included in the Codex Sinaiticus. Hermas is said by the author of the late second century canon preserved in the Muratorian Fragment of the Canon to have been the brother of Pius, bishop of Rome *c.* 140–50, but much of the book seems by its simple theology and reflection of a still primitive church to be earlier. Perhaps its composition occupied a long period. It is known as the Shepherd from the angel who appeared in the form of a shepherd to relate some of its contents. It is divided into five Visions, twelve Mandates and ten Similitudes, but the style is much the same throughout. Allegory presents the character of the Church, and moral teaching. Penance and post-baptismal sin are discussed at length.

Didache. The Didache (or 'Teaching', i.e. of the Twelve Apostles), known from a Greek manuscript from Constantinople published in 1883, is of an unknown origin and difficult to date, opinions ranging very widely. Most would agree that it must be placed somewhere in the second century and certainly not later, but the first century has been urged. A handbook of church discipline, it contains a summary of the Christian way of life, a treatise on the Two Ways (ultimately based on Deut. 30:15 and elaborated in intertestamental literature such as T12P), instruction on Baptism, Fasting and Prayer, and on the Eucharist, and a section on Church Order. It ends with an eschatological exhortation.

Letters of Clement of Rome. This Clement was bishop of Rome at the end of the first century and in the early Church many letters ascribed to him were circulated. The only genuine letter is the (First) Letter to the Corinthians and dates from the time of his episcopacy; it pleads earnestly for order, and for cessation of strife in the factious Corinthian church, showing knowledge of Paul's letters and of Hebrews. Rather obscure references are made to instances of strife in the early Church which had brought dire consequences. The Letter illustrates well the early Church's familiarity with and appropriation of the Greek Old Testament.

The so-called Second Letter of Clement is generally agreed to be falsely attributed to him; it is a sermon, rather than a letter, about the moral combat demanded of a Christian in the world.

Letters of Ignatius. Ignatius (*c.* 35 to *c.* 107) was the second bishop of Antioch (Peter being the first) according to Origen, the third according to Eusebius. He was arrested *c.* 106 and taken to martyrdom in Rome under a guard of ten Roman soldiers. Of his seven genuine letters he wrote the first four at Smyrna, three thanking the Christians of Ephesus, Magnesia and Tralles for sending representatives to greet him on his journey, the fourth to dissuade the Roman Christians from seeking to save him from martyrdom. The other three are from Troas where he heard that persecution at Antioch had ended, one each to Philadelphia and Smyrna, and one to Polycarp, bishop of Smyrna. Ignatius writes in a lively and individual style, expressing deep devotion to Christ and to the Church, and interesting doctrinal views.

Polycarp's Letter to the Philippians. According to Irenaeus, Polycarp had known 'John the Lord's disciple' and the latter's identity is much discussed. Polycarp was born *c.* 70, was bishop of Smyrna from *c.* 110 and martyred in *c.* 156. He was a Quartodeciman, that is, he celebrated Easter on 14 Nisan, whatever the day of the week. In 154 he conferred in Rome with the bishop Anicetus about the correct determining of Easter; they failed to agree, but amicably. In Rome Polycarp won over several heretics and rebuked Marcion (p. 206). His only extant writing is the Letter to the Philippians, now widely accepted as a conflation of two letters, the final chapters 13–14 forming the earlier and containing an enquiry about Ignatius and his followers; chapters 1–12 are then a later letter in which he thanks them for their reception of Ignatius and his companions, implying knowledge of their death. Chapters 1–12 include commendation of Paul's Letters, addresses to the groups making up the Philippian church, exhortations to keep the faith and to follow the life pattern of martyrs, and a note to say that he is sending with the letter the Letters of Ignatius which he possesses.

Letter to Diognetus. Author unknown, of third, perhaps second, century, so often classed with the Apologists. It commends the Christian way of life as superior to the Jewish or pagan, its code of conduct proceeding direct from God. The Christian is in the world as the soul is in the body.

Papias (*c.* 60–130). Almost nothing is known of Papias except that he was bishop of Hierapolis early in the second century, and that he wrote five books of *Expositions of the Oracles of the Lord* incidentally recording the tradition known to him of the origin of the gospels of Matthew and Mark. Fragments are recorded by Irenaeus and Eusebius, the work being otherwise not extant. Papias is also said to have known 'John' and Polycarp, and to have been a believer in the Millennium, that is, he expected the kingdom of God to be set up and to last for a thousand years on this earth immediately after the expected general resurrection.

THE APOLOGISTS

Apart from political persecution, a number of pagan writers attacked Christianity by argument. The three earliest known literary opponents were: Fronto (*c.* 100 to *c.* 166), a close friend of M. Aurelius and a famous orator; he made a speech accusing Christians of atheism, immorality and abominable practices (the stock accusations were of incest and child-eating); Lucian of Samosata (b. *c.* 120) who wrote mocking Christian beliefs and credulity; and Celsus (who wrote *c.* 178–80), the only one of the three to show any real ability and understanding of his subject. Celsus did not find a worthy antagonist until fifty years later, when Origen wrote his *Contra Celsum* from which what is known of the text of Celsus' attack has to be reconstructed.

Several Christian writers undertook replies to such pagan attacks. The earliest, Quadratus and Aristides, each addressed an Apology (i.e. Defence) to Hadrian, that of Aristides alone being extant. Aristo of Pella was the first to write an Apology against the Jews, but this, like the works of the later Miltiades and Apollinarius, is lost. The following are more important:

Justin Martyr. Born a pagan near the beginning of the second century AD at Flavia Neapolis (the ancient Shechem and modern Nablus), Justin became a Platonist and then a Christian, probably at Ephesus. He founded a school in Rome and was martyred there *c.* 163–7. He wrote two Apologies. In the first he refutes common charges against the Christians and attacks pagan ways of life. He gives a full account of the Eucharistic rite as known to him, both that for the newly baptized and that for a regular Sunday. He ends by quoting the rescript, *c.* AD 125, of Hadrian to Minucius Fundanus forbidding punishment of Christians other than for stated crimes. In the second and much shorter Apology he attacks Urbicus, the city prefect, for putting three Christians to death for being Christians, and denounces calumnies uttered by the Cynic philosopher Crescens. Any truth found in paganism is due to the presence in man of the seminal *Logos* revealed in full only in Christ. He wrote also a *Dialogue with Trypho*, a defence against Jewish criticisms. It is later than the Apologies and perhaps dates to AD 160. Other writings are lost.

Tatian. A Syrian disciple of Justin, after whose death he opened a school in Rome, but returned in 172–3 to the east. He founded the sect of the Encratites, being personally a severe ascetic. He is best known for his combination of the four gospels into one, the *Diatessaron*, but he was the author also of other books, of which only his *Discourse to the Greeks* survives. Like Justin he made use of the *Logos* doctrine, but not to explain any good in paganism, to which he was sharply opposed.

Athenagoras. Of the second half of the second century, but little is known of him. He wrote a *Supplication for Christians* addressed to

Marcus Aurelius and Commodus, making the probable date 177. He rebuts the usual charges against Christians, devoting most space to that of atheism. Like Justin he seems to use Greek philosophy sympathetically. In his *On the Resurrection* he defends the possibility of the resurrection of the body and seeks to prove the necessity of the resurrection.

Theophilus of Antioch. Eusebius says he was the sixth bishop of Antioch. His only surviving treatise of many writings is an Apology of *c.* 180, in which he developed the *Logos* doctrine and used the word 'Triad' of the Godhead. He too made a gospel harmony.

Sextus. In about 200 he put into Christian form a collection of 451 ethical sayings, teaching austerity, moderation and sexual asceticism.

Melito, Bishop of Sardis. What is known of Melito comes from Eusebius. He was a Quartodeciman (see p. 200) and was mentioned by Polycrates, bishop of Ephesus, in his dispute about Easter with Victor, bishop of Rome 189–99. Melito wrote an Apology to M. Aurelius, i.e. between 161 and 180; but, along with many other writings, it is known only by a quotation in Eusebius, though a few works have survived also in fragments. The great exception to fragmentary survival is an extended treatise *On the Pascha* (or Eucharist) known in Greek and Coptic as well as in fragments in these languages and Syriac. It appears to date between 160 and 170. The Passover anticipates the Gospel and is the historical beginning of the Eucharistic 'Mystery'. The exposition of this embraces the Fall of Man and the Saving Work of Christ. In the course of expounding the latter, Israel is bitterly reproached and the treatise ends with the triumph and exaltation of Christ.

THE EARLY GNOSTICS

Salvation is a paramount aim of all religion. Its meaning may be expounded in many different ways, but it always implies victorious deliverance from the enemy, whether moral, spiritual or physical evil, or all three. The victory is often conceived of as won by a saviour, and then for the individual everything depends on his relation to that saviour. This relation may be expressed by saying that he must *know* God or the divinely appointed saviour, or both, as in John 17:3. Such knowledge or *gnosis* (Gk. 'knowledge') is often held to include, or to be synonymous with, divinely revealed knowledge of the secrets of the universe, of God's action in it, of the true self and many other profound matters affecting the soul. Where there is a system which claims to impart to its initiates such special knowledge or gnosis as to guarantee salvation, it may justly be called gnostic.

Much new gnostic material has become available recently from Nag Hammadi, a site near the Nile sixty miles below Luxor, where in 1945 a library was discovered of thirteen papyrus codices comprising forty-nine religious treatises written in Coptic translated from Greek, most if not all gnostic. The works represented were first written at varying dates and only the most important of those thought to originate within our period are mentioned here. The importance of these finds lies in the fact that formerly a great deal of our knowledge of gnostic writings was derived from quotations in those of their opponents. These documents provide new and direct sources of information.

Irenaeus (p. 207) regarded all gnostic systems as deliberate anti-Christian heresies and he has strongly coloured subsequent thinking about them. Later discoveries and scholarly reflection tend now to show that a great many of the miscellaneous ingredients which produced the gnosticism opposed by Irenaeus were to be found in religions earlier than Christianity, e.g. in Judaism as it is found in Qumran, in Wisdom literature and in intertestamental 'pseudepigraphic' writings, in Iranian dualism, in oriental mysteries from Asia and Egypt, and in garbled versions of hellenistic philosophy. Indeed it is argued with increasing confidence that there were pre-Christian gnostic systems within both Hellenism and Judaism. Whether this is true or not, we are here concerned only with the chief gnostic writings of the first two Christian centuries.

The Fathers ascribed the beginnings of gnosticism to Simon Magus (Acts 8:9–24) but we do not know of any book by him, though he was credited with a Gospel of the Four Points of the Compass. Gnostics early tended to write gospels which distilled what seemed to them to be essential Christianity, and to claim that their books gave the true Christianity, were the true gospel. Both these and other of their writings are usually obscure, verbose and fantastic and lose touch with history, taking the form of private and esoteric discourse between Jesus (or some other authority) and his disciples.

Cerinthus (*fl. c.* 100), though not known by any writings, is important for his reputation as an early example of a thinker who believed two doctrines destined to have a long history, that the world was created by a lesser being than the supreme God (a *Demiurge*, or Workman), and that Jesus began life as a man on whom the 'Christ' descended at his baptism and left him before the crucifixion. Polycarp is credited with the story that John the 'disciple of the Lord' ran from a bath-house in which Cerinthus was for fear that the building would fall on such an enemy of the truth. Cerinthus was regarded by the Alogi, an obscure sect in Asia Minor in the later second century, as the author of the gospel of John and Revelation.

Basilides (*fl.* 120–40). An Alexandrian teacher who wrote among other things a gospel commentary and twenty-four books of *Exegetica*, all lost except for a few fragments. Evidence about his views is conflicting, but he seems to have emphasized the separation of the world from God, and according to Irenaeus believed in a hierarchy of spiritual beings issuing from God. He too shrank from believing the historic Christ suffered crucifixion, and said that Simon of Cyrene was crucified instead. Salvation depends on gnosis and is so much a spiritual matter that the fleshly sins of enlightened gnostics are outside the concern of God and may be disregarded.

Valentinus (*fl.* 140). A native of Alexandria who according to Irenaeus taught mainly in Rome in the years 136–65, enjoying considerable influence. His system envisaged a complicated order of beings (aeons) arranged in a succession of syzygies (lit. pairs yoked together) or couples whose ultimate product, due to the fall of Sophia, one of the lowest aeons, was the Demiurge, equated with the God of the Old Testament. The aeon Christ united with Jesus at his baptism and brought to men the necessary gnosis, imparted only to the truly spiritual, i.e. the followers of Valentinus, who are thus enabled to enter the higher sphere of being called the Pleroma, while others (ordinary Christians) attain only to that of the Demiurge, while the rest of mankind are lost. The Gospel of Truth discovered at Nag Hammadi (p. 204) may represent his teaching at an early stage or have been written by another. It retains only a residual contact with the canonical gospels, but contains some ingeniously if obscurely expressed spiritual convictions.

Among Valentinus' disciples Ptolemy and Heracleon are prominent.

Ptolemy (*fl.* 140). In his *Letter to Flora* Ptolemy discusses the value of the Mosaic Law after Christ and concludes that it was the work of the Demiurge.

Heracleon (*fl.* 145–80) wrote the earliest known commentary on the gospel of John. It survives mainly in the fragmentary quotations in Origen's Commentary on the same gospel.

Marcion (*fl.* 140, d. *c.* 160). A wealthy native of Sinope in Pontus, Marcion was active in Rome from 140. His teaching contrasted strongly the God of the Old Testament, the Demiurge, a God wholly of Law, with the God wholly of Love whom Jesus Christ came to reveal and whose purpose was to overthrow the Demiurge. This contrast had been understood only by Paul, so that Marcion's canon consisted only of the ten epistles by him, i.e. those other than Hebrews and the Pastorals, and his own version of Luke's gospel. His Christology was Docetic, i.e. Jesus' humanity only seemed to exist, so that his sufferings were not real. Marcion's writings are lost and known only through his opponents. He is usually classed with the gnostics through being an opponent of orthodoxy, but his doctrine, which is easily understood, is free from their fanciful speculations.

The following writings are by unknown authors and date from about the middle of the second century.

The Gospel according to Didymus Judas Thomas, usually abbreviated to the *Gospel of Thomas* (the title also of an apocryphal infancy gospel). This apocryphon was discovered at Nag Hammadi. It consists of a number of *logia*, sayings claimed to have been spoken by Jesus and written down by the 'Twin Judas Thomas'. They are of an allegorical, gnomic, even enigmatic character, but frequently recall canonical sayings, to which they give an esoteric meaning, implying the need for their true understanding, and the role of the disciples as a body of enlightened ones.

The Gospel of Philip. This may belong to a later date. The author evidently writes before the development in the Church of any consistent biblical theology. He uses some of the language of Paul without understanding it fully. He regards himself not only as a Christian but as a 'Christ', deriving 'Christian' from the chrism, or anointing, which he has received. 'The Father anointed the Son, the Son anointed the Apostles, and the Apostles anointed us.' He expresses some curious speculations as well as more usual gnostic convictions. Typical of the latter are the unreality of this world, which is under the power of hostile forces, and the reality of the other aeon or age. Peculiar to Philip is a rather obscure sacramental system embracing Baptism, Chrism, Eucharist, Redemption and the Bridal Chamber, the last being the means whereby the true gnostic is transformed into a unified resurrected being. Earthly marriage is a counterpart of the union of the Saviour with his bride Sophia. The precise nature of this last mentioned rite is obscure; it may have been entirely spiritual, though it was represented as scandalous by opponents.

The Gospel according to Mary (probably mid-second century). Mary Magdalen comforts the apostles in their loss by the departure of the Lord with a doctrine of the attainment of peace, which she claims was revealed to her by Christ.

The Gospel of Peter. An apocryphal gnostic gospel known to Serapion, bishop of Antioch from 199, only one section of which has survived. It is mostly legendary, anti-Jewish and Docetic.

The Apocryphon of John (mid-second century). John the brother of James receives in a vision instruction from a heavenly being, apparently a gnostic form of the risen Christ, about the Godhead and the aeons of heavenly beings and the liberation of souls.

CHRISTIAN WRITERS OF THE SECOND CENTURY

The main Christian writers of the period are more constructive, biblical and intelligible. They are:

Irenaeus (c. 130–202). Bishop of Lyons from 179 at a time of persecution, he sought to establish the authority of a New Testament canon, including that of the gospels. He developed a theology of Creation and Redemption through the Incarnation, and became the first great Catholic theologian.

Pantaenus (*fl. c.* 170–90). A converted Stoic philosopher who became head of the Christian catechetical school at Alexandria.

Clement of Alexandria (*c.* 150–215). The successor to Pantaenus, Clement argued that adherents of hellenistic philosophy could find, as he had, its crown and fulfilment in Christianity, the 'true gnosis'.

Origen (*c.* 185 to *c.* 254). Successor to Clement, biblical scholar, philosopher-theologian and spiritual writer, a most unusual thinker and prolific writer whose activity extended from textual criticism to metaphysical speculation, a faithful and courageous Christian. He had an immense influence on subsequent thinkers, but was condemned as heretical, and has never been canonized. He attempted a speculative and wide-ranging philosophy of all creation, and shows boldness and ingenuity in his exegesis of scripture, making frequent use of allegory, arguing that some passages must be so intended since in their literal sense they are false or unedifying.

The last three are representatives of the school of Alexandria with which that at Antioch is usually compared and contrasted; but the representative theologians of Antioch belong to the fourth century. In the meantime a number of important Christian writers were active in North Africa, writing in Latin, the only example within our period being *Tertullian* (*c.* 160–225) who wrote a number of strongly argued treatises against error and heresy and expounding orthodoxy within the Church, and an important and incisive *Apology* for Christians, pleading for universal tolerance within the Empire.

The Acts of the Martyrs. These are various accounts of martyrdoms, sometimes of individuals, sometimes of groups of Christians, the latter perhaps with a particular leader; very few which were written by eyewitnesses or near to the actual event have survived. The following, which have survived, are probably based on eyewitness accounts and are about events before AD 200.

The Martyrdom of Polycarp (bishop of Smyrna martyred *c.* 156), written from Smyrna by request to the church at Philomelium in Pisidia.

The Acts of St Justin and his Companions, whose martyrdom was about AD 165.
The Passion of the Scillitan Martyrs, on the martyrdom of seven men and five women of Scillium in north Africa, executed in 180 for refusing to renounce Christianity and swear by the 'genius' of the Roman emperor.

The Epistle of the Gallican Churches (or, *of the Churches of Vienne and Lyons*) is reproduced extensively by Eusebius in *Eccl. Hist.* v.i. In it the Christians of these churches give a vivid account of their recent sufferings in the persecution of 177–8 to their brethren in Asia and Phrygia.

12. Writers, other than Jewish or Christian, in the Roman Empire 200 BC to AD 200

This list includes the most important names. An asterisk marks those which are the most relevant to the history of Jews and Christians, usually because they illustrate contemporary attitudes to them. The language of each is noted or implied.

Acts of the Alexandrine Martyrs or *Acta Alexandrinorum* or *Acts of the Pagan Martyrs* (author or authors unknown), end of second or beginning of third century AD. About twelve fragments of Alexandrine patriotic literature in Greek describing appearances before various emperors of Alexandrian nationalistic leaders, usually just before their execution as patriots.

Aelian (Aelianus Claudius) of Praeneste, c. AD 170–235. His various Greek writings contain excerpts from previous writers and anecdotes, mostly of a moralizing kind, against a background of Stoicism. A popular writer much drawn on by Christian writers.

Aelius Aristides of Mysia, AD 117 (or 129) to 181. Wrote in Greek *The Sacred Teaching* as a result of his own religious experience through an illness.

Agatharchides, fl. c. 116 BC. Guardian of Ptolemy Soter II, known from Josephus and surviving only in extracts. Greek.

Alexander Polyhistor of Miletus, b. c. 105 BC. Came to Rome as a prisoner of war and was freed by Sulla. A writer in Greek who compiled from many different sources, including Jewish.

Antipater of Sidon, *fl. c.* 120 BC. Seventy-five epigrams in the Greek Anthology.

Apion of Alexandria, son of Posidonius. At Rome in reigns of Tiberius and Claudius (AD 14–37 and 41–54), after being head of the Alexandrian school. He wrote about Egypt, and his many

incidental attacks on Judaism provoked Josephus' *Against Apion*.
Greek.

⋆*Appian* of Alexandria. A Greek writer who experienced the
Jewish revolt of AD 116, and held office in Alexandria and in
Rome, under Antoninus Pius. He wrote of the growth of the
Roman Empire by describing in turn the races conquered, and
included the Civil Wars. Much still extant, preserving some valu-
able material.

Apuleius, b. *c*. AD 123 at Madaurus in Africa. Active at Carthage,
Athens and Rome. Wrote his *Apologia* when accused at law of
using magic; the *Metamorphoses* (*The Golden Ass*), a novel containing material of diverse kinds; and various oratorical and edu-
cational works, including translations from Greek originals. A
very influential author often quoted in antiquity.

Arrian (Flavius Arrianus), a Greek writer of the second century AD.
Governor of Cappadocia under Hadrian. His chief work is the
Anabasis, a history of Alexander the Great.

Athenaeus of Naucratis in Egypt, *fl. c.* AD 200. In the only extant
work collected a large number of excerpts from previous authors.
Greek.

⋆*Caesar, C. Julius*, 100–44 BC (see pp. 46–9). His *De Bello Gallico*
covered from 58 to 52 BC and was completed to 50 by Hirtius,
once an officer under Caesar. Caesar's *De Bello Civili* describes his
struggle against the Pompeians. Latin.

Calpurnius Siculus, perhaps of Sicily, *fl.* AD 50–60. Latin pastoral
verse.

Cato, M. Porcius of Tusculum, 234–149 BC. Wrote on agriculture
and *Origines*, seven books of Roman history, the first of its kind
in Latin literature.

Catullus, C. Valerius, b. Verona 84, d. 54 BC. An accomplished writer of lyric, minor epic and epigrammatic Latin
poetry.

Celsus. Wrote AD 178–80 against Christianity (see p. 201). Greek.

★*Cicero, M. Tullius*, 106–43 BC (see pp. 45–9). A prolific author of speeches, books on oratory, philosophical treatises, letters, and also of poetry of which little has survived. *Pro Flacco*, one of his many skilful professional speeches, provides evidence for the administration of the Temple tax, and contemporary prevailing attitudes to Jews. Latin.

Columella (Lucius Junius Moderatus) of Gades in Spain, *fl.* AD 36–60. Wrote on agriculture, the decline of which he deplored. Latin.

Cornutus, Lucius Annaeus of Leptis in Tripolitania, b. *c.* AD 20. A teacher of philosophy and rhetoric at Rome. Only extant work is a 'Summary of Traditions about Greek Mythology' in Greek, but he wrote also in Latin.

★*Dio Cassius* of Nicaea in Bithynia, praetor in AD 194 and consul 205. Wrote as well as some minor books a history of Rome from the beginnings to AD 229. Includes mention of the Jewish revolt of 115–16. Greek.

★*Diodorus Siculus* of Agyrium in Sicily, d. *c.* 21 BC. In *c.* 60–30 wrote in Greek his *World History*.

Dionysius of Halicarnassus, *fl.* 30 BC onwards when he taught at Rome. As a historian he supplements Livy (though writing in Greek); also a literary critic.

Ennius, Quintus of Rudiae in Calabria, 239–169 BC. Wrote a number of tragedies modelled on Greek originals, and other poetic works including an unfinished *Annales*, an epic history of Rome from earliest times. Latin.

★*Epictetus* of Hierapolis, *c.* AD 55–135. A Greek Stoic philosopher in Rome and Nicopolis; some of his teaching has been preserved by Arrian. Greek.

Eratosthenes of Cyrene, *c.* 275–194 BC. Appointed by Ptolemy III Euergetes as royal tutor and head of the Alexandrian Library. A versatile scholar, of whose writings only fragments survive. Greek.

★*Frontinus, Sextus Julius, c.* AD 30–104, Roman governor of Britain 74–8. Wrote in Latin practical books, especially on military affairs, his *Strategemata* running to four volumes. He notices Jewish insistence on keeping the sabbath. Latin.

★*Fronto, Marcus Cornelius* of Cirta, Numidia, *c.* AD 100–66. Much admired as an orator, a close friend of Marcus Aurelius. He wrote in Latin an anti-Christian treatise.

★*Galen* of Pergamum, AD 129 to *c.* 199. A Greek who rose from gladiator-physician to court physician in Rome under Marcus Aurelius. Wrote on human anatomy and physiology, and philosophical treatises. An ardent monotheist, mentioning both Jews and Christians.

Gellius, Aulus, c. AD 130–80. Native place unknown. Wrote *Noctes Atticae* in twenty books, a learned and mostly secondhand literary miscellany. Latin.

Germanicus, Julius Caesar, 15 BC to AD 19, son of Drusus and Antonia, brother of the emperor Claudius. His Greek comedies are all lost. He wrote also Greek and Latin epigrams and translated into Latin the *Phaenomena* of Aratus (315–240 BC).

Herodes Atticus of Athens, *c.* AD 101–77, consul at Rome 143. A wealthy Roman senator who was also both a patron of arts in his native Athens (where a theatre built by him survives) and an author. His Greek writings were highly regarded, but only a Latin translation of a story is extant. Friend of Hadrian, Antoninus Pius and Marcus Aurelius, of whom, as of L. Verus, he was tutor.

Herodian of Syria. Wrote in Greek a history of Rome in eight books from M. Aurelius to Gordian III (AD 180–238).

★*Horace (Quintus Horatius Flaccus)* 65–8 BC. A master of Latin verse in the time of Augustus; a protégé of Maecenas. For all his charm as a poet, his thought is shallow (mainly like that of Omar Khayyam), as is his knowledge of Judaism, to judge by his occasional references.

Juvenal (Decimus Junius Juvenalis), b. probably at Aquinum, *c.* AD 60–130. The last of the important Roman satiric poets, he reveals much of contemporary society with ruthless clarity. He refers quite often to Jews and their customs, showing no understanding or sympathy.

Livy (Titus Livius) of Patavium, 59 BC to AD 17 or 64 BC to AD 12. Wrote a monumentally comprehensive history of Rome in 142 books of which thirty-five survive. Latin.

Longinus, probably of first century AD. Wrote in Greek *On the Sublime*, a remarkably thoughtful and influential work of literary criticism and on the true function of literature.

Lucan (Marcus Annaeus Lucanus), AD 39–65. Nephew of Seneca, he studied at Rome and later at Athens. At first in favour with Nero, he was implicated in the Pisonian conspiracy and forced to commit suicide. He wrote the *Bellum Civile* or *Pharsalia* about the struggle between Pompey and Caesar. Latin.

Lucian of Samosata, b. *c.* AD 120. Probably from birth Aramaic-speaking, but learnt Greek well enough to become an advocate and lecturer. Famous for his *Dialogues* in which he criticized many of the accepted ideas of his time. Greek.

Lucretius (Titus Lucretius Carus), 94–55 BC. Native place un-known. His *De Rerum Natura* expands in six books of highly effective verse the philosophy and science of Epicurus (341–270 BC), who had adapted the views of the atomists Leucippus and Democritus. Latin.

Martial (Marcus Valerius Martialis) of Bilbilis in Spain, *c.* AD 40–104. A friend of Seneca and Lucan, but survived the Pisonian conspiracy. Known chiefly for his (mainly satirical) *Epigrams*, showing a penetrating insight into human nature. Latin.

Meleager, a native of Gadara who later lived in Tyre and Cos, *fl.* 100 BC. He spoke Greek, Syriac and Phoenician. Wrote satires (lost) and epigrams, editing a large selection of the latter, which he called the *Garland*. Greek.

Minucius Felix, Marcus, apparently an African, *fl.* AD 200–40. Wrote *Octavius*, a dialogue between a Christian so named and a pagan Caecilius who uses Fronto's anti-Christian treatise. *Octavius* is in fact a Christian apology and is related to that of Tertullian, whether as source or dependent on it. Latin.

Nepos, Cornelius, c. 99–24 BC. Came from Cisalpine Gaul to Rome. A small part of his *De Viris Illustribus* is all that has survived; it is interesting because Nepos dealt with foreigners as well as Romans among his famous men. Latin.

Nicander of Colophon, second century BC. A pharmacologist and zoologist who also wrote epics now lost; described as a grammarian, poet and doctor. Greek.

★*Nicolaus* of Damascus, *c.* 64 BC to AD 6. Court historian to Herod the Great. His *Universal History* is preserved only in part, mostly by Josephus. Greek.

★*Numenius* of Apamea, second century AD. A Pythagorean who combined in his teaching Greek and oriental elements. Shows some knowledge of Judaism and Christianity, which he interpreted allegorically. Influenced Plotinus, Origen and Porphyry, the later Neoplatonists. Greek.

★*Ovid (Publius Ovidius Naso)* 43 BC to AD 17. An Augustan poet, exiled by Augustus, perhaps partly for the licentious nature of his *Ars Amatoria*. Famous also for his poetic collection of mythological stories in the *Metamorphoses*. Latin.

Parthenius of Nicaea, first century BC. He went to Italy in 73 BC as a prisoner of war and was freed there. Influenced the 'new poets' and is said to have taught Vergil, being himself much admired for his own poetry. Greek.

★*Persius (Aulus Persius Flaccus)*, AD 34–62. Friend of Stoics of Nero's time; wrote satirical verse; his writings were edited by the philosopher Cornutus after his death. Latin.

★*Petronius*, first century AD. Perhaps to be identified with a courtier of the same name of Nero's court. Author of romances and of poetic works, especially the *Satyricon. Latin.*

Philodemus of Gadara, *c.* 110 to 40 or 35 BC. Came to Rome *c.* 75 BC through the First Mithradatic War and settled at Herculaneum through the protection of the influential Pisones. Philodemus had a great influence on literary and philosophical students, including Vergil, and wrote on many subjects. Greek.

Philostratus, c. AD 170–245. Studied at Athens and, under the influence of his patroness Julia Domna, wife of Septimius Severus (emperor 193–211), wrote his main work *Life of Apollonius of Tyana*, a wonder-worker to whom divine honours were accorded, seen by some as a deliberate attack on Christianity. Greek.

★*Pliny the Elder (Caius Plinius Secundus)*, AD 23/4 to 79, born at Comum. Had a military career and then followed literary and legal pursuits. He was also a historian and biographer, and author of the *Natural History*, a compendium of 'facts, histories and observations', reading at times like a gazetteer. Commander of the fleet at Misenum in 79, he sailed thence to see the eruption of Vesuvius, but stood too close and died from the fumes. Latin.

★*Pliny the Younger (Caius Plinius Caecilius Secundus)*, *c.* AD 61–112, nephew and adopted son of Pliny the Elder. He entered the senate and fulfilled a standard administrative course. His *Letters* are his main contribution to literature and include the correspondence with Trajan about Christians when he was governor of Bithynia. Latin.

★*Plutarch* of Chaeronea, *c.* AD 50–120. Industrious philosopher and biographer, he has left, especially in his *Lives*, much information about antiquity and its thought, including philosophical and religious. Greek.

Pollio, Caius Asinius, 76 BC to AD 4. One of the Augustan poets, but important for his history of Rome 60-42 BC. Latin.

Polybius of Megalopolis, *c.* 200 to after 118 BC. Able Greek historian of the rise of Rome (*c.* 264–146 BC).

★*Pompeius Trogus* from Gallia Narbonensis. In the Augustan period he wrote in Rome zoological books used by Pliny the

Elder, and a *Universal History*, of which only Justinus' 'Epitome' survives. Latin.

Posidonius, c. 135–50 BC. Born at Apamea, studied at Athens and in the western Mediterranean, and settled permanently at Rhodes. A strong supporter of Pompey, he wrote the very influential *Histories*, later used by Sallust, Caesar, Tacitus and Plutarch, in which he includes as well as history much teaching in the realms of philosophy, politics, religion and science, showing depth as well as breadth of interest. Greek.

Propertius, Sextus, b. between 54 and 47 BC at Assisi. A Latin poet of the coterie which included Ovid.

Ptolemy (Claudius Ptolemaeus) of Alexandria, *fl.* AD 127–48. Greek astronomer, mathematician and geographer. His *Almagest* (a hybrid Arabic–Greek word meaning 'the greatest') dominated all astronomical theory until Copernicus. Ptolemy is a great source for our knowledge of many other writers of the kind in antiquity.

Quintilian (Marcus Fabius Quintilianus) of Calagurris in Spain, b. *c.* AD 30–5. An orator and teacher of oratory in Rome; his writings are in the same sphere, especially the *Institutio Oratoria*. Latin.

Sallust (Caius Sallustius Crispus), 86–35 BC. For a time an associate of Julius Caesar. Wrote history, especially *Bellum Catilinae* about the Catiline conspiracy, and the *Bellum Iugurthium* which describes the rise of Marius in connexion with the Numidian succession. Latin.

★*Seneca, Lucius Annaeus* from Corduba in Spain, b. between 4 BC and AD 1, d. 65. Was Nero's tutor and adviser, forced to commit suicide in 65. A philosopher, mainly Stoic, he wrote a number of books of an ethical character, as well as poems and tragedies. Latin.

★*Sextus Empiricus, c.* AD 200. A Greek of place unknown. A physician, wrote on medicine, philosophy and mathematics, and is a good source for Stoic teaching.

Silius Italicus, c. AD 26–101. Wrote a long historical epic on the Second Punic War. Latin.

★*Statius, Publius Papinius* of Naples, *c.* AD 45–96. Became a very popular poet in Rome, writing epics of the legendary past as well as on contemporary themes. Much admired in the Middle Ages. Latin.

★*Strabo*, a Greek of Amaseia in Pontus, *c.* 64 BC to *c.* AD 21. A Stoic and admirer of the Romans, wrote on history and geography and for his posterity is a storehouse of historical geography. Greek.

★*Suetonius (Caius Suetonius Tranquillus)* of Numidia, b. *c.* AD 69. An advocate and historian. His works include the *Lives of the Caesars*. Latin.

★*Tacitus, Cornelius*, *c.* AD 56–115. Son-in-law of Agricola whose biography he wrote (largely about Agricola's governorship of Britain 78–84), and also a treatise on the Germans. His *Histories* covered AD 14–96 but only part survives, covering AD 69 and about nine months of 70. The *Annals* (parts missing) cover from AD 14 to the death of Nero. He writes at length about the Jews. Latin.

Tibullus, Albius, b. between 55 and 48 BC. A stylish poet of whose personal history very little is known. Latin.

Valerius Maximus of the reign of Tiberius. He wrote history in the form of illustrations of moral and philosophical sentiments, drawing on previous writers and so forming a compilation much used by later writers, including some in the Middle Ages. Latin.

Varro, M. Terentius from Reate in the Sabine country, 116–27 BC. A scholar and collector of books. Most of his own works are lost but some of his *De Lingua Latina* and all three books on agriculture survive. Latin.

Velleius Paterculus of Campania, *c.* 19 BC to after AD 30. His *Historiae Romanae* is a compendium of Roman history from earliest times to AD 30; a source for the reigns of Augustus and Tiberius, but its quality may be indicated by its being ignored by other ancient historians. Latin.

Vergil (Publius Vergilius Maro) from Andes near Mantua, 70–19 BC. Famous for his *Eclogues* (idyllic poems), *Georgics* (on husbandry) which are instructive as well as for pleasure, and especially for his monumental *Aeneid*, which used Homeric mythology to create an epic about the origin of Rome. Latin.

Vitruvius Pollio, fl. 43 BC to *c.* 25 BC. A Roman architect and military engineer who wrote the only surviving work from the period on architecture and related subjects. Latin.

Appendix I: Dates

Appendix I

	BC
Alexander III (the Great) king of Macedon and general of the Greeks	336
Assumed the title 'Great King', i.e. of Persian Empire	330
Died	323

Nominal Successors   BC

Philip Arrhidaeus (half-brother of Alexander)
Alexander IV (posthumous son of Alexander)   ruled jointly   323–316

Diadochi, or Effective Successors   BC

(Most important of Alexander's generals, listed with dates of their lives.)

Antigonus I	382–301	Lysimachus	350–281
Antipater	397–319	Ptolemy I	367–282
Cassander	356–297	Seleucus I	358–281

Antigonids of Macedonia   BC

(dates of accession)

	BC
Antigonus I king of Macedonia	319
(claimed to rule whole of Alexander's Empire as king from 306; killed 301 at Battle of Ipsus against Cassander, Ptolemy and Lysimachus; Macedonia ruled 305-294 by Cassander and his sons)	
Demetrius I Poliorcetes	294
(Macedonia partitioned 285 and part of Seleucid Empire 281-280; throne disputed 280-277)	
Antigonus II Gonatas	277
Demetrius II	239
Antigonus III	229
Philip V	221
Perseus	179
(Macedonia annexed by Rome 168)	

Seleucids of Persia   BC

	BC
Seleucus I Nicator	312–280
Antiochus I Soter (co-ruler 292)	280–261
Antiochus II Theos	261–246
Seleucus II Kallinikos	246–225
Seleucus III Keraunos Soter	225–223
Antiochus III the Great	223–187
Seleucus IV Philopator	187–175
Antiochus IV Epiphanes	175–164
Antiochus V Eupator	164–162
Demetrius I Soter	162–150

Appendix I

Alexander Balas	150–145
Antiochus VI Epiphanes	145
Demetrius II Nicator	145–139, 129–125
(in the hands of the Parthians 139–129)	
Antiochus VII Euergetes, Sidetes	139–129
(subsequent rulers ineffective owing to Hasmonaean success)	

Ptolemies of Egypt

	BC
Ptolemy I Soter I Lagi	304–283
(satrap of Egypt 323–304)	
Ptolemy II Philadelphus	283–246
Ptolemy III Euergetes I	246–221
Ptolemy IV Philopator	221–205
Ptolemy V Epiphanes	205–181
Ptolemy VI Philometor	181–145
Ptolemy VII Euergetes II Physcon	170–164, 145–116
	(king of Cyrene 163–145)
Ptolemy IX Soter II Lathyrus	b. 141, d. 81
Ptolemy X Alexander I	b. 140, d. 88
Ptolemy XI Alexander II	b. 100, d. 80
Ptolemy XII Auletes	80–58, 55–51
Ptolemy XIII and Cleopatra VII	51–48
Ptolemy XIV and Cleopatra VII	47–44
(The numbering and reigns of later Ptolemies are confused. See pp. 131–2.)	

Kings of Parthia

Arsaces I	245–210 BC
Arsaces II	d. 190
Priapatius	190–176
Phraates I	176–171
Mithradates I	171–138
Phraates II	138–128
Artabanus I	128–124
Mithradates II	124–87
Gotarzes I	90–80
Orodes I	80–78
Sinatruces	77–70
Phraates III	70–58
Orodes II	57–38
Mithradates III	57–55
Pacorus I	d. 38
Phraates IV	40–3
Tiridates I	30–25
Phraates V	3 BC–AD 3
Orodes III	AD 4–7

(The succession was often challenged in Parthia as the above indicates. See pp. 15ff.)

DATES IN ROMAN HISTORY

Rise and Expansion

BC

225	Rome supreme in Italy
218–201	Second Punic War (against Carthage) ends with Rome supreme in Mediterranean
206–197	Spanish provinces acquired
200–196	Second Macedonian War. Macedonia surrenders conquests. Greece declared free
188	Peace of Apamea with Antiochus III
146	Corinth destroyed and Achaean Confederacy ended. Macedonia a Roman province

Decline of Republican Constitution

BC

139–132	First Slave War
133	Tiberius Gracchus tribune
	Pergamum formed into Roman province of Asia
123	Caius Cracchus tribune
119	Marius tribune; at height of power 107–100
105	German victory at Arausio
104–100	Second Slave War
97–79	Career of Sulla
91–87	Social War

86	Death of Marius
73–71	Revolt of Spartacus
70	Crassus and Pompey consuls
63	Cicero consul
60	Alliance of Crassus, Pompey and Julius Caesar
59	Caesar consul
55	Crassus and Pompey consuls
53	Crassus killed at Carrhae
49	Caesar crosses Rubicon. Beginning of Civil War
47	Caesar celebrates triumph over Gaul, Alexandria, Pontus, Africa
44	Caesar assassinated
42	Battle of Philippi
40	Antony and Octavian in alliance
37	Antony in Egypt
31	Battle of Actium
27	Octavian entitled Augustus
23	Augustus accepts lifelong tribuneship. End of Republic and beginning of principate, i.e. monarchic rule of 'emperors'

Roman Emperors

Augustus	23 BC–AD 14
Tiberius	AD 14–37
Caius Caligula	37–41
Claudius	41–54
Nero	54–68
Galba	68–69
Otho	69
Vitellius	69
Vespasian	69–79
Titus	79–81
Domitian	81–96
Nerva	96–98
Trajan	98–117
Hadrian	117–138
Antoninus Pius	138–161
Marcus Aurelius	161–180
Lucius Verus	161–169
Commodus	177–192
Pertinax	193
Didius Julianus	193
Septimius Severus	193–211
Clodius Albinus	193–197
Pescennius Niger	193–194
Caracalla	198–217
Geta	209–212
Macrinus	217–218

Diadumenianus	218
Elagabalus	218–222
Severus Alexander	222–235
Maximinus	235–238
Gordian I and II, Balbinus, Maximus	238
Gordian III	238–244
Philip the Arab	244–249
Decius	249–251
Trebonianus Gallus	251–253
Volusianus	251–253
Aemilianus	253
Valerian	253–260
Gallienus	253–268
Claudius II Gothicus	268–270
Quintillus	270
Aurelian	270–275
Tacitus	275–276
Florianus	276
Probus	276–282
Carus	282–283
Carinus	283–285
Numerianus	283–284
Diocletian	284–305
Galerius	305–311
Constantine	312–337

RULERS OF JUDAEA

Hasmonaeans

(Josephus *Ant.* XII.6.1 (265) gives the descent: Hasmonaeus – Symeon – John – Mattathias, who in 166 began the revolt, and who had five sons, John, Simon, Judas, Eleazar and Jonathan, according to 1 Macc. 2:1–5. Of these Judas was the military leader, but Jonathan and Simon were the only two to adopt the title of high priest and thus to be regarded as official rulers.)

	BC
Jonathan	152–142
(Jonathan succeeded his brother Judas in 160 but was proclaimed high priest in 152)	
Simon	142–135
John Hyrcanus (I)	135–104
Aristobulus I (king?)	104–103
Alexander Jannaeus (king)	103–76
Salome Alexandra	76–67
Hyrcanus II	67, 63–40
Aristobulus II (king)	67–63
Antigonus (king)	40–37

Appendix I

Herodians

Herod the Great ruled Judaea, Samaria, Galilee, Peraea, Batanaea, Trachonitis	37–4 BC
Archelaus (son by Malthace) ruled Judaea	4 BC–AD 6
Antipas (son by Malthace) ruled Galilee and Peraea	4 BC–AD 39
Philip (son by Cleopatra) ruled Ituraea and Trachonitis	4 BC–AD 34
Agrippa I (grandson of Herod) ruled territory of Philip from 37, Judaea	AD 41–44
Herod of Chalcis (brother and son-in-law of Agrippa I) ruled Chalcis	41–48
Agrippa II (son of Agrippa I) ruled:	
Chalcis	48–53
and Batanaea, Trachonitis, Gaulanitis	from 53
parts of Galilee and of Peraea	from 61
(from 66 usually absent, d. *c.* 93)	

Prefects (Praefecti) — AD

Coponius	6
Marcus Ambibulus	9–11
Annius Rufus	12–14
Valerius Gratus	15–26
Pontius Pilatus	26–36
Marcellus	36–37
Marullus	37–41
(King Agrippa I	41–44)

Procurators — AD

Cuspius Fadus	44–46
Tiberius Julius Alexander	46–48
Ventidius Cumanus	48–52
Felix	52–60
Festus	60
Albinus	62–64
Gessius Florus	64–66

Legates

(Until *c.* 60 identical with commander of legion stationed in the province; list incomplete and dates approximate.)

AD

Sextus Vettulenus Cerialis	70–72
Lucilius Bassus	72–73
Lucius Flavius Silva	73–81
Cnaeus Pompeius Longinus	81–90
Sextus Hermetidius Campanus	93–96
Atticus	99–103

Caius Julius Quadratus Bassus	102–105
Pompeius Falco	105–107
Lusius Quietus	117
Quintus Tineius Rufus	132
Sextus Julius Severus	155

HIGH PRIESTS OF JERUSALEM

Simon	after 200 BC
Onias III	d. 171

(Numbering of high priests called Onias follows Josephus. It is sometimes held that he duplicated this Onias who was really Onias II)

Joshua (Jason)	175–172
Menelaus	172–162
(Onias IV, son of murdered Onias III, set up temple at Leontopolis	160)
Jacim (Alcimus)	162–159

(Intersacerdotium, period said by Josephus to be without a high priest but believed by some to be the period of a high priest of unknown name who was the Teacher of Righteousness of Qumran 159–152)

High priests from 152 were Hasmonaeans and the list follows that of those rulers until 37; but note that Hyrcanus II was high priest also during the reign of his mother 76–67

Ananelus (Hananel, deposed 36)	37 BC
Aristobulus III	35
Ananelus reappointed	35
Jesus, son of Phiabi (deposed 23)	?
Simon, son of Boethus	23
Matthias, son of Theophilus	6
Joazar, son of Boethus	4
Jesus, son of Sie	?3
Joazar reappointed	AD 5 or 6
Ananus, son of Seth (Annas)	6
Ishmael, son of Phiabi	)
Eleazar, son of Ananus	) 15–26
Simon, son of Camithus	)
Caiaphas, son-in-law of Ananus	)
Jonathan, son of Ananus	37
Theophilus, son of Ananus	37
Simon Cantheras	41
Matthias, son of Ananus	41
Elionaeus, son of Simon Cantheras	44
Joseph, son of Camithus	46
Ananias, son of Nebedaeus	48
Jonathan	c. 55

(murdered at the instigation of Felix; see p. 114)

Ishmael, son of Phiabi	*c.* 59
Joseph Cabi, son of Simon Cantheras	*c.* 61
Ananus, son of Ananus	62
Jesus, son of Damnaeus	62
Jesus, son of Gamaliel	63 or 64
Matthias, son of Theophilus	64 and 66
Phineas, son of Samuel	67–68

NOTE: The list from 37 BC is taken from E. M. Smallwood, 'High Priests and Politics in Roman Palestine', *JTS* XIII (1962), 14–34. See also J. Jeremias, *Jerusalem in the Time of Jesus*, p. 377.

NABATAEAN KINGS

It is impossible to compose a list of accession or regnal dates, as so little is known of these kings outside occasional references in historians. Dates have to be calculated from a mixture of these, with evidence from coins and inscriptions.

Aretas I   In 168 BC Jason the high priest sought refuge with him (2 Macc. 5:8)

Erotimus   *c.* 110–100 BC raided Egypt and Syria when both were weakened by wars; may be identical with Aretas II

Aretas II   *c.* 100 (Josephus *Ant.* XIII.13.3 (360–4)).

Obodas I   *c.* 93 repulsed an attack by Alexander Jannaeus. He or perhaps a king named Rabbel repelled Antiochus XII in 87

Aretas III   *c.* 85–62 took Coele-Syria and Damascus, sided with Hyrcanus II against Aristobulus II, but withdrew before Scaurus (first Nabataean contact with Rome)

Obodas II   *c.* 62 to *c.* 57

Malichus I   *c.* 56–28. In 47 provided Caesar's cavalry; in 40 refused shelter to Herod during Parthian invasion; in 39 paid tribute to Ventidius; in 34 M. Antony gave part of his territory to Cleopatra; in 32 he sent auxiliaries to Antony; in 31 defeated by Herod; in 30 promised to support Hyrcanus in plot against Herod

Obodas III   *c.* 28 king when Aelius Gallus campaigned against southern Arabs. Obodas left government to Syllaeus; died *c.* 9–8 BC

Aretas IV   *c.* 9 BC to *c.* AD 40. Secured execution of Syllaeus in Rome; in 4 BC provided auxiliaries for Varus. Herod Antipas married one of his daughters but divorced her to marry Herodias. War followed, won by Aretas. Escaped punitive expedition of Vitellius when Vitellius turned back on hearing of death of Tiberius AD 37. May be the king or the ethnarch of 2 Cor. 11:32 which suggests Damascus under control of Aretas, perhaps 37–41

Malichus II   AD 40–70. In 67 provided auxiliaries for Vespasian. Damascus no longer under Nabataean control

Rabbel II   AD 70/1–106

Arabia Petraea was made a Roman province by Trajan in AD 106.

Appendix II: The Literature

The lists which follow name the titles of the principal Jewish and Christian documents of the period covered by this book and the abbreviated forms in which they are customarily cited.

Standard abbreviations are given below in the order in which the books are printed in the English Bible. Where the full title is customarily used without abbreviation, no stop is printed.

The Song of Songs is sometimes called the Song of Solomon. Ecclesiasticus (Ecclus.) is also referred to as The Wisdom of Jesus son of Sirach, or as The Wisdom of Ben Sirach (or of Ben Sira) or simply as Ben Sira. This book of the Apocrypha should be distinguished from Ecclesiastes (Eccles.), a book of the Old Testament.

Old Testament

Gen.	1 Kings	Eccles.	Obad.
Exod.	2 Kings	Song of Songs	Jonah
Lev.	1 Chron.	Isa.	Mic.
Num.	2 Chron.	Jer.	Nahum
Deut.	Ezra	Lam.	Hab.
Josh.	Neh.	Ezek.	Zeph.
Judg.	Esther	Dan.	Hag.
Ruth	Job	Hos.	Zech.
1 Sam.	Ps.	Joel	Mal.
2 Sam.	Prov.	Amos	

Apocrypha

1 Esdras	Wisd. of Sol.	Susanna
2 Esdras	Ecclus.	Daniel, Bel and Snake
Tobit	Baruch	Pr. of Manasseh
Judith	Letter of Jer.	1 Macc.
Rest of Esth.	Song of Three	2 Macc.

New Testament

Matt.	John	1 Cor.	Eph.
Mark	Acts	2 Cor.	Phil.
Luke	Rom.	Gal.	Col.

Appendix II

1 Thess	Titus	1 Pet.	3 John
2 Thess.	Philem.	2 Pet.	Jude
1 Tim.	Heb.	1 John	Rev.
2 Tim.	Jas.	2 John	

JOSEPHUS

War	*The Jewish War*, or *De Bello Judaico*, hence often *BJ*
Ant.	*Antiquities of the Jews*
Apion	*Against Apion*, or *Contra Apionem*
Life	*Life of Josephus*, or *Vita Jos.*

PHILO

Abr	*De Abrahamo*
Aet Mund	*De Aeternitate Mundi*
Agric	*De Agricultura*
Cher	*De Cherubim*
Conf Ling	*De Confusione Linguarum*
Congr	*De Congressu Eruditionis Gratia*
Decal	*De Decalogo*
Det Pot Ins	*Quod Deterius Potiori insidiari soleat*
Deus Imm	*Quod Deus sit Immutabilis*
Ebr	*De Ebrietate*
Exsecr	*De Exsecrationibus*
Flacc	*In Flaccum*
Fug	*De Fuga et Inventione*
Gig	*De Gigantibus*
Jos	*De Josepho*
Leg All	*Legum Allegoriae*
Leg Cai	*Legatio ad Caium*
Migr Abr	*De Migratione Abrahami*
Mut Nom	*De Mutatione Nominum*
Omn Prob Lib	*Quod omnis Probus Liber sit*
Op Mund	*De Opificio Mundi*
Plant	*De Plantatione*
Poster C	*De Posteritate Caini*
Praem Poen	*De Praemiis et Poenis*
Quaest in Gn (Ex)	*Quaestiones in Genesin (Exodum)*
Rer Div Her	*Quis Rerum Divinarum Heres sit*
Sacr AC	*De Sacrificiis Abelis et Caini*
Sobr	*De Sobrietate*
Som	*De Somniis*
Spec Leg	*De Specialibus Legibus*
Virt	*De Virtutibus*
Vit Cont	*De Vita Contemplativa*
Vit Mos	*De Vita Mosis*

Appendix II

PSEUDEPIGRAPHA

ApAB	Apocalypse of Abraham
TAb	Testament of Abraham
ApAdam	Apocalypse of Adam
TAdam	Testament of Adam
LAE	Life of Adam and Eve
Ah	Ahiqar
AnonSam	An Anonymous Samaritan Text
LetAris	Letter of Aristeas
ArisEx	Aristeas the Exegete
Aristob	Aristobulus
Art	Artapanus
2Bar	2 (Syriac) Baruch
3Bar	3 (Greek) Baruch
4Bar	4 Baruch
CavTr	Cave of Treasures
ClMal	Cleodemus Malchus
Dem	Demetrius
ElMod	Eldad and Modad
ApEl	Apocalypse of Elijah
1En	1 (Ethiopic) Enoch
2En	2 (Slavonic) Enoch
3En	3 (Hebrew) Enoch
Eup	Eupolemus
Ps-Eup	Pseudo-Eupolemus
ApocEzek	Apocryphon of Ezekiel
ApEzek	Apocalypse of Ezekiel
EzekTrag	Ezekiel the Tragedian
4Ezra	4 Ezra
GkApEzra	Greek Apocalypse of Ezra
QuesEzra	Questions of Ezra
RevEzra	Revelation of Ezra
VisEzra	Vision of Ezra
HecAb	Hecataeus of Abdera
Ps-Hec	Pseudo-Hecataeus
THez	Testament of Hezekiah
FrgsHistWrks	Fragments of Historical Works
TIsaac	Testament of Isaac
AscenIs	Ascension of Isaiah
MartIs	Martyrdom of Isaiah
VisIs	Vision of Isaiah
LadJac	Ladder of Jacob
TJac	Testament of Jacob
JanJam	Jannes and Jambres
TJob	Testament of Job
JosAsen	Joseph and Asenath

231

PrJos	Prayer of Joseph
TJos	Testament of Joseph
Jub	Jubilees
LAB	*Liber Antiquitatum Biblicarum*
LosTr	The Lost Tribes
3Macc	3 Maccabees
4Macc	4 Maccabees
5Macc	5 Maccabees
PrMan	Prayer of Manasses
Ps-Men	Pseudo-Menander
ApMos	Apocalypse of Moses
AsMos	Assumption of Moses
PrMos	Prayer of Moses
TMos	Testament of Moses
BkNoah	Book of Noah
Ps-Orph	Pseudo-Orpheus
PH	*Paraleipomena Jeremiou*
PhEPoet	Philo the Epic Poet
Ps-Philo	Pseudo-Philo
Ps-Phoc	Pseudo-Phocylides
FrgsPoetWrks	Fragments of Poetical Works
LivPro	Lives of the Prophets
ApSedr	Apocalypse of Sedrach
TrShem	Treatise of Shem
SibOr	Sibylline Oracles
OdesSol	Odes of Solomon
PssSol	Psalms of Solomon
TSol	Testament of Solomon
5ApocSyrPss	Five Apocryphal Syriac Psalms
Thal	Thallus
Theod	Theodotus
T12P	Testaments of the Twelve Patriarchs
TReu	Testament of Reuben
TSim	Testament of Simeon
TLevi	Testament of Levi
TJud	Testament of Judah
TIss	Testament of Issachar
TZeb	Testament of Zebulun
TDan	Testament of Dan
TNaph	Testament of Naphtali
TGad	Testament of Gad
TAsh	Testament of Asher
TJos	Testament of Joseph
TBenj	Testament of Benjamin
ApZeph	Apocalypse of Zephaniah
ApZos	Apocalypse of Zosimus

Appendix II

The main writings are summarized on pp. 180–3 and the principles governing the accepted abbreviations are explained there. The list is summarized here with a few additions. The initial figure denotes the number of the cave where the scroll or fragment was found.

Biblical Documents

1QIsa^a	St Mark's Isaiah
1QIsa^b	Hebrew University Isaiah

Other MSS of biblical books will be readily recognized since their abbreviations include a traditional abbreviation – or full name – of the book concerned, e.g. 5QAmos denotes a fragment from Cave 5 of the book of Amos, 6QCant a fragment from Cave 6 of the Canticum Canticorum Salomonis, or Song of Songs.

Note also:

4QLXXLev^a	Greek Fragments of Leviticus 26:2–16
4QLXXLev^b	Greek Fragments of Leviticus 2–5
4QLXXNum	Greek Fragments of Numbers 3:40–2; 4:6–9, 11–12
11QPs^b	Psalms Scroll

Other Documents

Cave 1

1QpHab	Commentary on Habakkuk
1QS	Rule of Qumran
1QSa	Rule of the Congregation (also known as the Messianic Rule)
1QSb	Collections of Blessings
1QapGen	Genesis Apocryphon
1QM	War Scroll, or Scroll of the War of the Sons of Light with the Sons of Darkness
1QH	Thanksgivings Psalms or Hymns
1, 4 or 6QEnGiants	Book of Giants fragments

Caves 2–3 and 5–10 are called 'Minor Caves', since few finds were made in them compared to those in other caves and these are all very fragmentary. The Copper Scroll (Cave 3) is an exception.

Cave 2

Fragments of Old Testament, apocryphal, juridical and liturgical texts.

Cave 3

Fragments of Old Testament, apocryphal, and other texts hard to identify, including one commentary fragment:

3QTreasure	Copper Scroll

Cave 4

4QpIsa	Commentary on Isaiah fragments
4QpNah	Commentary on Nahum fragment
4QpPs^{a,b}	Commentary on Psalms fragments
4QFlor	Florilegium, or Midrash on the Last Days
4QTestim	Testimonia, or Messianic Anthology

Cave 5

Fragments of Old Testament and apocryphal texts, including the Qumran Rule and Damascus Document.

Cave 6

Fragments of Old Testament, apocryphal and Qumran texts.

Cave 7

Very small fragments of biblical (?) texts, all in Greek.

Cave 8

Very few fragments of Old Testament texts and one of a hymn.

Caves 9 and 10

From Cave 9 one unidentified fragment and from Cave 10 one piece of inscribed pottery.

Cave 11

11QtgJob	Targum of Job
11QMelch	Melchizedek Fragment
11QTemple	Temple Scroll

From the Cairo Geniza (with fragments in some Qumran caves):

CD	Damascus Document or Rule

Abbreviations denoting Qumran texts of Pseudepigrapha will be recognized by their containing the accepted abbreviation for the Pseudepigraphon concerned (pp. 231–2), e.g.

4QEn^{a,b,c}	Fragments (in Aramaic) of the book of Enoch

For a full list of abbreviations of the Qumran writings see J. A. Fitzmyer, *The Dead Sea Scrolls: Major Publications and Tools for Study*.

RABBINIC WRITINGS

Tractates of the Mishnah

Ab.	Abot	Bek.	Bekorot
A. Zar.	Abodah Zarah	Ber.	Berakot
ʿArak.	ʿArakin	Beṣ.	Beṣah
B.B.	Baba Batra	Bikk.	Bikkurim

234

B.M.	Baba Meṣ'ia	Nid.	Niddah
B.Q.	Baba Qamma	Oh.	Oholot
Dem.	Demai	'Orl.	'Orlah
'Ed.	'Eduyyot	Par.	Parah
'Er.	'Erubin	Pe'ah	Pe'ah
Giṭ.	Giṭṭin	Pes.	Pesaḥim
Ḥag.	Ḥagigah	Qid.	Qiddušin
Ḥal.	Ḥallah	R.Š.	Roš ha-Šanah
Hor.	Horayot	Šab.	Šabbat
Ḥul.	Ḥullin	Šabu.	Šabu'ot
Kel.	Kelim	Sanh.	Sanhedrin
Ker.	Keritot	Šeb.	Šebiit
Ket.	Ketubot	Šeq.	Šeqalim
Kil.	Kilaim	Soṭ.	Soṭah
Kin.	Kinnim	Suk.	Sukkah
Ma'as.	Ma'aserot	Ta'an.	Ta'anit
Mak.	Makkot	Teb. Y.	Tebul Yom
Makš.	Makširin	Tam.	Tamid
Meg.	Megillah	Tem.	Temurah
Me'il.	Me'ilah	Ter.	Terumot
Men.	Menaḥot	Toh.	Tohorot
Mid.	Middot	'Uqs.	'Uqṣin
Miq.	Miqwa'ot	Yad.	Yadaim
M. Qat.	Mo'ed Qatan	Yeb.	Yebamot
M.Š.	Ma'aser Šeni	Yom.	Yoma
Naz.	Nazir	Zab.	Zabim
Ned.	Nedarim	Zeb.	Zebaḥim
Neg.	Nega'im		

Further Abbreviations

Tos.	Tosephta
A.R.N.	Abot deRabbi Nathan
b	Babylonian Talmud
M	Mishnah
Mid. Tan.	Midrash Tanna'im
Meg. Ta.	Megillat Ta'anit
Mek.	Mekilta deRabbi Ishmael
Mek. SbY.	Mekilta deRabbi Simeon ben Yoḥai
R.	Rabbah
y	Yerushalmi (Palestinian Talmud)
S.'Ol.R.	Seder 'Olam Rabbah
M.M.	Mishnat ha-Middot
Neof.	Neofiti I (Targum)
Targ.	Targum
P.R.	Pesiqta Rabbah
P.R.K.	Pesiqta deRav Kahana

P.R.E.	Pirqei deRabbi Eliezer
Tanḥ.	Tanḥuma
Mid.	Midrash
Targ. Ps. J.	Targum Pseudo-Jonathan
P. Targ.	Palestinian Targum
Targ. Onq.	Targum Onqelos

Not abbreviated are: Sifra (Midrash on Leviticus); Sifre (Midrash on Numbers and Deuteronomy).

Appendix III: Chronological Tables

Notes to fig. 2 (p. 239)

★ *'Herod', Herodias and Antipas.* The 'Herod' of these three is the son of Herod the Great and Mariamme II. *Ant.* XVIII.v.I. (109–11) tells how Herod the tetrarch (i.e. Antipas) fell in love with Herodias, wife of his half-brother, also called Herod, son of the high priest's daughter (i.e. Mariamme II). See *War* I.XXVIII.4 (562) for list of descendants of Herod the Great which includes this 'Herod'. Herodias as a consequence left her husband and married Antipas, who divorced his wife, daughter of Aretas IV of Nabataea. It was for this that John the Baptist rebuked Antipas. According to Mark 6:17 Herodias' first husband was called Philip, and it is often assumed that his full name was Herod Philip. He should not be confused with Philip the tetrarch, son of Herod the Great and Cleopatra of Jerusalem.

† *Agrippa II* (Acts 25: 13, 23; see p. 67)
†† *Drusilla, Felix* (Acts 24: 24; see p. 114)

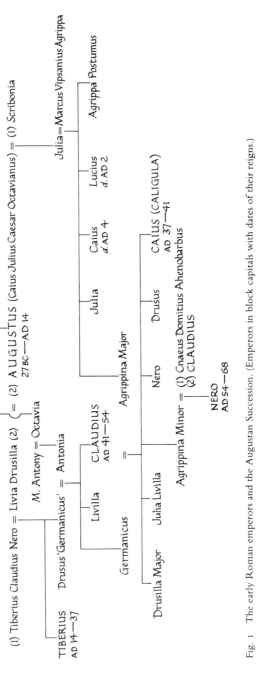

Fig. 1 The early Roman emperors and the Augustan Succession. (Emperors in block capitals with dates of their reigns.)

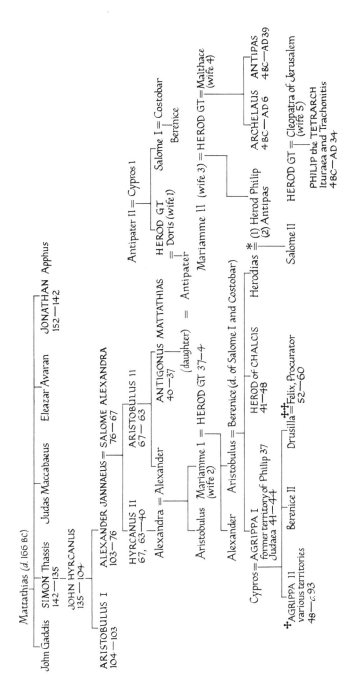

Fig. 2 Hasmonaeans and Herodians. (A select list. Rulers, in capital letters with dates of reigns, are of Judaea except where otherwise indicated.)

Bibliography

I BIBLE AND BIBLE HISTORY

Austin, M. M. *The Hellenistic World from Alexander to the Roman Conquest, A Selection of Ancient Sources in Translation*, Cambridge University Press, 1981

Bartlett, J. R. *Jews in the Hellenistic World*, Cambridge University Press, forthcoming

Bell, H. I. *Egypt from Alexander the Great to the Arab Conquest*, Oxford University Press, 1948

Beyerlin, W. (ed.) *Near Eastern Religious Texts relating to the Old Testament*, SCM Press and Westminster (Philadelphia), 1978

Bickerman, E. J. *Chronology of the Ancient World*, Thames and Hudson, rev. edn 1980

Bright, J. *A History of Israel*, SCM Press, 3rd edn 1981

The Cambridge History of the Bible, Vol. 1 (eds. P. R. Ackroyd and C. F. Evans), *From the Beginnings to Jerome*, 1970, paperback 1975; Vol. 2 (ed. G. W. H. Lampe), *The West from the Fathers to the Reformation*, 1969, paperback 1976

Carpenter, C. *Kings, Rulers and Statesmen*, Guinness Superlatives Ltd, London, 1978

de Vaux, R. *Ancient Israel* (trans. J. McHugh), Darton, Longman and Todd, 2nd edn 1965

Eissfeldt, O. *The Old Testament: an Introduction* (including the Apocrypha and Pseudepigrapha, and also the works of similar type from Qumran) (trans. P. R. Ackroyd), Blackwell (Oxford), 1965

Gowan, D. E. *Bridge between the Testaments*, Pickwick Press (Pittsburgh) and T. and T. Clark (Edinburgh), 1976

Hayes, J. H. and Miller, J. M. (eds.) *Israelite and Judaean History*, SCM Press, 1977

Hengel, M. *Jews, Greeks and Barbarians*, SCM Press, 1980

Hengel, M. *Judaism and Hellenism*, SCM Press, 1981

Jeremias, J. *Jerusalem in the time of Jesus*, Eng. trans. of 3rd German edn (1962), SCM Press, 1969

Josephus, *The Jewish War* (trans. G. A. Williamson), Penguin Classics, rev. edn of 1970, with new introd. by E. M. Smallwood, 1981

Mellor, Enid B. *The Making of the Old Testament*, Cambridge University Press, 1972

Noth, M. *The History of Israel*, A. and C. Black, 2nd Eng. edn 1960

Bibliography

O'Connor, J. M. *The Holy Land*, Oxford University Press, 1981

Pritchard, J. B. (ed.) *Ancient Near Eastern Texts relating to the Old Testament*, Princeton University Press, 3rd edn 1969

Safrai, S. and Stern, M. (eds.) *The Jewish People in the First Century*, Van Gorcum (Assen), 1974

Schürer, E. *The History of the Jewish People in the Age of Jesus Christ* (new English version rev. and ed. by G. Vermes and F. Millar), T. and T. Clark (Edinburgh): Vol. 1, 1973; Vol. 2, 1979

Smallwood, E. M. *The Jews under Roman Rule*, Brill (Leiden), corrected edn 1981

Stone, M. E. *Scriptures, Sects and Visions: A Profile of Judaism from Ezra to the Jewish Revolts*, Fortress Press (Philadelphia), 1980

Tarn, W. W. and Griffith, G. T. *Hellenistic Civilization*, Arnold, 3rd rev. edn 1952

Thomas, D. Winton (ed.) *Documents from Old Testament Times*, Harper and Row (New York), 1961

Wiseman, D. J. (ed.) *Peoples of Old Testament Times*, Oxford University Press, 1973

Yadin, Y. *Bar-Kokhba*, Weidenfeld and Nicolson, 1971

Yadin, Y. (ed.) *Jerusalem Revealed*, Yale University Press and Israel Exploration Society, 1976

Yadin, Y. *Masada*, Weidenfeld and Nicolson, 1966

2 GREEK VERSIONS, APOCRYPHA AND PSEUDEPIGRAPHA

Charles, R. H. (ed.) *Apocrypha and Pseudepigrapha of the Old Testament*, Vol. 1, *Apocrypha*, Vol. 2, *Pseudepigrapha*, Oxford University Press, 1913

Charlesworth, J. H. *The Pseudepigrapha and Modern Research*, Scholars Press (Montana), 1976 (reissued with Supplement, 1981)

de Jonge, M. *Outside the Old Testament*, Cambridge University Press, forthcoming

Eissfeldt, O. *The Old Testament* (see above, under 1 Bible and Bible History)

Jellicoe, S. *The Septuagint and Modern Study*, Oxford University Press, 1968

Nickelsburg, G. W. E. *Jewish Literature between the Bible and the Mishnah*, SCM Press and Fortress Press (Philadelphia), 1981

3 QUMRAN

Fitzmyer, J. A., s.j. *The Dead Sea Scrolls, Major Publications and Tools for Study, with an Addendum*, Scholars Press (Montana), 1977

Knibb, M. A. *The Qumran Community*, Cambridge University Press, forthcoming

241

Bibliography

Vermes, G. *The Dead Sea Scrolls in English*, Penguin Books, 1962
Vermes, G. *The Dead Sea Scrolls: Qumran in Perspective*, Collins (London), 1977; rev. edn Fortress Press (Philadelphia), 1981

4 EARLY RABBINIC JUDAISM

Bonsirven, J., S.J. *Textes Rabbiniques*, Pontificio Istituto (Rome), 1955
Bowker, J. *The Targums and Rabbinic Literature*, Cambridge University Press, 1969
Danby, H. *The Mishnah*, Oxford University Press, 1933
Maccoby, H. *Early Rabbinic Writings*, Cambridge University Press, forthcoming
Montefiore, C. G. and Loewe, H. *A Rabbinic Anthology*, Meridian Books (New York), 1963
Neusner, J. *First Century Judaism in Crisis*, Abingdon Press (New York), 1975
Neusner, J. *There We Sat Down: Talmudic Judaism in the Making*, Abingdon Press (New York), 1972
Sandmel, S. *Judaism and Christian Beginnings*, Oxford University Press, 1978
Strack, H. L. *Introduction to the Talmud and Midrash*, Meridian Books (New York), 1959

5 EARLY CHRISTIAN WRITINGS

Cross, F. L. *The Early Christian Fathers*, Duckworth, 1960
Cross, F. L. and Livingstone, E. A. (eds.) *Oxford Dictionary of the Christian Church*, Oxford University Press, 2nd enlarged and rev. edn 1974
Eusebius, *The History of the Church* (trans. G. A. Williamson), Penguin Classics, rev. edn 1981
Hennecke, E. *New Testament Apocrypha*, 2 Vols. (trans. R. McL. Wilson), SCM Press, 1974
Quasten, J. *Patrology*, Vol. 1, *The Beginnings of Patristic Literature*, Spectrum (Utrecht), 1950
Stanton, G. N. *Outside the New Testament*, Cambridge University Press, forthcoming
Stevenson, J. (ed.) *A New Eusebius*, SPCK, 1965

Hammond, N. G. L. and Scullard, H. H. (eds.) *The Oxford Classical Dictionary*, Oxford University Press, 2nd edn 1970

Bibliography

Millar, F. et al. *The Roman Empire and its Neighbours*, Weidenfeld and Nicolson, 1967, 2nd edn Duckworth, 1981
Scullard, H. H. and Van der Heyden, A. A. M. *Shorter Atlas of the Classical World*, Nelson (Edinburgh), 1962

7 CLASSICAL LITERATURE

Rose, H. J. *Handbook of Latin Literature*, Methuen, 3rd edn 1954
Rose, H. J. *Handbook of Greek Literature*, Methuen, 4th edn 1957
Whittaker, M. *Jews and Christians: Graeco-Roman Views*, Cambridge University Press, forthcoming

Index

(Figures in brackets indicate dates or biblical references)

Amel-marduk (Evil-Merodach), 1

Amora (teacher), 195

anachoresis, definition of, 135

Ananus (Annas of Luke 3:2, John 18:13, 24, Acts 4:6), high priest appointed by Quirinius, 109; and death of James, brother of Jesus, 115

Ananias, converted Izates and others, 27

Ananias, high priest, murdered in revolt, 116

Anilaeus, Jew of Nehardea, 29

annona, corn supply, 53f, 126

Antigonus I, Alexander's successor in Macedonia, 8, 127

Antigonus II, struggle with Egypt, 129f

Antigonus Mattathias (40–37 BC), last Hasmonaean, 17, 25, 99; ruled with Parthian support, 17, 97; titles on coins of, 98; killed Herod's brother Joseph in battle, 99; beheaded, 99

Antioch in Syria, capital of Seleucid empire, 8; staging post, 23; Jewish population of, 82

Antiochus III, the Great (223–187 BC), defeat of Ptolemy V at Panion (200), 13, 83, 130; peace with Rome at Apamea (188), 13; death in Elymais, 13, 85; transportation of Jews to Phrygia, 35; confrontation with Rome, 41f; financial and material aid to Jews, 79, 85

Antiochus IV, Epiphanes (175–164 BC), 13; enemy of the Jews, 14, 87; attack on Mithradates I, king of Parthia (166/165), 14; expelled from Egypt, 42, 87; split in Seleucid dynasty, 85; dedicated altar to Zeus Olympios in Temple, 87f; death, 88

Antiochus VII (c. 139–129 BC), 14f; lost Parthia, 89; death, 90

Antipas, Herod (4 BC–AD 39) (Luke 3:1), 106; hosted negotiations between Rome and Parthia, 18, 107; tetrarch of Galilee and Peraea, 105; relations with Aretas IV of Nabataea, 106f; marriage to Herodias, 107; beheading of John the Baptist (Mark 6:17–28), 107; buildings, especially Tiberias, 107; unsuccessfully claimed Philip's territory and a royal title, 107; banished to Gaul, 107

Antipater of Sidon, 210

Antipater, son of Herod, designated heir, 104; disgrace and death, 105

Antipater, the Idumaean, and Pompey, 74; support for Hyrcanus II, 93, 95; support for Caesar, 96, 136; procurator of Judaea, 96; murder by Malichus (43 BC), 97

Antoninus Pius (AD138–161), excellent relations with senate, 69; character, 69; relations with Jews, 125

Antonius, Marcus (Mark Antony), campaign to Media and death, 17, 51, 101, 133; joins Caesar, 48; triumvir with Octavian and Lepidus (43 BC) 49; marriage to Octavia, 50; and to Cleopatra, 50f, 132; friendship with Herod, 50, 97f; in command of Asia, 97; frees Jewish slaves, 97

Apamea, peace of, 13, 42

Apion of Alexandria, provoked Josephus' *Against Apion*, 210f

Apocalypse of Abraham, 168

Apocalypse of Adam, 169

Apocalypse of Zosimus, 170

Apocrypha (hidden), periods of writing, 31f; definition of, 155; changes in meaning, 155f; list of books in Septuagint Apocrypha, 156f; Vulgate Apocrypha, 158; English Apocrypha, 158; fragments from Qumran, 182; NT Apocrypha, 198f

Apocryphon of John (brother of James), gnostic vision, 207

apologists, replies to attacks of pagan writers, 201ff

Appian of Alexandria, historian, records three destructions of Jerusalem, 123; 211

Apuleius, 211

Aquila (c. AD 117–38), revision of OT translation, 154, 193, 196

Aramaic, as common language, 20f, 81

Archelaus of Cappadocia, and Herod the Great, 34

Archelaus (4 BC–AD 6), son of Herod, 34; ruler of Judaea, 105; cruelty and banishment, 106

Aretas, support for Hyrcanus II, 93

Aristeas, Letter of, origins of Septuagint, 153; content of, 159

Aristides, early apologist, 202

Aristo of Pella, first apologist against Jews, 202

Aristobulus I (104–103 BC), high priest and possibly king, 91, 98, 147

Aristobulus II (67–63 BC), 25f; and

Index

Index

defeated at Carrhae (53 BC), 16f, 46, 95; crushed slave revolt, 45; plundered Temple, 95

Croesus (*c.* 560–46 BC), 33

crucifixion, first Jewish use of, 92; of Jesus, 110

Ctesiphon, 23; referred to in Josephus and the Talmud, 24, 30

culture, influence of Greek, 42; Jewish opposition to 'alternative', 87

Cumanus, Ventidius (AD 48–52), procurator of Judaea, suppression of Jews, 113

Cuspius Fadus (AD 44–6), procurator of Judaea, suppression of rising under Theudas (Acts 5:36), 113

Cyprus, Phoenician colonies in, 82; decree against Jews following revolt, 143

Cyrene (Cyrenaica), 6; history and extent of, 140f; Jewish relations with Rome in, 141f; restoration of, 142

Cyrus, king of Persia (550–530 BC), 2, 7; conquest of Babylon and extent of empire (539), 9f; policy, 21f, 25; defeated Croesus of Lydia, 33

Cyrus Cylinder, the Restoration of the Jews, 3, 10, 21f

Damascus, staging-post, 23; capital of Syria/Aram, 79; Jewish population of, 83; Paul's visit to, 83

Damascus Rule or Damascus Covenant, historical introduction of, 175f; dating from, 176; varying attitude to foreign domination, 176f; description of, 181

Darius I (522–486 BC), extent of empire, 7; inscription at Behistun and defeat at Marathon (490), 10

Decapolis, 94, 116

Decius, C. Messius Quintus (AD 249–51), first general persecution of Christians, 72; killed in battle with Goths, 72

Decretum Gelasianum, 169

Delos, early inscription referring to synagogue, 147

Demetrius I (162–150 BC), 85; attacks on Judas Maccabaeus and death, 89

Demetrius II (145–139, 129–126 BC), imprisoned by Mithradates I, 14, 89; death, 90; intrigue with Ptolemy VI, 131

Demetrius III, support for Pharisees, 92; mention in Commentary on Nahum, 177, 179

Demiurge (workman), gnostic doctrine of, 205f

Deuteronomic history, 31

Diadochi, Alexander's successors, 8, 127

Diaspora (dispersion), 4ff

Didache (teaching), dating and content of, 199f

Dio Cassius of Nicaea, historian, coup against Hadrian, 68, 71, 122ff; ban on Jews in Cyprus, 143, 212

Diocletian (Diocles) (AD 284–305), 37; successes of, 72f; persecution of Christians, 73; reforms of tax system, 135

Diodorus Siculus of Agyrium, 212

Dionysius of Halicarnassus, 212

Domitian (AD 81–96), 65–8

'Donations', vision of Eastern empire by Antony and Cleopatra, 132f

Drusilla, sister of Agrippa II, wife of Felix (Acts 24:24), 67

Drusus, stepson of Augustus, 55

Dura-Europos, 15, 23; excavation of site, 30, 126, 147

Ebla, (Tel Mardikh), discoveries at, 81

Egypt, 6; Jewish mercenaries in (455 BC), 11; Roman infiltration of, 42; Tiberius' attitude to religion of, 74; Caesar's war with Ptolemy XIII, 48, 96; relations with Greek overlords, 127f; establishment of independence, 129f; later Ptolemies, 131f; civil war, 131; settlement by Augustus, 133; commerce, 133; Roman administration and taxation, 133ff; influence of Greek culture, 134, 138; defeat of Jews (AD 119), 139

Elagabalus (AD 218–22), 70

Eleazar, captain of Temple Guard, 115f; at fall of Jerusalem, 119

Eleazar b. Azariah, and Gamaliel II, 189, 192

Elephantine, 132, 136; temple at, 145

Elephantine, papyri, date of Nehemiah and Ezra, 3f; evidence of Jewish settlement, 136; folk tale of Ahiqar, 166f

Eliezer b. Jacob, 191

Ennius, Quintus, of Rudiae, 212

1 Enoch (Ethiopic Enoch), content of, 163; fragments from Qumran, 182

2 Enoch (Slavonic Enoch), 163

Epictetus of Hierapolis, 212

Index

haggadah (story-telling), 32, 165, 168, 197

Haggai, on rebuilding of Temple, 4

halakah (way), legalistic teaching, 26, 32, 103, 185, 197

Hananel, Babylonian Jew, high priest, 25, 100

Hanina (or Hananiah), 191

Hannibal, flight to Antiochus (202 BC), 13, 41; suicide (*c.* 183 BC), 13

Hanukkah, 187

Harran, 17, 20, 27

ḥasidim (pious ones), 91; origin and beliefs of, 172

Hasmonaeans, Parthians show favour to, 14, 25; revolt against Seleucids, 14, 88, 157; as high priests, 89ff; links with Rome, 91; Herod's attitude to, 99f; fortresses of, 103; links with Qumran period, 171

Hecataeus, Egyptian historian, 84

Helena of Adiabene, conversion of, 26ff; became Nazirite, 28f; burial in Jerusalem, 28f

Hellenism, values of, 85f; influence on Judaism, 86f, 103, 138, 176; Parthian attitude to, 14; Herod's support for, 102; in Egypt, 127f, 134; elements of in Essene teaching, 174f; gnostic systems in, 204

Heracleon (*fl.* AD 145–80), gnostic teacher, 206

Herod of Chalcis, given right by Claudius to appoint high priest, 113, 115

Herod the Great (37–4 BC), besieged Jerusalem (37), 17; and Babylonian Jews, 25f; patronage of Athens and other cities, 36, 102f; friendship with Antony, 50, 100; governor of Syria, 97; co-tetrarch of Judaea, 97; fled to Masada, 97; recognition by senate as king of Judaea, 98; reign of, 99ff; attitude to Hasmonaeans, 99f; marriage to Mariamme I, 99f; relations with Octavian, 101; execution of Hyrcanus, 101; family intrigues, 101f; building activity, 102f; Temple of, 102; rebuilding of Hasmonaean fortresses, 103; respect for Pharisees and Essenes, 103; expansion of territories by Augustus, 103f; relations with Agrippa, 104; designated Antipater as successor, 104; quarrels amongst sons, 104f; opposition from Syllaeus of Nabataea,

105; council at Berytus, 105; death and will, 105f

Herodes Atticus of Athens, 213

Herodian of Syria, historian, 71, 213

Herodias, wife of Herod Philip and Antipas, 107

Herodotus of Halicarnassus in Caria (*c.* 484–424 BC), 33; reference to Syria, 78

Hexapla, of Origen, 155

Hezekiah, received envoys from Merodach-Baladan, 20; Testament of in the Martyrdom of Isaiah, 160

high priests, descent from Zadok and importance of office, 83, 166; covenant of Phinehas (Ecclus. 45:23f), 85; Menelaus, non-Zadokite, 87; Jonathan, first Hasmonaean, 89f; Antigonus, last Hasmonaean, 17; political appointments of, 109; appointment by Herod of Chalcis, 113; murder of Jonathan, 114; cessation of office, 121; and *ḥasidim*, 172

Hillel, 26, 188f; school of, 190; dominant halakhic interpreter, 190

ḥiṣonim (outside), rejected books from the canon, 155

Historia Augusta, biographies of emperors, 71; unrest in Diaspora, 122f; 125

Hiyya, rabbi editor of *tosephta*, 197

Horace (Quintus Horatius Flaccus) (65–8 BC), 74, 213

Hyrcanus II, 25; and Pompey, 74, 93; appointed high priest by Salome, 93; ruler (67, 63–40 BC), 93, 97; support from Aretas of Nabataea, 93; power restricted, 94f; support for Caesar, 96; ethnarch of Judaea, 96; made unfit for high priesthood, 98; taken prisoner to Parthia, 98; execution of, 101

Ignatius (*c.* AD 35–*c.* 107), Letters of, 200; 201

Intersacerdotium, 178

Irenaeus (*c.* AD 130–202), fragments from Papias, 201; opposition to gnosticism, 204f; teaching of, 207

Isaiah Scrolls, 180

Ishmael b. Elisha (d. AD 135), 193

Isidorus, Alexandrian Greek nationalist, 139

Issus, battle of (333 BC), 7, 12

Italy, 6; Jews in, 37ff; subjugation to Rome, 43f

Izates of Adiabene, conversion, 26f; burial in Jerusalem, 28

Index

Jamnia, 26; historical importance of, 120; establishment of academy in, 120; Council at, 151

Jannes and Jambres (2 Tim.3:8), 169

Jason, high priest (175–172 BC), support for Jerusalem as hellenistic city, 86; Zadokite, 87; usurped by Menelaus, 87

Jerusalem, respect for, 4f; destruction of (597 and 587 BC), 20, (37 BC), 99, (AD 70), 67, 119; under Seleucids and Ptolemies, 79f; capture of by Pompey, 94; ruled by aristocratic council, 95; walls rebuilt, 96; Herod's buildings in, 102f; internecine war, 116ff; renamed Aelia Capitolina, 122f; 'ploughing up' or marking of *pomerium*, 124; colony with three toparchies, 124; idealized in Letter of Aristeas, 159

Jesus, active in reign of Tiberius (Luke 3:1ff), 58; visited Phoenician cities (Matt. 15:22 and Mark 7:26), 82; crucifixion, 110; references to in Vision of Isaiah, 160f; Son of Man sayings in 1 Enoch, 163; parallel sayings in Ahiqar, 167; relations with Pharisees, 184, 186f; and 'traditions' (Oral Law), 186; possible references to in Talmud, 192; gnostic teaching about, 205f

Jewish revolt, outbreak of (AD 66), 63, 115; extent of, 116ff

Jews, attempt to set up places of worship within *pomerium* of Rome, 73; relations with Caesar and Pompey, 73f; relations with Augustus and Tiberius, 74; relations with Caius and Claudius, 74f, 138f; expulsion from Rome, 73, 75; catacombs in Rome, 75; known as Antiochenes, 79, 82; in Syria and Phoenicia, 82f; in Judaea, 83ff; privileges granted by Antiochus III, 85; uprisings against Rome, 95; Caesar's protection of, 96; united with Samaritans against Archelaus, 106; granted privileges by Vitellius, 111; revolt of (AD 66), 63, 115ff; return to Palestine, 126; in Alexandria, 128f, 136ff; defeat in Egypt (AD 119), 139; rebellion in Cyrenaica against Rome (AD 115), 141; Diaspora in later centuries, 143ff; defence against hatred of in 3 Macc., 161

Johanan b. Zakkai, 26; established academy in Jamnia, 120f, 189; and Oral Law, 186; establishment of

Judaism centred on community, 191; disciples of, 192

John Hyrcanus (135–104 BC), 15; high priest, 90f, 94; Qumran dating, 171; possible 'Wicked Priest', 179; mentioned in Josephus, 184f

John of Gischala, assistant to Josephus, 117; in Jerusalem, 118f

John the Baptist, beheaded by Antipas, 107

Jonathan (160–142 BC), 89; possible 'Wicked Priest', 90, 178f

Jonathan b. Uzziel, 191

Joseph and Asenath, 169f

Josephus, the Restoration, 3, 22f; Demetrius II and Parthia, 14; meeting hosted by Herod Antipas, 18; Hananel, high priest, 25; Herod's private army at Bathyra, 26; conversion of rulers of Adiabene, 26ff; Antiochus III's transportation of Jews to Phrygia, 35f; forecasts Vespasian as emperor, 65, 117; favourable measures to Jews in Alexandria, 75; life of, 76, 117; writings of, 76f, 81, 211; Jewish population in Syria, 82; Hezekiah and Onias II, 84; Jewish privileges from Antiochus III, 85; delegation of 'the nation' to Pompey, 94; building of Herod's Temple, 103; incidents relating to Pilate, 109f; riot under Cumanus, 113; murder of high priest Jonathan, 114; abolition of sacrifice on behalf of Caesar, 115; in charge of Galilee, 116f; siege of Jotapata, 117; Onias III (IV) in Egypt, 136; refutation of anti-Jewish slanders, 137; instructions to pray, 146; synagogues, 147f; fixed list of the Writings, 150; details of canonical books, 152; Essenes, 173ff; Intersacerdotium, 178; Pharisees, 184f

Jotapata, siege of, 117

Juba II, king of Mauretania, 52f

Jubilees, 160; fragments from Qumran, 182

Judaea, under Romans, 94ff; settlement by Pompey, 94; divided into five districts, 95; Caesar's restoration of, 96; Herod appointed king of, 98; earthquake in, 101; Archelaus last Herodian ruler, 106; became Roman province (AD 6), 108; military colonies established, 120; Bar Kokhba revolt, 123f; became Syria-Palaestina, 125

251

Index

Judah ha-Nasi' I (AD 135–219) (*nasi'* = chief), rabbi, restoration of religious observances, 125; in Beth She'arim, 126; relaxed laws on sabbatical years, 127; chief compiler of Mishnah, 189, 197; life and work, 194f

Judaism, formation as system of belief and practice, 1; influence of priests from Babylon and Jerusalem, 31; piety of Jews in Phrygia, 35f; Roman attitude to, 74; hellenistic influence, 86f, 103, 176f; Antiochus' outrages against, 87f; emergence of Pharisees, 92; opposition to census (cp. 2 Sam. 24), 109; after destruction of Temple, 120ff; centred on Galilee in later centuries, 147; commendation of in Wisdom of Solomon, 156; exaltation of in Letter of Aristeas, 159; traditions of Stoicism, 162; Essene teaching, 174; early rabbinic, 184ff; establishment of community view of, 191; gnostic systems in, 204

Judas Maccabaeus (*c.* 166–160 BC), guerilla warfare led by, 88f; death at Elasa, 89

Judas of Galilee, armed protest against census, 109, 116

Judas of Sepphoris, popular leader during war of Varus, 106

Jude, brother of Jesus, Eusebius' story of grandsons, 122

Jupiter Capitolinus, supported by Jewish Temple tax, 121

Justin Martyr, apologist, Bar Kokhba's persecution of Christians, 123; life and works, 202, 209

Juvenal (Decimus Junius Juvenalis), dislike of Jews, 74, 214

Kittim (Cypriots), 82, 179f

Laenas, C. Popillius, in Egypt, 42

Lampo, Alexandrian Greek nationalist, 139

laographia, definition of, 138

Law, composition of the Pentateuch, 149; emphasis on validity of in Jubilees, 160

Legatio ad Caium, list of places inhabited by Jews, 5f, 36; reason for, 59; pogrom under Flaccus, 138, 140

Leontopolis, Jewish temple and settlement established by Onias IV, 136, 145, 179

Lepidus, triumvir with Antony and Octavian, 49; retirement of (36 BC), 50; death (12 BC), 54

Letter of Barnabas, 199

Letter to Diognetus, 201

Liber Antiquitatum Biblicarum (or *Pseudo-Philo*), 170

Life of Adam and Eve (and Apocalypse of Moses), 166

Lives of the Prophets, 170

Livy (Titus Livius) of Patavium, 214

Longinus, 214

Longinus, C. Cassius, commander in Judaea, 95

Lucan (Marcus Annaeus Lucanus), 214

Lucian of Samosata (b. *c.* AD 120), opponent of Christianity, 201, 214

Lucilius Bassus, capture of Herodium and Machaerus, 119

Lucius Verus (joint emperor with M. Aurelius, AD 161–9), 69

Lucretius (Titus Lucretius Carus), 214

Lusius Quietus, legate of Judaea (AD 117), 122, 143

Maccabees, *see* Hasmonaeans

3 Maccabees, 161

4 Maccabees, 161f

Macedonian empire (*c.* 333–320 BC), 7

Macrinus (AD 217–18), 70

Maecenas C., friend of Augustus and patron of arts, 50

Manetho, author of Egyptian chronicle, 128; reports hostility to Jews, 137

Manichaeism, 182

Marathon, battle of (490 BC), 10

Marcion (*fl c.* AD 140, d. *c.* AD 160), 201; teachings of, 206

Marcus Antonius Aurelius (AD 161–80), joint emperor with L. Verus (161–9), and with Commodus (177–80), 69; Stoic philosopher, 69; campaigns, 69; *Meditations*, 69; opposed by Avidius Cassius, legate of Syria, 126; 201; 202f

Marduk, god of Cyrus, 21f

Mariamme I, wife of Herod, 99f; execution of, 101

Marius C., military reforms under, 44

Martial (Marcus Valerius Martialis) of Bilbilis, 214

Martyrdom of Isaiah (and Ascension of Isaiah), 160f

Martyrs, Acts of the, 208f

Masada, Herod at, 97; rebuilding of, 102;

Index

Onias II, high priest (*c*. 245–220 BC), refused tribute to Ptolemy III, 84

Onias III, high priest, deposed and murdered (171 BC) (2 Macc. 4:32–4), 85, 87, 179; flight to Egypt, 136

Onias IV, temple and settlement at Leontopolis, 136; 145; 179

Oral Law, 149f; origin of, 186; Jewish traditions regarding, 187; 197

Oreine, one of toparchies of Jerusalem (Luke 1:39, 65), 124

Origen (*c*. AD 185–255), Symmachus' translations of Scriptures, 154f; Hexapla, 155; 169; 200; teaching and influence of, 208

Orodes II (57–38 BC), battle of Carrhae (53), 16f

Orosius, expulsion of Jews from Rome, 75; 139

Otho (AD 69), 64

Ovid (Publius Ovidius Naso), 215

Oxyrhyncus, literary fragments found at, 134

Pacorus (d. 38 BC), raid into Syria (51), 17; support for Antigonus, 17, 97; death, 17

Palestine, 6; under Ptolemies and Seleucids, 8; derivation of, 78

Palestinian Talmud (or Yerushalmi), 195

Pallas, financial secretary of Claudius, 61; brother of Felix, 114

Palmyra, 23, 72

Panion (Panias, later Caesarea Philippi), battle of (200 BC), 13, 83, 130; added to Herod's territories, 104; rebuilt by Philip (Mark 8:27), 108

Pantaenus (*fl. c.* AD 170–90), Christian teacher at Alexandria, 208

Papias (*c*. AD 60–130), fragments of *Expositions of the Oracles of the Lord*, 201

Parthenius of Nicaea, 215

Parthia, the Diaspora, 5; period of Jewish history (*c*. 140 BC–*c*. AD 226), 7; Mithradates I, king of, and the Seleucids, 14f; struggle with Rome, 16ff, 41, 50; support for Antigonus, 97f; conquered by Ventidius and Antony, 98; peace with Rome, 18, 107

patres, patrician senators, 37

Paul, native of Tarsus, 34; contests Essene heresy among Colossians, 36; persecution with Peter under Nero, 63;

earliest sure testimony to Christians in Rome, 75; visit to Damascus (Acts 9), 83; before Felix and Drusilla, 114; Letters of, 198, 201; Marcion's canon, 206

Pentateuch, priestly recension of, 31

persecution, of Jews in Babylonia and Seleucia, 30; of Christians in Rome, 63; of Jews and Christians under Domitian, 67f; of Christians by Decius and Valerian, 72; Maccabaean response to, 88; of Christians, 123

Perseus (179–168 BC), contacts with Rome, 42

Persian empire (539–333 BC), 7

Persius (Aulus Persius Flaccus), 215

Pertinax, Publius Helvius (AD 193), attempts at reform, 69

Perusine War, under Augustus, 49f

Pescennius Niger, rival to Septimius Severus, 69

pesher (meaning or interpretation), in Qumran fragments, 177, 180f

Petronius, 215

Petronius, legate of Syria, preparation of Caius' statue, 112

Pharisees, emergence of, 91; political power of, 92; peace with Salome Alexandra, 92f; Herod's respect for, 103; 177; comments on from Josephus, 184; oral teaching of, 186f; list of the 'Fathers', 188f

Pharsalus, battle of, 48, 96

Phasael, Herod's brother and co-tetrarch of Judaea, 25, 97; suicide, 98

Philip (4 BC–AD 34), tetrarch of Gaulanitis, Trachonitis, Batanaea and Panias, 105f; coinage inscriptions, 107f; wise rule of, 107f; marriage to Salome who danced before Antipas (Mark 6: 17–28), 108; died without heir, 108

Philip II (359–336 BC) of Macedon, 11

Philip V (221–179 BC) of Macedon, confrontation with Rome, 41f

Philip the Arab (Julius Philippus) (AD 244–9), led thousandth anniversary of foundation of Rome (248), 71; good relations with senate, 71f; pressure from Goths, 72

Philippi, battles of, deaths of Brutus and Cassius, 49, 97

Philo (*c*. 15 BC–AD 45), *Legatio ad Caium*, 5f, 36, 59, 78, 138; Agrippa's letter on Pilate, 109; incident of shields, 110;

Against Flaccus, pogrom under Flaccus, 138, 140; life and works of, 140; mention of synagogues, 147f; description of Essenes, 172f

Philodemus of Gadara, 216

Philostratus, 216

Phoenicia, 6; cities of, 80; shared Canaanite culture, 80; commerce of, 81; alphabetic writing in, 81; colonial foundations by, 81f; Jesus' visits to, 82

Phraates II (138–128 BC), defeated Antiochus VII, 15

Phraates III (70–58 BC), alliance with Tigranes (64), 16

Phraates IV (40–3 BC), 25

phylacteries, from Qumran, 183

Pirqe Abot, *see* Abot

Pliny the Elder (Caius Plinius Secundus) (AD 23/4–79), 169; description of Essenes, 175; 216

Pliny the Younger (Caius Plinius Caecilius Secundus) (AD 61–112), criticism of Domitian, 68; approval of Trajan, 68; 216

Plotinus, Neoplatonist philosopher, 72

Plutarch of Chaeronea, 216

politeuma, definition of, 137; Jewish in Alexandria, 137f; 143

Pollio, Caius Asinius, 217

Polybius of Megalopolis, 216

Polycarp (*c.* AD 70–*c.* AD 156), *Letter to the Philippians*, 200f; and Cerinthus, 205; 208

Pompeius Trogus, 216f

Pompey (Cnaeus Pompeius) (d. 48 BC), fixed boundaries with Parthians (64 BC), 16; consul with Crassus (70 BC), 45; member of first triumvirate, 46; death, 48, 95, 161; relations with Jews, 74; siege of Jerusalem, 80, 94; negotiations with Hasmonaeans, 93f

Pontius Pilate, prefecture of (AD 26–36), 58, 109ff; adverse comments on by Philo and Josephus, 109f; crucifixion of Jesus, 110; character in gospels, 111; dismissal owing to massacre at Mount Gerizim, 111

Posidonius of Apamea, 217

Praetorian Guard, emperor's bodyguard, 58; importance of prefect of, 58, 59, 62, 64, 70, 72; size reduced, 67; opposed to reforms of Pertinax, 69

prefect (*praefectus*), definition of, 108

Probus (AD 276–82), 72

procurators, of Judaea, Jewish revolt against, 63; definition of, 108; Coponius and successors, 108ff; Cuspius Fadus and successors, 113ff; misgovernment under Albinus and Gessius Florus, 115

Propertius, Sextus, 217

prophetic books, formation in Babylon, 31; composition of, 149f

proseuche (prayer), changes in usage, 146, 147

Psalm 151, 167

Psalms of Solomon, 161

Psalms Scroll, from Qumran, 167, 182

pseudepigrapha, definition of, 158; preservation in various languages, 158; main books of, 159ff; Martyrdom of Isaiah, 160f; Psalms of Solomon, 161; Odes of Solomon, 161; Odes or Canticles, 162; Sibylline Oracles, 162; 1 Enoch, 163; 4 Ezra, 164; 2 Baruch, 164; 3 and 4 Baruch, 165; Testaments of the Twelve Patriarchs, 165f; Ahiqar, 167; modern rearrangements of, 167f; haggadic midrash, 168; fragments from Qumran, 182

Pseudo-Phocylides, 170

Ptolemy (*fl.* AD 140), gnostic *Letter to Flora*, 206

Ptolemy (Claudius Ptolemaeus), of Alexandria, 217

Ptolemy I (304–283 BC), extent of empire, 8; worship of Sarapis, 128; 129

Ptolemy II (283–246 BC), struggle with Macedonia and Syria, 129f; origins of Septuagint, 153, 159

Ptolemy III (246–221 BC), Library at Alexandria, 129; extension of empire, 130; synagogues under, 147

Ptolemy IV (221–203 BC), victory at Raphia, 83, 130; 161

Ptolemy V (203–181 BC), defeat at Panion, 13, 130; loss of Syria–Palestine, 130

Ptolemy VI (181–145 BC), intrigue with Alexander Balas and Demetrius II, 131

Ptolemy VII (Euergetes II) (170–164, 145–116 BC), attempts at reform, 131; king of Cyrene (163–145), 141; 162

Punic War, Second (218–201 BC), 44

Purim, 187

Index

Index

48; of Augustus (29 BC), 52; of
Pompey, 94; of Titus, 119; of Marcus
Aurelius, 126
Trypho, pretender to Syrian kingdom,
supported by Jonathan, 89f

Ugarit, *see* Ras Shamra
Ur of the Chaldees, 20

Valentinus (*fl.* AD 140), gnostic teachings
of, 205f
Valerian (AD 253–60), defeated at Edessa
(260), 19; persecution of Christians by,
72
Valerius Maximus, 218
Varro, M. Terentius of Reate, 218
Varus, suppression of Judaean rebellion
(4 BC), 56, 106; suicide (AD 9), 56f
Velleius Paterculus of Campania, 218
Vergil (Publius Vergilius Maro) of Andes
(70–19 BC), 52, 218f
Vespasian (Titus Flavius Vespasianus)
(AD 69–79), in Judaea, 63, 65;
campaigns in Britain, Africa and
Judaea, 65, 117ff; support for imperial
candidature of, 65; claim to accession,
66, 118f; building in Rome, 66;
restoration of military discipline and
other successes, 67; establishment of
military colonies in Judaea, 120

Vision of Isaiah, *see* Martyrdom of Isaiah
Vitellius, legate of Syria, 18, 107; ordered
Pilate to Rome, 111; granted privileges
to Jews, 111
Vitellius, Aulus (AD 69), 64f, 118f
Vitruvius Pollio, 219
Vologeses I (AD 51–76), reaction against
Hellenism, 18; 28
Vonones I (AD 7–12), 17

Wall, Hadrian's (AD 23), 68
War Scroll, 181f
Weidner Tablets, 2
Wicked Priest, the, 90; possible identity
of, 177ff

Xerxes (486–465 BC), son of Darius I, 10,
22

Zealots, origin of, 98; attacked Romans
in Masada, 115; supremacy in
Jerusalem, 118; at fall of Masada, 119f;
contrast with *hasidim*, 172
Zechariah, rebuilding of Temple, 4
Zenon papyri, Zenon's visit to Tobias, 84
Zerubbabel, governor of Judah, 4, 10
Zeugma, 23
Zeus Olympios, altar to ('Abomination
of Desolation' Dan. 11:31; 12:11; 1
Macc. 1:54; Mark 13:14, etc.), 87f

259